GIVE THE MAN ROOM

BY ROBERT J. CASEY

Travel
Four Faces of Siva
Baghdad and Points East
Easter Island
The Land of Haunted Castles
The Lost Kingdom of Burgundy
The Black Hills
The Texas Border

Personalities
Such Interesting People
More Interesting People
Mr. Clutch

War
The Cannoneers Have Hairy Ears
I Can't Forget
Torpedo Junction
Battle Below
This Is Where I Came In

Mystery
The Secret of No. 37 Hardy Street
The Secret of the Bungalow
Hot Ice
News Reel
The Third Owl

Romance
The Gentleman in Armour
Cambodian Quest

Satire
The Voice of the Lobster

Technical
Manual of Radio Interference

Verse
The Vest Pocket Anthology

BY MARY BORGLUM (Mary W. Montgomery)
Told in the Gardens of Araby (with Izora Chandler)

GUTZON BORGLUM

GIVE THE MAN ROOM

The Story of Gutzon Borglum

By ROBERT J. CASEY
and MARY BORGLUM

THE BOBBS-MERRILL COMPANY, INC.

Publishers

INDIANAPOLIS   NEW YORK

First Edition

To
LINCOLN and LOUELLA,
MARY ELLIS and DAVID

Beauty is like a soul that hovers over the surface of form. Its presence is unmistakable in Art or in Life. The measure of its revelation depends on the measure of our own soul-consciousness, the boundaries of our own spirit.

—GUTZON BORGLUM

CONTENTS

CONTENTS—*Continued*

LIST OF ILLUSTRATIONS

GIVE THE MAN ROOM

CHAPTER ONE

MOUNTAINTOP

IF YOU ARE STUDYING the history of Gutzon Borglum, the place to stand is at Stone Mountain, Georgia.

It is an impressive spot, quiet, little visited, a vast bubble of granite rising abruptly some 800 feet out of a grassy plain, and thousands of feet long. Good roads lead to it from Atlanta. There is, or used to be, a little information office at the foot of its towering cliff, and usually there is someone about to sell souvenirs or to give a sketchy and bewildering account of the mountain's history. High on the cliff there is a flat place from which several acres of surface rock have been removed; and to the left of the flat is the somewhat unidentifiable head of a man. The guide will tell you that this is the representation of Robert E. Lee, as indeed it might be—Lee or anybody.

There is little left to mark the handiwork of man in this neighborhood. Grass and brush have covered the fallen rock. The scaffolds are down, the tool sheds and storehouses vanished. The steel hooks are gone from the face of the cliff. There are no great funds in the hands of the local patriots. But this is the place. It was because of his work here, because of what he discovered about granite at Stone Mountain, and because of his carving of the head of Robert E. Lee, which today nobody can rightfully attribute to him, that Gutzon Borglum's memory will be a long time in dying.

Stone Mountain's story is often repeated and seldom—very seldom—authentic. What you see of the place today is mostly what was here on one dire day in February 1925 when Borglum's work on it came to an end—forever. But there is much about it that anyone who cares may know.

Mrs. Helen Plane, an aging Daughter of the Confederacy, had dreamed one night that the history of the South's Great Cause might be carved in vast figures on the surface of this cliff, General Robert E. Lee, President Jefferson Davis and a list of towering generals marching forever across the granite at the head of the defiant troops. She brought the matter to the attention of Borglum, and he was probably the one artist in the world who would understand what she wanted done and would find a way to get it done. That was in 1915. Borglum made a trip from Washington to Atlanta and inspected the mountain.

In 1924 this fantastic undertaking was no longer anybody's dream; it was well under way. The first group of figures, Lee and Davis and Jackson and the generals, had been outlined on the mountain, following the flag to perpetual glory. Lee himself was appearing in a stature that Art had never before given to anyone anywhere.

Machinery was in place for diagram projection, power, hoisting, drilling, carving, hauling, dynamiting. The business of high-explosive carving had been brought to a point of almost unbelievable fineness and accuracy. After years of money shortage the Stone Mountain Confederate Memorial Association was looking into a debt-free future with a million or two dollars of surplus cash in the treasury. The last march of the Confederacy was definitely on its way. . . .

Up in Pierre, South Dakota, State Historian Doane Robinson, a scholar with patriotism, an extraordinary love for beauty and very little knowledge of magnificent finance, looked at the news photographs of the Stone Mountain project and studied the roto-gravure outlines of what the sculptured cliff would look like when Gutzon Borglum finished with it. And he wondered that nobody had ever thought of trying a similar scheme in the mountains of South Dakota, the Black Hills. He wrote a letter to Borglum inquiring why.

The sculptor wrote that he was perfectly willing to look into the sculptural possibilities of the Black Hills if anybody in South Dakota was willing to provide the necessary expenses. A few months later Robinson wrote, somewhat erroneously, that the state of South Dakota would underwrite this not too considerable sum; so Borglum came out, looked at the Hills and toured their hinterland late in the summer of 1925.

In February 1925 the sculptor had a bitter disagreement with some of the executive committee of the Confederate Memorial. He thought these men careless in handling public funds. They made complaints and fired him. He broke up his models and went away from Georgia. Without him the mountain stayed uncarved.

That same year a group of Black Hills patriots guaranteed a fund of $25,000 for a patriotic mountain carving. Gifts of $5,000 each were received from Senator Coleman DuPont, Charles E. Rushmore—who gave his name to the peak later selected for the memorial in the Black Hills—The Chicago and North Western Railway, the Chicago, Burlington and Quincy Railroad, The Chicago, Milwaukee and St. Paul Railway and the Homestake Mine. Herbert Myrick contributed a donation of $1,500. The Northwestern Public Service Company of Huron, South Dakota, had offered a power plant. Doane Robinson sent out another call to Borglum, and Borglum made a second trip to the Black Hills.

In the summer of 1927 Calvin Coolidge, President of the United States, dedicated the Rushmore Mountain project. And before the ending of the Second World War the carving of this peak was finished—the only thing of its kind on the face of the earth.

From the top of Mount Rushmore four Presidents of the United States—Washington, Jefferson, Lincoln and Theodore Roosevelt —gaze out from an unbelievable block of hard rock into glowing sunlight, placid but remarkably alive. Hundreds of thousands of persons have come from the far corners of the world to look at them, and are still coming in expanding companies. The money spent by the Treasury of the United States for the carving of this peak has long since been returned to its source through the gasoline tax of the tourists. The faces of four men important in the history of the country will be preserved to us, barring some unpredictable catastrophe, until the mountains are worn as flat as the surrounding prairies. And an interesting feature of all this is that there were only a handful of people in the world who believed it possible until it was done.

It is safe to say that the carving of Mount Rushmore would never have been attempted and could never have been carried out save for the early experiment on Stone Mountain. Borglum had to learn how to remove large masses of rock—more than 50,000 tons in his first twenty months in Georgia. So he had learned how to carve with dynamite and had trained stone workers so well that they could blast down to within three inches of the surface to be chiseled. He learned about drills and their sharpening. He learned how to suspend his workmen on slings that were easily maneuvered and entirely safe. He found out how to project patterns from a distance onto the rock to be carved. And he knew how to do all these things quickly when, eventually, he moved on to Rushmore.

On the South Dakota memorial his fame now rests and probably will continue to rest until the end of time. He might possibly have felt bitter about that. The sculpture into which he poured his greatest enthusiasm was undoubtedly the Confederate memorial. It had movement instead of stasis. It told a story in a language that no man could fail to understand. The piece of his carving that he himself loved best may have been the seated Lincoln at Newark, New Jersey. None of his other works—nor any sculpture in the world—is as big as the work on Rushmore. But not at this time will any expert in sculpture come to select one of the carvings of Mount Rushmore as Borglum's masterpiece.

That is not to say that the Four Faces are not well done. They are. Lincoln's has the same pathos that marks Borglum's head of him in the Capitol at Washington. Jefferson and Washington come to us out of the unphotographed past of more than a century ago as real men. Theodore Roosevelt many of us knew when he was alive, and he is himself. But all four of them are overpowering because of their size. They are the product of an art that few men ever attempted before and none accomplished.

It is a striking thing about Borglum that nobody knew very much about him, even his friends. More people know of him now than ever did when he was living, and to most of them he is a man whose sole work was the carving of Mount Rushmore. Few of them know of the tragedy of Stone Mountain. Virtually none has ever heard of his Wars of America Memorial in Newark— forty-two human figures and two horses cast in bronze.

Some of his pieces that few people know about—his horses, his figures of Lincoln, whom he devoutly loved, his statue to James McConnell on the University of Virginia campus at Charlottesville, his simple tribute to Edward L. Trudeau—show his genius as a sculptor. His other pursuits are in dozens of record books, already dusty and forgotten.

For example, he was a member of the New York City Parks Association for a dozen years, and until the day he quit he was a factor in keeping the parks free from injurious exploitation. He organized a bus company in Stamford. He somehow became a leader of the Progressive party in Connecticut. He conducted an investigation of airplane manufacture during the First World

War. In the same war he gave the use of his grounds and what money he could raise for the recruiting of a Czecho-Slovak expeditionary force. He designed roads and reconstructed historic old buildings. He contrived waterways and beautified highways and rivers. He designed coins and medals. He invented projection apparatus and hoisting machinery. He wrote magazine and newspaper articles and built up an amazing file of information about sculpture. He invented an airplane. He laid out a breakwater for Corpus Christi, Texas. He experimented with dynamite so long that he could calculate stone removal in ounces. And as he continued his work of mountain carving he made himself an engineer in a new and difficult trade.

It is interesting to note that he did all of these things well. Some have said that he had a touchy temper, but those of us who knew him, say, over forty years didn't think so. He could never understand that money might have a different value to other people than it had to him. He would get annoyed when the treasurer of one of his projects would hesitate to empty the treasury for a power plant or some other machinery at the moment he needed it. He got genuinely angry only at people he suspected of being dishonest.

Neither did he make many enemies. One man, long a member of the executive committee of the Mount Rushmore National Memorial Commission, probably knew him longer in irritating circumstances than anyone else on earth. Once he came down from Mount Rushmore to Rapid City frothing at the mouth.

"All he knows about money for this business is that somebody has to dig it up," he roared. "He thinks I make it out of something just because he needs it. He'd bust the whole state of South Dakota in two weeks just because he needs some dynamite or an A-rig."

"But," someone inquired, "do you think he'll get this memorial finished?"

"Hell, yes!" he roared. "And nobody else could do it either!"

One is surprised that such a diversified character could have had much time left to spend in sculpture. As a matter of fact, he probably did more of it than any other individual in his profession and time. He was a prodigious worker as well as a talented dilettante in fields where he thought his influence needed. His paintings between 1890 and 1901 seem to have been virtually numberless. Many of them are appearing now and then, more valuable than ever.

Some of his better sculpture has disappeared. One of his pieces was used by a lady as security for a loan. It has gone from human ken. His study of Woodrow Wilson at Poznan, Poland, was uprooted and no doubt melted by the Nazis in the Second World War. A second artist took the hat off Robert E. Lee on Stone Mountain "because Lee would never wear a hat in a place where ladies were present." The face as one sees it today was altered in this thoughtful improvement. Much of Borglum's early work seems to have passed through similar vicissitudes.

However, most of what he did throughout his creative years seems to be with us still—statues in a dozen states, small ones, grand ones, but always anatomically perfect ones. If he had never done anything but the Newark Lincoln and the Wars of America group, he would have done enough to put him among the leaders of his art. But beside those and a generous scattering of bronze and marble all across the United States, there is still Rushmore. His own criticism of Rushmore is still the most apropos: "They'll be a long time wearing that one down."

CHAPTER TWO

THE DIM BEGINNING

THE BEGINNINGS of Gutzon Borglum are not easy to trace. Until more than fifty years after his birth nobody seems to have cared where he came from or when. Nobody was much interested in who his parents were or how or where he was brought up. By that time the evidence of his boyhood was far away and hazy.

When in middle age he turned his head toward the Far West he had known shortly after the Civil War he saw a past that was exciting, colorful and glamorous. He was lyrical in talking about it and wrapped up in memories of unbelievably noble inspiration. But the oddest feature of his reminiscence is that, except for his stylistic urge, he never wandered far from historic fact.

Gutzon Borglum was born in a frontier town in Idaho. His early childhood was spent in Fremont, Nebraska, jumping-off place of the covered wagons, haunt of wild Indians. And whatever hints he conveys about Gutzon, he is probably telling the truth. He was never anybody but Gutzon.

He intended, when he sat down to recall his youth, to write an autobiography. But writing an autobiography was just one more task that took its place in a tremendous program of brass casting, airplane design, mountain dressing, sea-wall building, picture projection, boxing promotion, park improvement, old-building restoration, motor-bus operation, horse raising, politics and—every now and then—colossal sculpture. When he died he had written two chapters and several hundred thousand words of notes and journals, an astonishing record, presenting a picture of an old warrior battling for youth against a cynical world.

He said in his introduction:

This story is told to lend an encouraging, believing hand to all lonely, creative souls who are wandering into the uncharted, untraveled wilderness of God's greater universe, finding through their own understanding new and undreamed worlds; and to those who continue alone to pour into unpeopled space their cry —unafraid, expecting no answer. Courage to stand alone; courage to master, to know, to do alone. Courage to spurn the tradesman's reward and popularity. Courage to be without great approval, in spite of government, in spite of today's laws, tomorrow's threat—every threat—in spite of Heaven. God's greatest gift to us and His supreme test is courage bestowed only on those He trusts entirely.

There are two points in this worthy of attention: his recognition of the need for courage and the stressing of his loneliness. He had the courage. No one in half a century of continuous battling had more. His loneliness must have been in his soul, not literal. With friends and enemies who included a line of Presidents of the United States, senators, congressmen and public officials, artists, writers, singers, politicians, sheriffs, policemen and such, all of them in vast numbers and continuously present throughout the years, he could have been lonely only in his more detached moments. He certainly had a full life. The portions of it unfilled with other people were of his own choosing. In his chronicle he wrote:

I should like to begin this story with Eric the Red, the great warlike Dane, driven from Denmark to Norway, from Norway to Iceland, and finally from Iceland. From there he drifted with the tide before the chill winds southward in his Viking ships, dodging the ice in the Atlantic Flow, the cooled Gulf Stream, circling up by Greenland which he claimed and named. Or even better to have been with our fellow Danes who invaded Greece and gave that people their heroic age, left in their bloodstream the blue in the eyes of Pericles, the gold of Helen's hair, the short nose of Socrates and the one blue eye of Alexander the Great. For I am as certain as I am of anything, that the spirit and the ancient Danish or Borglum blood were with and in the raiders of the Mediterranean who roused the geese in Italy's imperial city and awoke drunken Rome.

The fact that he had lived long enough to write these stirring words probably justifies his admiration for his forebears. He must have sprung from hardy stock. He had come through fifty years, part of it in the parlous times of the new West, where only the good started and only the strong survived. The family of which Gutzon was a part must have had good ancestry. There were nine of them—six of them boys—and they lived as the pioneers did, a routine without much luxury, and all of them rounded out good long lives.

Gutzon doesn't seem to be sure about their origins and early development any more than he is sure of his own. He never gave a thought to such things until he was about fifty years old and inquisitive admirers began to ask questions. Somewhat confused, he gave some ill-assorted answers, many of which remain puzzling today. In his notes, for instance, he says that he was born on March 25, 1867. This, according to some evidence given by his brother Solon, seems to be correct. Yet the biographical sketch in *Who's Who in America,* which he himself wrote, says that he was born in Idaho on March 25, 1871. One must leave it at that.

Borglum was a man of great imagination, and he built up a fine character for the men of the hardy North country from which his ancestors had come. In his mind they came from "the North of Denmark, the land bending eastward under the cruel winds from Greenland and Iceland, the rendezvous of Vikings and high-sea rovers. There we have what are called Black Danes. . . . They are unquestionably an exchange token from Spain, Rome or Greece. . . . In our own family of blonds there are always some with fine dark eyes and hair to remind us of our ancestral wanderings."

The best Borglum's father did for this family research was to locate a prospective Borglum with Frederick of Sweden in his crusade to the Holy Land. This man seems to have been named Reinhardt. But he saved the prince from a charging goat in the south of France and was given the title *de la Mothe,* "the one of courage." This forebear returned to Denmark and, Borglum's father reported, "his arms carry the crusader's shield in the center." The founder of the modern branch of De la Mothes was a priest who, in due course, joined Luther and married a nun. Gutzon wrote:

The menfolk became priests, soldiers, adventurers, and I have books left by them in their own scripts. In this black dune, the wind-swept northern part of Denmark, there is an ancient Norman pile called the Borglum Kloster which, in the nineteenth century, was a hunting lodge for the kings and nobles. The De la Mothe family was closely connected with this cloister. On a visit not so long ago I found in the great chapel, buried in its floor, the only memorial tablet to our ancestors extant.

Some years ago, after the unveiling of Gutzon's statue of Woodrow Wilson in Poznan, he took his wife and two children on a flying visit to Denmark. They arrived in Copenhagen about 8:00 A.M., and by 8:15 Gutzon was a sensation. He was a great sculptor by that time, and he had an international reputation. But the baggage carriers, the cabdrivers and the early passers-by did not know that. He was interesting to them only because he spoke to them unhesitatingly in archaic Danish, the Danish of a hundred years ago. "I learned it at my mother's knee," he explains, "and she had learned it in her youth, now a century past." He was linguistically one with the Danes of 1800. The romantic swashbucklers of crusading times no longer seemed quite so close to him.

The King of Denmark saw the Borglums after their return from Borglum Kloster and "the black duneland of the North." He sent his chamberlain to the hotel with an invitation because Gutzon, fifteen years before, had made a three-quarter bust of the king's grandfather. It was proudly displayed on a gilt mantel.

"Is it a good portrait?" asked the sculptor.

The king smiled. "Yes, it is," he said. "It is a good portrait with just a touch of American vigor."

His Majesty then presented Gutzon with the Order of the Knights of Danenborg. "Interesting," the king said as he draped the ribbon about Borglum's neck, "to think that your people killed one of our kings."

"I had heard of some disturbance in the old days at Borglum Kloster," Borglum said. "There was violence. . . ."

"That was it. The king was seized. They took him to a prison and a week later they hanged him. But you, of course, hadn't much to do with that."

"No," admitted Borglum, "I hadn't. I don't know what to say."

The king smiled again. "I'll forgive you," he said. "You know, Borglum, your people, the Jutlanders, may be said to have saved Denmark. They were the only ones the Swedes could not defeat."

"That makes me feel better," declared Gutzon.

But the king seemed not to have heard him. "Yes," His Majesty went on, "the Swedes took virtually all the country. They overran the villages and cities. They captured Copenhagen. They took everything valuable. But, of course, they never took Jutland. That's where your people were."

The financial situation in Denmark in the middle of the nineteenth century was what caused James Borglum, Gutzon's father, to come to the United States. The markets were bad, the crop yield had been none too good and there was discontent in the family

over the probable division of what little would be left of Grandfather Borglum's estate.

James de la Mothe Borglum at twenty-three was a Latin-and-
Greek scholar in his last year as a medical student. He took
passage with his sweetheart on a freighter from Esbjerg across the
North Sea to London. They were married in London and immediately afterward took passage in a three-masted sailing ship on
a voyage from Liverpool to New York. Of this voyage Gutzon
writes:

The trip was a nightmare. The ship was dismasted in a violent
storm. The passengers helped to clear away the wreckage and
drop it overboard. Then with a few spars for masts and sails made
out of bedding they gathered wind enough to carry them to the
New World. They were six weeks on the way, most of the time at
the mercy of the mad sea.

The honeymooners lingered only a day or two in New York.
Steam trains took them to Nebraska City on the west bank of
the Missouri River. There they joined an expedition of 126 wagons
starting out for Oregon.

They were months on the road, rarely traveling more than ten
miles a day. The day's course depended on the distance between
water holes. They traveled without incident until they came into
the land of the Cheyennes at the confluence of the North and
South Platte rivers. The team boss had died. James Borglum, who
was an able doctor and popular with the people in the train, was
chosen to converse with some visiting Indians. One of them asked
permission to examine Borglum's pistol and shot himself with
it. The chief blamed the mishap on the white spokesman because
he had owned the pistol. He demanded the surrender of Borglum's person and was refused. The Indians, loudly muttering,
went away.

They spent a restless night, but the expected attack did not
come. Toward midnight a band of wild horses rushed into the

expedition's herd of mules, horses and oxen. These animals were well tied and guarded and there was no alarm save for the sudden screaming of a woman. Nothing amiss was discovered until a check was made toward morning and the wife of a teamster was found to be missing. Twenty years later she was found in Montana, the wife of a chief, with grown children. She refused to leave her adopted people or to return to the whites.

James Borglum never forgot the tragedy of this long trip. The desperate hardships came near the end. There was scarcity of everything. It is hard to realize the amount of food consumed by some 450 men, women and children in four months, or the amount of water necessary daily on a dry plain in midsummer to keep horses and oxen on their feet. Borglum used to tell of a small group of voyagers who had joined his party in Wyoming. They had been living on mule harness which they boiled to give salt and "some strength" to the water.

James de la Mothe Borglum crossed the line into Idaho and reached Bear Lake on the road to Oregon. There, literally, he dug in—half the house in the ground, then sod, then log. That was in 1862—or maybe 1863. John Gutzon de la Mothe Borglum joined the family there most likely, as his unfinished autobiography says, in 1867.

Gutzon remembers his mother (Ida Michelson Borglum) as a great woman, gifted and beautiful. She had one other son, Solon, born on December 22, 1868, the boy to whom Gutzon frequently referred as his little brother.

Not many years after Solon was born, Gutzon recalls, "She left us. I was five. She turned to see me as she lay ill. There were tears in her eyes and she was trembling as she took my hand. . . . And she told me to take care of little Solon.

"I never forgot it, but I wondered why. I thought she was going to stay with us. She and Father had always been with us. I could not understand. . . ."

Gutzon was a baby. He was at the age when children are said

to be only slightly interested in family changes, but he seems to have realized that something had happened.

"By the time I was seven," he says, "I knew what it meant not to have a mother of my own. I thought I didn't want to stay around things that reminded me of her any more. So I ran away."

CHAPTER THREE

ALONE

GUTZON BORGLUM was seven years old; so the time must have been roughly 1874. In the twelve or thirteen years since James de la Mothe Borglum's caravan had come to Bear Lake, Idaho, he had been singularly restless. Gutzon had been born in Idaho, Solon a year later in Ogden, Utah. Father Borglum had moved back eastward. He had another wife. He had acquired horses and cows, a home and an office. When Gutzon ran away, home was in Fremont, Nebraska.

The child left suddenly, accompanied only by his dog. He hadn't thought to provide himself with food. He had heard of Omaha; so he started in that direction. He was three days on the way and had gone what seemed to be miles and miles when the sheriff caught up with him and brought him home. The sheriff dropped him at the Borglum house and went away. Fearful and hungry, Gutzon slept that night in the dog kennel.

Next morning he had a memorable return to the bosom of the family. His father was somewhere out of town, and his grandfather on his mother's side had come for a visit. The grandfather was a martinet who felt that children should be taught that it is wrong to run away from home. He took charge of Gutzon and Gutzon never forgot him.

"I was only seven," the sculptor remembered, "but I made up

INTERIOR OF 38TH STREET STUDIO

At the left is "I Have Piped and Ye Have Not Danced" and at the right is the "Mares of Diomedes."

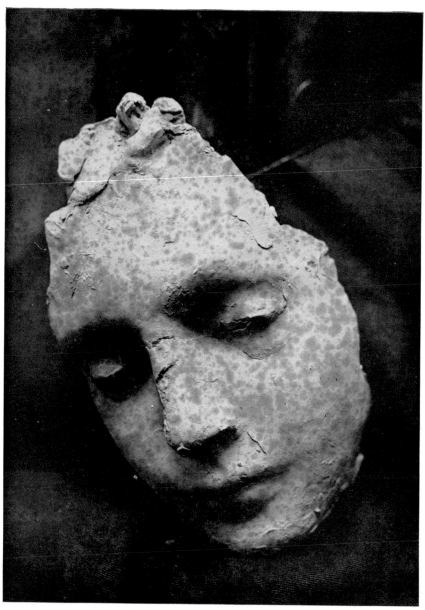

MODEL OF ANGEL'S FACE

This is one of the offending feminine faces.

my mind that I would get away from there and that I would keep trying until I succeeded . . . and, eventually, that's what I did."

For all his muddled childhood, Gutzon loved his father. James Borglum was kind, tolerant and a philosopher. He sensed his son's unhappiness, even though he would have had trouble explaining it, and a great bond developed between them. The boy went everywhere with him when not in school, even on his sick calls out in the country. Gutzon remembered that they would ride along for miles and miles in sunshine or cold or wet, sometimes talking, sometimes silent, but always in perfect peace.

One afternoon the doctor called to him and asked him to help hitch the horse. Gutzon at the time was a little over eight years old, but he did what he could with the harness and thereafter believed that he had been just as skilled and agile as any professional horse handler.

"I want you to come with me," his father said. "There is a wounded man out on Rawhide Creek and I may need some help." And Gutzon saw nothing wrong about that, either.

"We'll fix him up fine," he said. "Maybe we'll have to sew him up."

"Sure," said the doctor as he lifted Gutzon into the buggy.

Rawhide Creek was a stream with a sorry reputation. It had taken its name from an English hunter who had turned away from slaughtering buffalo long enough to murder a young squaw. Other squaws had tied him to a cottonwood tree near the creek and skinned him alive. Gutzon recalled in his chronicle:

As for our call for medical help, we found our man in the cabin armed. He was stern, fine looking. I admired him greatly and what followed made us lifelong friends. He was an outlaw on the run who had been in some shooting scrape and had received a charge of goose shot in his arm. Father had no anaesthetic for him. I doubt if at the time there was more than a pint of it in the whole state of Nebraska. The wounded man was bleeding terribly, his arm resting on some blood-soaked blankets. A piece of rope, tightly drawn about the elbow, partly stanched the flow. He was alone with two inscrutable Pawnees. After they had washed the arm in warm water, my father turned to me and said, "Gutzon, you will have to help hold his arm."

The Indians gripped the man's hand; my job was to keep the lacerations open so that Father could find the shot. We were still working when there was a sharp knock at the door. Sheriff Gregg, with a deputy at his heels, came in and put our patient under arrest. Gregg and Father were friends and Father said, "He stays here till this job is done, Bob." And we went on doing what we had to do.

The man, whose name was Fielding, was then taken to jail to be held for trial. There I visited him frequently with Father and later alone with the permission of the sheriff who liked me. Fielding was an excellent draughtsman and I brought him red and blue pencils. He loved to draw the American Eagle and the flag as we saw them on the older coins.

Weeks later when his arm was well healed there was a sudden alarm of "Jailbreak!" Fielding and another man had sawed through one of the bars with a hacked table knife. It must have been the work of many days. I prayed that he would escape. But posses went out and caught him as he was crossing the river in an open skiff. Report came back that the sheriff had killed him in midstream with a lucky shot.

Fielding was a kindly man. He told me of his shooting trouble. He'd been wronged, robbed and shot at. Why he broke jail I never knew. He dreaded imprisonment. I shall always feel that he had a great deal to do with awakening my interest in drawing and developing my ability in that direction, although I really had no idea of becoming an artist until I was fifteen. We never know where little unsuspected impulses for good may lead, or what is back of them.

Often in a family of five or six children there is one who does not want to work. He would like to write on birch bark, examine a flower, get a little color on a board or canvas . . . and there is an artist. All very simple and natural, but it comes out of the lives and struggles of perceptive men and women who follow these impulses along. I believe music first started when some mother was trying to get her little child to sleep when he was scared to death about something. She found that certain tones were pleasant when she repeated them. And thus the thing that is behind all instrumental music—woman's voice—brought harmony and sweetness to life.

Not all of Dr. Borglum's errands had to do with wounded men, and the little boy found that some of the simpler ones were more terrifying. Once they went on a long quest that had something to do with a baby. Gutzon stayed outside the house. He sat on a knoll, looking at the moon across a ravine. Of this incident Gutzon writes:

I had watched it come out of the grass in front of me. It was about three times its usual size as it came above the dull blue horizon.

My father came and I asked him, "What is the moon?" And without waiting for him to answer I told him how beautiful she was and how I loved the moon better than the sun, better than anything in the world. He picked me up and said, "I'll give her to you if you promise never to take her away from us."

I wriggled out of his arms and ran toward her. I stumbled, fell, rose up, ran on, began to cry but kept on, faster and faster, Father slowly following. . . . But the moon was retreating faster than I could move. And then the knowledge came to me—I could not have my moon. I stood weeping my heart out. . . . That moon has hung in my heaven for well over half a century with the child fable written all over it. . . . I have never reached it.

Fremont was a town of bewildering experiences. It was filled with fantastic excitement—Indian alarms, the coming and going of prairie schooners, visits of parties of Cheyenne and Sioux chiefs, gun fights beyond the hills and reports of Indian massacres on the Niobrara. Against all this the simple village life of the Swedes and Danes looked like that of quaint foreigners. Yet there were tragedies among Gutzon's own people—sickness and death and evil times, thin crops and blizzards, high winds and floods.

There was a brief school life at home, then school life at a distance. Each year when the boy returned he would find that some of his Fremont had vanished. Not exactly *vanished,* he felt; rather, the town had grown and he had grown, and somehow they had parted. The doctor moved his family after years of this to Omaha. There didn't seem to be much difference.

He had been gone a long time—or so it seemed to him—when he was eighteen years old. The thought came to him that he must see his old playground and playmates, swim in the old Rawhide, go graping or be once more with the boys and girls with whom he had grown up. He bought a train ticket for Fremont and long remembered how he could hardly wait to reach the town.

The train slowed down at the platform and he was off before it stopped. He looked at the crowd of strangers pressing about, and tried to catch a glimpse of a familiar face. At last he found a few . . . but very few.

He went into town and to the homes of friends. He found the girls he had known. Their hair was piled high on top of their heads; their dresses were long, their manners awkward. The boys stared at him and didn't say anything. He couldn't tell what had happened to these people, and, he realized later, they were puzzled in the same way about him. All of them had grown.

There was no longer any school from which to play hooky, no occasion to hang one's clothes on a cottonwood and dive into mud from an old stump. Gutzon was now a stranger to all that. And, though he refused to see it, so were these close friends of a few years ago. None of them could understand. He wrote:

I turned like one frightened and hurt and brokenhearted and ran back to the station. There on the platform I sat for hours waiting for any train to get away from Fremont. No—away from the reality that had blotted out my magic world, the world that a boy of from six to twelve lives in. And I have never had the courage to return.

The Fremont, Nebraska, of my boyhood days has gradually reconstructed itself and still lives in my memory with its two little streets and a half. Its quaint old citizens I know are still trading, spinning yarns—the occasional Indian or more, single file, quietly moving about. There are some prairie schooners and the annual one-ring circus. And as I pass the town, as I have done many times, it has always been at night—for which I have been strangely glad. I watch in the dark for all the old ways and byways I know so well, and the dark has always helped me to believe that they are all there just as I left them.

Thus far the words of Gutzon Borglum. He ceases to comment on his life in the forbidding period of early youth. He is hopeless about what has gone by and terrified at what lies ahead. But he need not have been. He was alone, a child of the night, only in his imagination. Actually, he was one of the very few human beings of his period who were singularly popular. He might have succeeded at anything he tried.

CHAPTER FOUR

CALIFORNIA

Dr. James de la Mothe Borglum is somewhat difficult to see as he moves briefly and grayly through the background of Gutzon Borglum's records. But it is quickly obvious that the restless-footed doctor never moved anywhere without being noticed. He assuredly left one heritage to his son: an inquiring, seldom satisfied mind.

Eventually this adventurous, nervous, eager spirit settled down in Omaha to a long, useful and almost uneventful life as a general physician. He was much loved and quite successful, but few of the mourners who turned out for his funeral had any idea of his questing past. He had come from Denmark to the settlement called St. Charles-on-Bear-Lake, Idaho. He had moved with his family from there to Fremont and on to Omaha. From Omaha he had moved to Los Angeles and finally back again from Los Angeles to Omaha.

His journey to Los Angeles in the middle eighties seems to have been of little importance except that Gutzon was started definitely on his art career. This was the father's last gift to his son. Ever after, Gutzon was independent and lived his own life.

The doctor, in his earnest search for religious truth, found time for the less argumentative features of a good education. He tried to give a firm basis in Greek and Latin classics to his son Solon

36

Hannibal. He sent two other sons, Gutzon and August, to St. Mary's, a Jesuit college in Kansas. He studied the Sanskrit Vedas and the doctrine of Mormon, and once served as president of the Theosophical Society of Nebraska.

During his investigation of Theosophy, Madame Blavatsky, Russian-born founder of the Theosophical Society of America, came touring from India. She visited the Borglums in Omaha and sat for a portrait by young Gutzon. This portrait hung for many years in the Borglum home, and the brooding eyes of the lady seemed to follow the Borglums about the room wherever they moved. Gutzon used to explain that this was a familiar trick in painting and not hard to achieve.

Gutzon was interested in art while the family still lived in Fremont. His schoolmates there recalled that the margins of his books were covered with sketches and that he liked to draw maps and make caricatures of his teachers or of local men in public life.

His teachers at St. Mary's had readily noticed his talent. They had set him to drawing saints and angels—subjects of which, at the time, he was not particularly fond. He refers to his Kansas experience in an article written in 1919:

My interest in the beautiful began before I came to St. Mary's, but it was due to encouragement there, and to a definitely expressed desire on the part of two young men who were graduated the year I left that the determination was awakened in me to treat seriously what I had previously considered a delightful trick.

One of these men was named Murphy, and I shall never cease to remember with profoundest gratitude his earnest talk to me as we walked up and down during the evening recess. He talked to me of the great masters. He got books for me. I came to know the whole Italian school, painters and sculptors. And for years it seemed that I knew little else. As a result I have never gone to Italy. [Nor did he until 1931.] As I grew older I found I had a powerful bias toward Italian art and its melodrama. But I did not want to go there, even though I admire Italian and Grecian art more than all else.

Murphy went out of my life and I have never heard of him since. He may not—doubtless does not—remember what he did for me. But in those evenings at school he set me afire. And the goal he painted seems bigger, better, more wonderful and worthwhile now than it did, even then. So he served. He may never have known it, but I owe everything to his inspiring words.

The whereabouts of Murphy was never traced because his first name apparently had been forgotten, and hundreds of Murphys passed through St. Mary's before it surrendered its charter and became a Jesuit seminary sometime after the First World War. People who knew the place in the eighties are not surprised at Gutzon's declaration that his real inspiration came from there. It was a small school that had grown out of an early mission to the Potowatomi Indians, but it had few characteristics that identify the tank-town college. Out of it in half a century came a singular troop of famous persons, many of whom no doubt crossed Gutzon's path without realizing that he was a fellow alumnus. Judges, lawyers, bishops, educators, engineers, builders, doctors, merchants, chiefs, sailors, soldiers, politicians, inventors, musicians and all the rest of them are included in the list. It is interesting to note that Borglum is the institution's only offering to sculpture.

His life at old St. Mary's seems to have been perfectly normal. He had several fights which he remembered ever after. He remembered, too, that he was always in the right, which is likewise perfectly natural. His chief exploit in fisticuffs was a wrangle with three rather hard lads in the dining room, and there is a tradition that he won. At any rate, he learned how to protect himself with his bare fists—a skill that he always counted as a major asset.

He finished the academy course—the equivalent of high school —when, at that period in the West, he was considered sufficiently adult to find a job. Dr. James suddenly moved his family to California. Gutzon quit St. Mary's and went to work as a lithographer's apprentice in Los Angeles, and studied engraving and designing on stone. At the end of six months he was producing work that he thought was good. That, of course, was nothing to cause any emotional outbursts among the lithographers, because Gutzon thought that everything he produced was good.

The young man wanted better pay, but he didn't get it. The lithographer said that if he stayed at his work he would someday be an experienced hand. But Gutzon sacrificed this opportunity. He went to work for a fresco painter, and he got more money. He rented a little studio and did part-time work as he pleased.

On a ranch somewhere in the vicinity was Solon Borglum. Of all the family he was closest to Gutzon because he had shown interest in art. Gutzon eventually got him to leave the ranch and to take up the study of painting and sculpture seriously. He contributed to Solon's support and, in time, to his tuition in a Cincinnati art school. But there is little mention of this in his written record, for he was shy about such things.

California was a constant surprise to him. He was by himself and supporting himself. He felt free and able, and he was proud of himself. His father had gone back East with a family that in time totaled nine. Someplace with that brood was August, Gutzon's companion at St. Mary's. It was to be a long time before Gutzon would see some of his other brothers and sisters. But no matter! California was warm in the winter, and it didn't cost much to get things to eat. And he kept meeting people who interested him. While he was still with the lithographer he met an artist named Eberlie, a really good painter of the Düsseldorf school. Eberlie turned out beautiful ensembles that seemed perfect in color and design. Gutzon yearned to do the same thing.

Something had awakened in him. He went on and on with his work in the tiny studio, producing little that looked like anything, learning slowly what was wrong. He couldn't have quit. He was still there even after Dr. Borglum and the family had moved back to Omaha.

Information about his early years in this paradise, however, doesn't come so much from him as from strangers. Charles F. Lummis, whom he knew well and with whom he later wrangled extensively, wrote a piece about him in *The Land of Sunshine* (later, *Out West*) magazine in 1906. He said:

It was a matter of nine years ago. Los Angeles was a country town, just emerging from adobehood. This writer found a green, serious lad belaboring canvas in a bare room on what was then Fort Street. He had no money and not many friends. The painting he was at had many shortcomings and showed his lack of art education. Yet there was in them a creative breath that promised to make him heard from. . . .

He was born in the West and was Western in every fibre. Soon after graduation from seminary he came to Los Angeles, and presently began the long, hard struggle of an unbefriended artist. By and for himself, by sheer dint of pluck and brains, he hewed his way. At last his pictures attracted the attention of one of the few connoisseurs then here. . . . A couple have been sold to Easterners at good prices. . . .

Gutzon, however, was not long friendless. He appears to have been discovered by George Butler Griffin, who had married a Castilian lady from Colombia and lived in Los Angeles. They had several gifted children, one of whom was the mother of the actress, Bebe Daniels. Another daughter, Mrs. Eva Griffin Turner, herself a painter, was among Gutzon's early heralds. She met him first in the eighties and never forgot a detail of their meeting.

She was twelve years old at the time and for a year or more had been sketching and painting in her own fashion with a child's color box. She was allowed to trail along with him and a class he was instructing, and she never forgot what he said as the pupils gazed at a sunset beyond Los Angeles.

"The artist," he declared—and it seemed to her that he was talking to himself—"The artist should approach nature with great reverence."

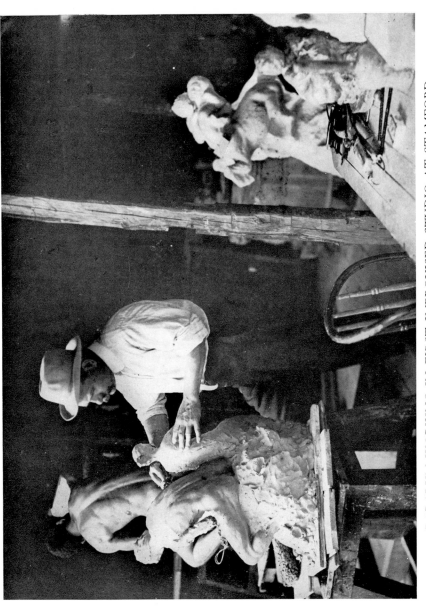

BORGLUM WORKING IN FIRST IMPROVISED STUDIO AT STAMFORD

"DR. TRUDEAU" THE BELOVED PHYSICIAN

He left the class for a while when he went to work with William Keith, an artist in San Francisco. Gutzon was an extravagant admirer of Keith, who was called the "Grand Old Man of California Painting." He stayed in his class for several months. During that same period he took a short course under Virgil Williams.

Mrs. Turner vividly remembered his home-coming and how his old students reassembled with him for outdoor sketching. But he was not long for his old ways. He had painted a picture called "Stage Coach" and some rich man had seen it. There was an immediate furor over the picture and Gutzon. And so presently he went to Paris to study.

"He won prizes," Mrs. Turner mentioned, "and he was greatly admired."

And then we have the memory of Bob Davis, onetime editor of *Munsey's Magazine* and a columnist for the New York *Evening Sun*. In his California days he was a printer's apprentice with a job near Gutzon's studio. Davis describes Gutzon's studio thus:

His walls were the most fascinating thing in my life. They were hung with pictures of stage coaches and horses leaping at you from every direction. These things were painted in oils and I thought they were the finest things in California. He also modeled in clay and chiseled a bit in stone. During the lunch hour I visited his studio and struck up a friendly acquaintance. He confided that his ambition was to excel in sculpture and that he painted only to get the sinews with which to go on.

One noon I entered his studio and found him in high spirits. He was rigging a large canvas on the easel and making great preparations for something important.

"I'm going to do a life-size, seated portrait of General Frémont in military regalia," he told me. "Mrs. Frémont is bringing him around this afternoon for the first sitting. Come around tomorrow at lunch time and I'll have the figure rounded in. He has a strong face and I think I can make a pretty good picture."

I saw the painting from the first touch of the brush. Frémont always came in on the arm of his wife who seemed to be the one person he wanted to please. She brought with her a military coat adorned with gold fringe and epaulets, a garment the great Indian fighter wore with dignity.

And it was a good picture. Day after day it assumed more life and grandeur until it was finished and taken away to be exhibited in an art gallery on Spring Street. I went to see it there. And I boasted about my acquaintance with the artist to anybody who would listen to me.

There seems to be no doubt that the Frémont portrait was one of the most important works of Gutzon's youth. It got him attention and acclaim. But more than that it got him the friendship and advice of Mrs. Frémont. The general was nearing death when Gutzon first saw him. The portrait was finished in 1888 and Frémont died in Washington, D. C., in 1890. But the motherly interest of Jessie Benton Frémont in the artist went on unbroken for many years. She helped him with letters to important people and with advice on how and where to sell his works. Some of these letters were still in Gutzon's effects when he died.

The most discriminating patron of the young artist in California was, perhaps, Spencer J. Smith. Smith bought enough canvases to give Gutzon a start toward his training in Paris. These pictures, tenderly cared for, are still in the possession of Smith's widow in the same house where the artist saw them hung some sixty years ago. As then the house, surrounded by gardens, stands like an oasis in the heart of busy Los Angeles.

Shortly before going abroad in 1889, Gutzon married Mrs. Elizabeth Putnam, whom the family called "Lisa," a painter of ability and a teacher of art. Unfortunately, the details of the romance are lacking. Gutzon never talked about such intimate matters. His father and other members of the family met her only after the marriage.

Lisa seems to have loved her husband. At any rate, his worries during the early years in Europe made little impression on her—

nor on him. Yet, that there was some difficulty in their relationship is evidenced in letters written to Gutzon by friends of both of them. A young sculptor pupil, Arthur Putnam, who lived with them at Sierra Madre, mentioned the vague unhappiness he sensed in Gutzon and tried delicately to probe into the matter. But, unfortunately, only the question of Putnam is extant. Gutzon's reply to his letter has not been kept.

From the sculptor's diary, a sporadic and sketchy document, it is plain that he was passionately anxious to have a child. It is probable that the impossibility of this was the basis of whatever trouble he had with Lisa. Moreover, she was twenty years his senior and did not care much for his strenuous way of life.

Such was Gutzon's fear of hurting her, and his almost abnormal dread of publicity in so personal a matter, that the legal tie was not broken for several years. Few of Gutzon's friends of later years knew of this marriage, and his own children were in their teens before they heard of it.

A French servant, Jeanne, who had lived with the Borglums in Europe, accompanied Lisa to California to live with her until her death. In 1931 she wrote to the sculptor about certain of his paintings that he had given to Lisa and closed her letter with a significant and touching thought.

"You have two beautiful children," she said, "and you are at last happy. You deserve it. . . ."

Gutzon and Lisa bought a little house among the orange groves in Sierra Madre, near the base of the mountains back of Pasadena, not far from where the Santa Anita race track now stands. "Lucky" Baldwin, who had a horse ranch on land that included the site of the race track, was a great friend and allowed Gutzon to use his horses as models. Gutzon loved this place. His favorite subjects for sculpture were horses, and he never tired of looking at them. Mrs. Frémont, after seeing his equestrian casts and drawings at his studio in 1889, summed up his future with the gift of prophecy: "The boy is spirited. Here is one sculptor who will ride to fame on horseback!"

That wasn't quite true, but it was near enough. Within the year he was moving. And never thereafter did he recognize the existence of anything that could hold him back.

CHAPTER FIVE

OVERSEAS ART

GUTZON LEFT California in 1890 accompanied by his wife and forty unsold canvases. He was fairly happy. He had made a little money, he had learned something about art and he had a growing circle of friends in California. On the other hand, he gave little evidence that he might be something other than one more simple art student from the Pacific coast. That is what makes his progress remarkable.

He stopped in Omaha to visit with his father and, almost unaccountably, left a pile of his canvases with a Mr. Leininger, a dealer and patron of art. It is a little difficult now to identify or appraise these works. This is a pity, for, good or bad, expensive or cheap, they all seem to have found somebody who loved them. They never came back to haunt his garret, nor, for that matter, did the ones we are told he sold "at an exhibition in New York."

There is little known about the "exhibition in New York" except that Mrs. Frémont, the general's widow, had been informed of it. She wrote a note to the one person in New York who might be able to give a lift to the young artist. And that's how Gutzon met Theodore Roosevelt, then Police Commissioner, who became a lasting friend.

Through some similar effort Gutzon also met Collis P. Huntington, one of the builders of the Southern Pacific railroad. Their encounter would be of no interest here save for the example it gave of the young man's purpose and directness and of his confidence in himself. Huntington, impressed by Gutzon's work and charm as well as his friends, wanted to know what he could do to help him. Gutzon shook his head and smiled. "Nothing," he said. "When I get through with this exhibition I'm going to Paris to study art."

This was something new to Huntington—as it would have been to any art patron in New York. "I am amazed," he said. "Almost nobody comes to see me that doesn't want me to do something for them." He bowed and went away and Gutzon never saw him again.

Gutzon sailed on the *Bourgogne* with plenty of hope and the proceeds of his art sales in Omaha and New York. He admitted that he felt proud of himself. He had been out of St. Mary's seven years.

In 1891 a description of him was included in a passport issued by the U. S. Embassy in Paris and signed by Whitelaw Reid. It gave his age as twenty-four years; stature, 5 feet, 8½ inches; forehead, broad; eyes, gray; nose, regular; mouth, medium; chin, round; hair, dark; complexion, dark; face, oval—and it is a matter of great puzzlement to one who knew Gutzon for forty years. It shows the picture of a somewhat thin, energetic young man of dark complexion, regular features, broad forehead and no great height. Yet, not until he had read this record did an old friend realize that Borglum's complexion was anything save that contrived by weather and wind. Even more astoundingly came the revelation that Gutzon was less than six feet in height. He looked to be taller.

Nobody seems to have found much about Gutzon's art studies in Europe worth recording. He passed two years in Paris, studying at the Julien Académie, at the École des Beaux Arts and under individual masters. He exhibited in the Old Salon as a painter in 1891 and 1892. His picture called "Clouds" attracted some attention. In 1891, through a deliveryman's mistake, a piece of bronze was taken to the New Salon. It was accepted by the New Salon, which made him a member of the society.

The notice informing him of this unexpected honor was followed by a personal letter of congratulation written by the celebrated painter Puvis de Chavannes, who had succeeded Meissonier as president of the Salon. Borglum's work of sculpture was called "Death of the Chief" (*Mort du Chef*) and represented a horse with lowered head beside the body of a dead Indian. A copy of the group was unveiled in Los Angeles in 1947.

The great experience of Gutzon's life in Paris was meeting and forming a friendship with Auguste Rodin. He said afterward that it wasn't a new experience. "It was rather a feeling of coming home," he said, and finding something he had dimly sensed in himself and was trying to express. Rodin at the time was having trouble with the Academicians and would follow a long road before being acclaimed the great master the world now recognizes. Gutzon's attitude toward life was much the same. He was also committed to a long quarrel with that state of mind which accepts stereotyped standards and resists change or improvement. Gutzon wrote this about Rodin:

I hold Rodin to be one of the great individuals of history. He was one of the rarest souls of whom we have any record during the last 3,000 years. He is passing and there will be nothing left to speak for this man, who stands with Phidias, Donatello, Rembrandt and Shakespeare, but a trail of broken fancies. The nineteenth century has made no adequate use of his incomparable gifts.

He quoted Rodin's remarks as recorded by M. Gsell in his book about the master:

To any real artist worthy of the name, all nature is beautiful, because the eyes, fearlessly accepting all exterior truth, read there, as in a book, the inner truth. Not a feature deceives him. Hypocrisy is as transparent as truth. The beauty of the Greek ideal is ever present and there is as much loveliness in the human form today as when Phidias immortalized his race. But this loveliness is passing into oblivion unrecorded, because the artists of today are blind. That is all the difference.

Whether or not we follow what Rodin said, there is no doubt that Gutzon did. He brought home with him from Europe nothing that so continuously affected his life. Again he writes of Rodin:

Rodin meant more. He meant what I will add. The artists have not seen, nor felt, nor understood the present, although they still seem to appreciate the beauty of the Greek.

Great emotion, with great understanding, again united with mastery over medium, are indispensable in the production of masterpieces in song, form or color. Prophetic insight, coupled with great love and trained to be a master in one of the mediums which the human race has invented or discovered to express itself, is lost in our day, as Rodin laments.

This paragraph seems to sum up Gutzon Borglum's position on the matter of art expression, and it explains his reaction to much of what is called Modern Art. Years afterward he augmented it with another bit of learning out of his two years of study in France. At a meeting in honor of the French during the First World War he said:

France has been a foster mother and I shall always remember her, as Hugo put it, as my second birthplace, because to be "educated in another place is to be reborn there."

So I was born in France at Auvers-sur-Oise. Here at Auvers I had a quiet little home and for three years grubbed and labored with my stubborn Americanism.

Finally I returned to America after having tried while there to acquire French art. And then it came to me in an hour. I shall never forget that hour. It came to me that the value and greatness of French influence are in their superiority and their devotion to the "inspiration" and not special concern for technique.

France has taught me respect for the sincere effort of other men, courage in my own, and that originality lies in being true to one's self.

I learned that what is known as "French Art" is not the art which has placed France as art mistress of the modern world. Rather, it is Millet, Corot, Rousseau, Chavannes. It is not the Parisian article, any more than it was Falguière or any other dozens of masters of the technique, but Rodin and Dalou who helped French sculpture to its high place in our century and fixed France with the ancients.

Gutzon was not a pupil of Rodin, but he was a frequent visitor in his studio. He used to tell of watching Rodin make quantities of water-color sketches of his model, who was allowed to sit at ease and to change her position as she wished. He gave Gutzon some of these sketches, which have been preserved. They are inscribed "A mon ami, Borglum" and signed "Rodin." Letters from him across the years have also been kept. During the First World War, when Paris was being bombed, Gutzon invited Rodin to come to the United States and use his studio in Stamford. Rodin declined and said he had decided to find refuge in Rome.

During this early period in Europe, Gutzon also passed an interesting year in Spain about which his American friends seem to have known very little. As a record of his stay, many spirited sketches of bullfights are still extant. One of them is owned by O. R. McGuire, the art connoisseur of Washington, D. C. He also made a copy of Velasquez' portrait of the court jester, and a wood carving done by Gregory Pardo, pupil of Michelangelo, in the Toledo cathedral. His studies of Cortez' conquest in Mexico and the tragic fate of the Aztecs made a deep impression on him.

He prepared background sketches for a large painting which he started on his return to California. It depicted the gray dawn on the broken causeway of Mexico City when the soldiers of Cortez were floundering against the Aztecs in the gap. The episode, known to history as *noche triste,* was a subject that haunted Gutzon through his life. But although he first planned his picture of it for exhibition at the Columbian World's Fair in Chicago in 1893, he seems never to have finished it.

Other sidelights of his year in Spain are found in a letter to Mrs. J. Seddon of Hollywood who bought a painting labeled "Don T., Toledo, Sept. 1892." She had written to him for information about it, and his reply to her query was this:

I am very much interested in the picture, and I have wondered what had become of it. It ought to be in good condition, for it was honestly and well painted.

It is the portrait of a Catholic priest, Don Tomas, pronounced To-mass. He was the canon in charge of the great cathedral in Toledo, a remarkable little man, very kindly and friendly, but he belonged to the period of Philip II. He was extremely fond of bullfights. He and I attended them regularly.

I first started to paint him smoking a cigarette, but when he saw it, he threw the cigarette away and said it was undignified for a priest. He is sitting in the outer room, the library room, which forms the entrance to the Council Chamber where some 250,000 more or less heretics and Protestants were tried, burned, exiled or condemned to the galleys. The chamber beyond was like a court, surrounded with seats against the wall in which the judges sat. Into the middle of the room, the victim, or the accused, was brought.

I don't remember much of the carving of the background, but the room was richly carved by Gregory Pardo, pupil of Michelangelo. The work was done between 1549 and 1551, and this particular chamber is called the Sala Capitula and was executed under orders of the Archbishop of Toledo and in the reign of Philip II.

Gutzon returned from Spain to California in 1893 and brought a bit of the Old World with him. He arrived to find a matter seemingly awaiting his attention, as most matters did—the restoration of California's Spanish missions. It cannot be said that Gutzon

Borglum ever came to lavish his indignation over affairs with which he was unfamiliar, and admittedly he was indignant over no small number or variety of them before he died. In this instance he found a battlefield made to order, because he had been studying the old records of the Spanish missions in Spain.

His argument about the course and methods of the restoration became his first recorded controversy, and was dragged out and redebated every time he had a disagreement with somebody about something else. But, for all that, it wasn't much of a fight.

Charles Lummis, the editor, was at the head of a group of Californians interested in restoring the ruined missions. He appears to have been somewhat irritated when Gutzon came home from Spain and demanded an important share in the work. The reconstruction plans, the sculptor declared blithely, were prodigiously wrong. Incensed by this, Lummis wrote several angry letters to Gutzon. Gutzon, never at a loss for words, replied in kind. Unfortunately, some steps in the correspondence seem to be lacking. There is no indication of how this battle came to be resolved; however, the strong language presently ceased. Gutzon got his way about the methods that should be pursued in restoring the buildings, and he and Lummis became close friends. It appears that many of Borglum's arguments turned out that way.

Gutzon's most important comment on the California missions never saw the light until some time around 1927, when he was discussing the missions of Texas. He wrote:

In the winter of 1893-1894 we organized in California the Association for the Preservation of the Franciscan Missions, founded or built by the followers of Junípero Serra. In preparing for that work I made a trip to Spain and spent a year there studying the Spanish civilization and securing the records of Junípero Serra's work in the New World, some original publications and the records of the building of the missions.

On my return I recovered and re-established the boundaries of perhaps the most beautiful ruins in America, San Juan Capistrano, thirty or forty miles from Los Angeles and the only mission I hold that is comparable to the San Jose Mission near San Antonio, Texas. With the help of Indians who carried the dirt on their backs, I removed the debris from the dome of the main church which had fallen in during the earthquake of 1812, destroying some life. Under the debris we found diamond-shaped flagging that formed the floor. I made careful drawings of all the buildings, the pilasters and cornices in place, cut beautifully by the Spaniards, much of it of limestone.

In this work we came suddenly face to face with the very serious question of how far we could go in the matter of reconstruction— what constituted human rights in the work of restoration, retouching and rebuilding, how much of our work would immediately become vandalism—how far could we go without meddling with the form and design and the actual work of the men who built these fine structures. After much debate, the kind of debate that took place in Rome many years later, it was determined that we must do nothing more than save and preserve the work as we found it.

Where we found a stone that clearly had fallen out and where it was recognizable, we might replace it. But to rebuild or in any way reconstruct or restore what we conceived might have been the character of the building at the time, all agreed would be vandalism. There is no question that the Franciscan missions are still a live subject of interest because they are not buried under modern debris of cement and make-believe restoration. The late Charles F. Lummis, president of the association since 1894, was adamant in his resolution against any meddling with the ancient methods of the work.

Of his art studies during this formative period Gutzon wrote:

As I became acquainted with the masterpieces in the fine arts, I soon became aware that a landscape painter could not draw or paint horses, cattle or sheep; that a cow painter could not paint a convincing landscape equal to his cow painting as a matter of creative production. The same applied to figure painting. I made up my mind that I should master each of these subjects, and I began at once. As I painted and drew almost exclusively in my first twenty years of art work, I drew and painted incessantly dogs, cattle, horses, portraits, figures, and never had to turn to a fellow artist and ask him to draw my figure or cow or horse or sheep.

Reflection on this caused me to note that most men, as well as artists, were one-track minded—that the average layman knew nothing of art, nor the place in civilization held by the masters of the fine arts, or even that civilization in its crudest forms was solely the product of the arts, or that the reaching urge in all civilization was the expressed mood of nature, seeking through them an outlet.

The reaching, enveloping soul of musical harmonies is the prelude to an understanding of the creative impulse. And again, who is insensible to the tremendous power of words? The marriage of words? The Milky Way of words which language conjures up and creates? Who has not been conscious of the strange beauty of words ancient as Lancelot—of heart, love, soul loneliness, craving and conflict? And as these thoughts grew on me I became aware that the circle of any human group was too small to live deeply within; that all moods of life were something alive in the cosmic in which the creative mind moves in limitless orbit, sensitive to every impression; that the larger the spoken language, the greater, more comprehending became one's expression.

Gutzon, in this period, was no finished sculptor. He did some work with stone and metal—but sporadically—for some three years. He painted tirelessly. He was back at Sierra Madre, and life was placid and pleasant.

His friends made much of the Baldwin ranch. Mrs. Frémont had already sent to him there, before he went abroad, young Philip Rollins, who became his lifelong friend. Rollins was much interested in horses and in pictures. He had seen a painting of Gutzon's in Mrs. Frémont's possession which he said was worth a thousand Corots. "I have never looked so far into the sky in any painting," he said. And he brought that admiration into his friendship.

In San Francisco Gutzon had a little trouble with the estate of

Leland Stanford. Mr. Stanford, during his lifetime, had ordered three pictures from Gutzon, who was then in Paris. One of these was a small canvas priced at $500, accepted and paid for. The others were larger. Stanford accepted them but died before any payment had been made.

Rollins brought suit against the estate for Borglum, but the claim was rejected. The widow declared that there was no written contract. Mrs. Frémont was much incensed and wrote Gutzon a very gossipy letter about the worth of widows who needed written contracts.

In 1896 Borglum left California again, expecting to settle in England. His last act before leaving was to model a bust of his dear friend and patron Mrs. Frémont. A photograph of the bust is the frontispiece of Mrs. Phillip's biography of Mrs. Frémont and is credited to "John Gutzon Borglum, 27 years old, painter and sculptor, recently returned from Spain, following his triumphs in the Paris salons of 1891 and 1892."

What Borglum thought of this credit he does not say. He was headed for a permanent berth in a foreign country, and for once he didn't seem to be quite certain of where he was going.

CHAPTER SIX

ENGLAND

THERE ARE not many people alive in the United States today who remember "the panic of 1893" and the "hard times of '94, '95 and '96," but the histories point out briefly that they were with us. Depression had begun to spread in 1890. The banking house of Baring, badly entangled with Argentine investments, closed its doors. The British began to dump American securities. The gold reserve began to disappear. And, in general, that is how things went for five or six years.

Nowhere in Gutzon's record of the times is there much mention of panic or money shortage. This may be a good place to record that in London he did show some concern about dollars—what they were and how they were kept. One gathers, indirectly, that he liked to be working. That he really enjoyed the pleasure of others in the things that he painted or carved was fairly obvious. Against that, he knew all that was to be known about hunger. His movement to England at a time when living in California was beginning to look difficult may indicate that somebody was taking thought.

Life in England appears to have been no complete idyll. Gutzon himself was quite happy. There was work for him to do and he had plenty of English friends, but one gathers that Mrs. Borglum found the exile a bit painful.

In 1897 Jessie Frémont wrote this to him:

If you come away or go away from London, I shall be sorry and disappointed in you. English people *demand* stability. And there is to be no talk even of preference for any other place. The time will surely come when you can put your preferences into execution, but it does chill and turn away interest to have a vanishing prospect.

Mrs. Borglum has too much sense and far too much affection for you not to see that this is for your true interest. You cannot re-cast a national mold and England is set to its "slow-and-sure," sure being its complement to slow. I do not blame Mrs. Borglum's American impatience, but "stay where the money is."

The artist's prevailing mood during 1897 seems to have been one of profound melancholy and disillusionment regarding Europe. He kept a diary at this time which, with his letters from Mrs. Frémont, is the chief source of information concerning his life in England.

Mrs. Frémont's letters gave him great cheer and comfort. General Frémont had an artistic and sensitive nature with frequent ups and downs of mood. Circumstances beyond his control had ruined his dreams for developments in California. The United States government itself had taken land from him for war purposes in 1861, and he had never been paid for it. His widow was still hoping to have her claim settled thirty-six years later. She knew the value of money, the need for patience and diplomacy; and she could sympathize with a struggling artist in language that he could understand.

Gutzon's diary opens with an indication that he needed the sympathy. He begins:

Now, at last! I feel some—enough—desire to make notes of steps and landings in this, this curious life that we are doomed for a certain time to bear. I must be honest with myself—else why record? Lies, trivialities and the daily doings of the body are not worth thinking of much less making memoranda of. But it's not

"GENERAL SHERIDAN"

This statue is in Washington, D.C.

"WARS OF AMERICA" MODEL

for the public—not for one single soul. For I am alone and who would understand?

Six years ago I said to myself, "I'll be great at thirty, or never." I am thirty. I have had the disturbing pleasure of being called "master" by the French critics and some Americans, yet at the moment I cannot spend sixpence without wondering where the next one will come from. Art is not self-sustaining until it becomes commercially valuable, and a man is not to be counted until he is in popular demand.

Gutzon's reach was far beyond his grasp, and his Heaven was far away. Undoubtedly he was extravagant. He loved beauty and costly things, rare books, rich stuff and tapestries. But the problem of where the next dollar was coming from began to worry him less and less. He got big commissions in America, in England and all through his life. His trouble was not that he failed to make money but that he never learned how to keep it.

He never seemed to know the value of a dollar, nor did he care. His real extravagance was in putting into commissioned work added richness of detail or extra figures that he thought would add to the effect. That was why he rarely came out of an undertaking with any great profit to himself and was hounded by debt all his life.

He rarely spent money on his person, except for small lovely things that he could carry in his pocket. He often had holes in his shoes, and his unpressed clothes were always a distress to his friends. To emphasize the sacrifices of a struggling artist, he used to tell of buying baked potatoes on the street corners of London to keep his hands warm. The potato-buying story was undoubtedly true, but it was hardly a record of a typical condition.

Building was his chief delight—always. In London, after he had lived for months in a studio apartment in West Kensington, he rented a villa in St. John's Wood and proceeded to make repairs and additions to it, regardless of cost. The villa had a rose garden, and he frequently talked of how he mowed the lawn early in the morning before starting the day's work. All his life he enjoyed the work of beautifying his surroundings. During the years he built at least six other studios and houses for himself without ever being satisfied. His ideal home, which he was always ready to describe in detail and with feeling, was a fabulous sort of place that existed only in his restless mind.

In his diary he mentions having gone shopping with the painter Frank Brangwyn to consider taking over Sir Edward Leighton's studio. They decided it was too pretentious. In Paris he rented a studio in the Boulevard Arago. He still found some of his old friends and business acquaintances in the neighborhood when he visited it in 1931, thirty years after he had moved out of it. It was a place of rare memories. He had fitted the little stove with a red isinglass front, and he had burned a solitary candle in it in those freezing days to give the illusion of rosy warmth.

In Gutzon's reminiscences it seems always to have been cold in the neighborhood of Boulevard Arago. A sculptor, living in one of the garrets with which the region seems to have been plentifully supplied, fashioned a masterpiece. It was still in the wet clay when the thermometer dropped below freezing. The artist was frantic. In the bitter cold of night he began to fear for his statue. He got up and wrapped it in rags of clothing and finally in his only blanket to keep the ice away. He died of the cold. But the statue for which he froze to death now reposes in warm, serene quarters in the Luxembourg.

Frank Brangwyn, some of whose work may be seen in Rockefeller Plaza in New York City, was the one artist who made a deep impression on Gutzon in England. The Borglum diary is filled with notations such as this: "November 19, 1897—Short half hour with Brangwyn. . . . He belongs to *art* and will do work that will live." And the feeling was mutual. In later years Brangwyn wrote, "I admire those strong virile things of yours. It is like a strong sea breeze on a hot and listless day to see your honest works. . . ." Each foresaw for the other a greatness that he could not hope for himself.

The sculptor met Ruskin briefly and was so impressed with his features that he made a statuette of him. The figure is seated with a rug over the knees and was one of Borglum's most successful pieces. A copy of it is now in the Metropolitan Museum in New York.

He also met George Bernard Shaw, although little of art figured in their association. In a letter years later he mentioned Shaw's attendance at meetings of what he called the "Kingsley Society." "This," wrote Gutzon, "was a lively debating society and we visited once a week at one another's homes. I debated with Shaw on 'The Ignorance of Educating Me.' I forget which side. Shaw likes to play smart, but at heart he is a serious, lovable, great man."

Gutzon may have been right about most of these points, but he made an error in naming the club. It was probably the Fabian Club. Shaw denied that he had ever heard of the "Kingsley Society," and mentioned that for that matter he had hardly heard about Kingsley.

Gutzon remained in England until the turn of the century which, considering the intensely modern impact of his life, seems like a long time ago. The days of quick success had become fewer in 1897, and they lessened rapidly thereafter. There was trouble on the horizon and the people of England were uneasy and crotchety.

In the controversy preceding the Boer War, which broke out in 1899, he was loudly critical of the British for their oppression of "the intrepid band in the Transvaal," and freely forecast that they would pay for it dearly. And they did. General Baden-Powell, another of Borglum's friends, was besieged with his troops in Mafeking, a little town north of Kimberley. There, holding what appeared to be a hopeless position, they came closer to starvation daily while England prayed.

Years afterward, in an article about the Boy Scouts, which Baden-Powell founded, Borglum recalled the turning point of that war:

I was in London. I was sitting in the New Globe theater. Duse, the magnificent, was giving one of her superb performances. And during one of the curtains the director came onto the stage with an announcement.

At first he said, "I hope that everyone will remain in his seat. I hope that you will be quiet and let the play go on." The audience was dead still, trying to understand. And then the man said: "Mafeking has been relieved."

The play ended right there. I never saw a sedate audience so completely surrender to joy. Believe it or not, every man everywhere in the theater kissed the others, kissed the women, shouted and cried. They poured into the streets and jumped up and down. They crawled onto the tops of buses and danced. And then and there Mafeking became historic.

Mafeking had been relieved, and that relieved the heart of Great Britain. The siege, with General Cronje commanding the Boers, had lasted about six months. It was lifted by Lord Methuen and sixteen thousand troops, and it brought a new day to England. . . .

Gutzon's work in England was widely talked of though little of it now remains. One of his principal commissions came to him after he had left the country, and the work was executed in the United States. A somewhat incongruous product of the Thirty-eighth Street studio, it was a series of murals for the Midland Hotel in Manchester, England, nearing completion with advertising accompaniments that said it would be the finest in the British Isles. The order, placed by the Midland Railway Company, owners of the hotel, was remarkable in that it broke what had long been considered an untouchable precedent. It was the first large order for fine art work ever placed by England in America, and brought the painter wide publicity at a time when it seems to have been considerably needed. Twelve panels were included in the series, and the Midland Railway Company agreed to pay $25,000, a sum almost incredible in those hard times; but the fee was payable on delivery.

The Midland's art committee knew what it was getting. In 1898 Borglum had painted a series of panels for the Queen's Hotel in Leeds, another property of the railroad. They were a graceful, joyous group, and Gutzon admitted in his diary that he was a little proud of them.

They represented the four seasons with lithe, slender maidens as the central figures. They were pleasant-looking and the critics liked them. For "Spring," they danced with garlands of flowers, the trees and background shrubbery in harmony with pale spring colors. For "Summer," the same girls were shown relaxed on the bank of a bubbling pool with young Pan playing his pipes for them. The "Autumn" panel pictured them dancing out the juice of the grapes. And in "Winter," Pan, now old and gray, sat on a bleak shore gazing at the hardly visible wraiths of the maidens as they pirouetted away over the ocean. These panels are still extant.

The group of murals for the Midland Hotel in Manchester was finished in 1903, and it seems to have pleased the critics even more than it did Borglum, who admitted that he was pleased with it.

The central figure in a panel twenty-seven feet high showed Sir Lancelot escorting Guenevere to King Arthur's court. Lancelot, "the chief of knights and darling of the court," and Queen Guenevere, the loveliest of the ladies, were in the foreground on horseback, traveling through a leafy English wood. Mounted men in armor followed at a distance.

The eleven paintings that accompanied Lancelot and Guenevere back to England were scenes from *A Midsummer Night's Dream*—Queen Titania asleep with Oberon's love potion in her eyes; Titania's encounter with Bottom, the weaver; her adventures with Quince, the carpenter, Starveling, the tailor, Snout, the tinker and Flute, the bellows-mender—all in a fine, fantastic humor. Gutzon was still at work on this group on June 30, 1903, which was the day before he started for England to make delivery and supervise installation. He was very ill with typhoid fever that year, and his cash had disappeared. Friends about the studio took up a collection to pay his steamship fare to Liverpool.

Borglum's last years in England were marked by a tremendous emotional depression. His journal, in places, becomes almost incoherent as he attempts to analyze mental suffering. He found relief in work, and he worked incessantly.

He painted murals for private homes and made the illustrations for at least two books, *The Spanish Main,* with pictures of old war galleys, and *King Arthur,* with especially fine drawings of oak trees a thousand years old. He had some success as a portrait artist. He painted the likenesses of a large number of the aristocracy at whose country houses he was entertained. One of these was the portrait of Lord Mowbray, which was exhibited at Liverpool with the Lord Mayor taking part in the ceremonies. He mentions in his diary the painting of the composer, Clarence Lucas, who thought it a good portrait "that possibly might also be a work of art."

There is also some evidence that during the late nineties he was doing more and more work with sculpture. In his journal he mentions a lost piece, "The Return of the Boer," which brought considerable attention to his carving. It showed a man on horseback returning to his ruined home. He was a figure of complete dejection, his shoulders drooping, his head bent down. His rifle was before him across the saddle. The horse was sniffing at the burned bits that remained of a house. The statue brought plenty of criticism and discussion but no money. The Parisian who cast the group said it was *trop personnel* to be a financial success. Gutzon's only copy of it was borrowed by the dancer Loie Fuller for an exhibition and later left by her in a New York bank as security for a loan. Presumably it lies forgotten in some vault.

Another bronze group, "Apaches Pursued," had greater public appeal and was exhibited in several shows in Europe. It was decidedly popular in Turin, and a copy was bought for Kaiser Wilhelm II. It shows two horses in full gallop, one of the riders holding to a third man whom he has lifted off the ground in his flight. The critics were pleased by its composition, which was as striking as its animation.

Oddly enough, this group came back into public view in 1946 in an art dealer's window in Fifty-seventh Street, New York City. It was found to have been purchased by a Philadelphian at an auction sale of the effects of "Diamond Jim Brady." A copy made from this is now in the Witte Art Museum, San Antonio, Texas.

All in all, in 1900 Gutzon Borglum was one of the most popular artists in England. He lived in a comfortable villa, he had plentiful work, and what he did was enthusiastically received. And mental dejection did not keep him from having a rather full and varied social life.

In a letter to Mrs. Frémont he mentioned meeting a Madame Helen Bricka, who brought his work to the attention of the Duke and Duchess of Teck of whose household she was a member. Gutzon visited the Duke and Duchess and so met, and threw into the air, a little boy who grew up to be the Duke of Windsor and, for a time, the King of England.

Through Madame Bricka he was summoned by Queen Victoria to bring his work, both painting and sculpture, to Windsor Castle for an exhibition. But for a young man born on the shore of Bear Lake, Idaho, the invitation was not clear enough. One may be permitted a bit of speculation as to what might have happened if he had caught the meaning—if he had paraded with his work under royal patronage before the aristocracy of Great Britain. But it is futile thought. He sent his art to Windsor for an exhibition, but he never met the queen. It never occurred to him that a queen might want to see him.

He had a very successful one-man show at Macmillan's in Bond

Street, and he made many friends in England and France, some
of them American artists. Some of these appeared later in his life
and in his correspondence in the United States. One of them was
Carl Sobieski, descendant of the famous Polish general. Another,
who noted his experience entertainingly, was the writer R. M.
Eassie. He told Gutzon of hearing of his connection with the
Angels of St. John the Divine, in the heart of Africa, thirty-five
miles from the nearest whites.

One of Gutzon's last entries in his London journal tells of a
party in 1901 at his home, "Harlestone Villa," in St. John's Wood.
It is worth mentioning in that it honored Isadora Duncan and
marked her debut as a dancer.

Gutzon had known the Duncans in California. Isadora's father
had recently been in London and was on his way back to America
when his ship, the *Mohegan* foundered off the Irish coast. The
sculptor had gone from England to take charge of Duncan's
body and to see that he was properly buried.

Isadora, her brother and sister had come from California after
their father's death. August Borglum, Gutzon's brother, was a
guest at the party and always recalled the impression Miss
Duncan made as she danced out from the studio onto the lawn,
scattering red rose petals that she had been gathering in the villa
garden. Isadora, Gutzon observed, brought an active revival of
memories from home. "The fresh western breeze that came with
her," he said, filled him with nostalgia.

Very likely it did. Shortly afterward he had gone over to Paris
and was standing idly on a street corner. It was a day like any
other in his life except that he had had a brief meeting with a
casual American tourist in a café, and that there was an unusual amount of cash in his pocket.

Suddenly there came to him an irresistible urge to return to
the United States—to go home. All his pent-up irritation over
spiritual repressions and his grievance over decadent art conditions in Europe surged over him at once. He leaped at a passing

"ABRAHAM LINCOLN"

This statue, in front of the Newark courthouse, was Borglum's own favorite.

cab, offered double fare if he could get to the Gare du Nord in time for the boat train . . . and so, presently, he had passed through Cherbourg and was on a ship headed for America.

This ended an era in his life and marked, definitely, the beginning of another. He was never to return to Europe except for the placing of work he had produced in the United States.

CHAPTER SEVEN

QUIET IN NEW YORK

THE FIRST THING Gutzon Borglum did in New York was to join—or, perhaps, originate—a movement whose object was to make American art distinctive and national. This was a bit out of the ordinary. Gutzon, so far as he had expressed himself, hadn't much concern about American art. What he had seen of it annoyed him, and he didn't intend to give much time to its promotion. He was presently to return to England . . . but somehow he could never find time to book a passage.

In the early days of the twentieth century his journal mentions, and many of us unfortunately remember, European and classic influences were dominant in art. Our public buildings were often Greek or Roman temples adorned with sculpture right out of Homer's mythology. In New York the extreme example of this tendency was a building erected by some art society on Lexington Avenue which was decorated across the front with a frieze from the Parthenon in Athens. The New York version of the frieze was so exact as to include all the mutilations that the march of hundreds of years had inflicted on the original.

Artists—painters, sculptors, musicians alike—had to have studied abroad before they could get a hearing in America. But, unfortunately, most of the people who patronized art learned about the subject from a few simple home rules. They were break-

ing out of the awesome, gewgaw-enveloped homes of the eighties
and nineties and moving into chateaus imported by the boatload
from France. But there is no record that any art dealer ever succeeded in selling an American house to some customer in Paris.

It often happens that a convert to a religious sect is more fanat-
ical in his beliefs than one born into the fold. Gutzon's father
had come to the United States from Denmark to escape the ancient fetters of thought, and Gutzon himself had become thoroughly disillusioned by his years abroad. He considered America
to be the last stronghold of freedom for the spirit. And he believed
that the time had come for the country to express itself culturally.
He had a theory that many people are born Americans though
their physical birthplace might have been Denmark or Poland
or Timbuktu. He insisted that although America was compara-
tively a young nation, the significance of her discovery, coloniza-
tion and development offered rich sources for the painter or
sculptor seeking decorative themes. He wanted architects to stop
copying classic models.

He was a great admirer of Louis Sullivan's individual art, and
he understood it. Once, driving through a small town in Ohio
that he had never seen before, he suddenly stopped the car and
went back to look at a red-brick building. "Built by Sullivan," he
said. And so it was.

The subject of the Prix de Rome scholarships, in his opinion,
was debatable. He thought it a mistake to send talented young
artists to Rome during their most formative period and expose
them to the overpowering influence of the great masters. He
lived his theory, for he did not see Italy until late in life, rather
than lose his individuality in the presence of those giants, Michelangelo, Da Vinci and Donatello, whom he deeply revered.

Borglum came to America a sculptor. He painted very little
after 1901. Among his first direct contacts with American art
methods on the Atlantic coast was a competition for an equestrian monument to General Grant to be placed in Washington.

He devoted a great deal of time and thought to the making of a model and worked it out in fine detail. Grant and two other officers on horseback were mounted on a high pedestal, Grant a little higher than the other two. Around the base of the pedestal and extending out on both sides was a rich frieze of figures more than life-size, showing events leading to the Civil War, the struggle itself and the period of reconstruction.

Gutzon was told afterward that Augustus Saint-Gaudens, all-powerful in the selection, had thrown out the model because he felt that no sculptor in America could carve so elaborate a frieze and that he suspected foreign help.

Subsequent steps in the contest are interesting as an indication of how memorials were sometimes produced in those days. The jury could not decide which of the two remaining models was best, so each sculptor was asked to submit a second model. It happened that Solon Borglum had made the horse on which the principal figure was riding in both models. The two sculptors called for help and Solon said that he would do what he could for whichever one got to his studio first.

The disappointed contestant went to Gutzon and asked him to provide a horse, but Gutzon refused to compete with his brother. As it turned out, the one who received Solon's help a second time was given the commission.

Neither of the brothers thought that Gutzon's unwillingness to enter a contest was anything but routine. Solon and he were devoted to each other. Gutzon had called him away from ranch life to develop an art sense that became remarkable. Gutzon had instructed him personally and had helped to finance his career in Cincinnati. He believed himself personally responsible for giving Solon a chance at a sculptor's career; he could never consider himself free to accept any commission in which he thought that his brother might have an interest.

Only once again, in Cuba, did Gutzon Borglum enter a competition. He steadfastly refused to accept attractive offers on the ground that the principle was wrong. A sculptor, he said, should be selected for his known ability to do what was asked of him and should be allowed to offer a variety of designs, if necessary, until he produced one that was satisfactory to the committee. He declared flatly that it was unjust to ask an artist to risk his best effort on a gamble, to ask him to spend his time, energy and money on something that might only be thrown away. It is interesting to note that his ultimate declaration on this subject was made after his Cuban experience. That was something that he failed to talk about.

The question of talented artists losing their identity in work for other artists, sometimes of less or even mediocre ability, was a grievous one to him and caused many heartaches with which he frankly sympathized. Often talented artists could not even *get* a job in another studio, no matter what their ability. Such a one was Paul Nocquet.

Paul Nocquet was a Belgian of real ability who had known Gutzon in Paris and had come over to be near him. Eventually he lost his life in a balloon ascension which he had undertaken in sheer despair. In an open letter to the *Evening Sun* he called attention to the humiliating role played by unrecognized artists in this country, all of which gave Gutzon Borglum new voice. Borglum wrote:

I have read with astonishment and pleasure the letter by Paul Nocquet pleading for the sculptor's art in America. It is no exaggeration to say that a large part of the sculpture in this country is produced under false pretenses. Much of it is from the studios of celebrities, the labor, the thought and even the basic ideas of poor devils who are paid so much a day.

That the abuses Mr. Nocquet speaks of exist, there is abundance of proof. A glamor has been thrown about sculpture here that is not deserved. For a century the bulk of us have ambled along timidly, following a single lead, sniffing the trail, only to assure our questioning souls that we were on the beaten path. We fear a new lead. We placard our homes with safe, old sentiments. We permit no passion, no action, nothing to disturb the even tenor of a puritanism that has hardly warmth enough or blood enough to produce great sculpture and that rarely ventures beyond the meaningless nudes that disgrace our museums.

If this were not so, Mr. Nocquet would have no complaint. If character and individuality were even tolerated in American sculpture, our production by proxy would cease in a fortnight. Let the people have what they feel the need of. There is something deep in the souls of all of us which seeks the real thing. Then our ideals, our lives and our passions will be expressed in our art. When that is done each man will express himself, and a new value will be placed on every work of art.

Such outspoken criticism inevitably brought from the caves all the winds of controversy. They merged in a tempest in 1908 when the sculptor wrote in *The Craftsman:*

With the passing of Saint-Gaudens the standard of good work was taken from us. . . . Not *great* work, for he was not a great artist like Rimmer, Rodin, or Meunier, nor was he a great poet. Nor was he a great technician like Falguière or a dozen other Frenchmen. But he had a quality that persisted to the end and wrought, with few exceptions, something beautiful, often noble, something that left the whole world better because it was made. He gave us Farragut (in Madison Square) and one or two other great statues. Then he dropped to the architect's standard, the lay figure, and there he remained. Curiously his Farragut contains figures in the base that appear to have been made years after the figure of the Admiral, so quickly does he seem to have lost his youthful spontaneity.

Saint-Gaudens' sense of refinement led to conventions, and his lack of imagination to a repetition of these conventions. Another thing—I do not recall in all his work one single group of creation that may be called a "pipe dream." In other words, I do not know of one work of Saint-Gaudens that was not commissioned, that was not suggested to him and produced for another.

I speak thus because I believe few people realize how little sculptural art is shown in this country that is purely the output of the sculptor's imagination, produced creatively because the sculptor has something he must say. Saint-Gaudens, master that he was, was a great workman; he was not a creator. It is but natural that his following should, in their effort to catch his spirit, acquire only his style. His reserve becomes in their hands more reserved, his architectural and impersonal manner more mannered, and we have a pseudoclassic school which for dull mediocrity is without a rival in the whole field of art.

This analysis of another man's work did incalculable harm to Gutzon's position in New York art circles. The controversy became nationwide when the newspaper headlines announced, "Borglum Attacks Saint-Gaudens." Partisans joined the argument with more zeal than discretion, and the wrangling went on without end.

Another controversy that swirled about George Gray Barnard and his undraped figures on the Pennsylvania Capitol in Harrisburg caught up Gutzon in its progress. Borglum had a wholehearted respect for Barnard and took up cudgels in his defense, thus further antagonizing the "sourdoughs," as he called the Academicians.

Long afterward when Barnard was excluded from his studio on the Billings estate, which had been bought for a public park, Gutzon offered him his Stamford studio to work in and, at Barnard's request, appeared before the New York City Board of Aldermen in an effort to iron out his troubles with the city.

Barnard's "Two Natures" and Gutzon's "Mares of Diomedes" were the first pieces of American art purchased for the Metropolitan Museum. Of the former, the sculptor wrote:

"The 'sourdoughs' took 'Two Natures,' perhaps the finest marble in its dimensions by an American in our country, and as quickly and quietly as possible relegated it to the basement. Not long after my 'Mares of Diomedes' followed the same descent."

His antipathy to the National Academy was based on his observation that there was too little fraternity about it and always a lack of *esprit de corps*. It followed too much the general tendency of all academic organizations against anything new, he said. It was probably his undiplomatic manner of expressing his convictions that aroused the enmity of the older set, who successfully kept him out of any monumental work in New York City.

One grievance the younger artists did have. There was no place where they could exhibit their work. In harmony with Gutzon's desire to establish a fairly representative American art was his crusade to obtain a fair deal for young American artists. In 1912 he helped organize a new Association of American Painters and Sculptors which would provide exhibition space for new and unknown youngsters.

A novel feature of the constitution of the new society was that it declared against juries. Every member was entitled to exhibit; only the amount was to be decided by a committee. A certain amount of space was reserved to invited work and no work not invited might be shown. Should any member wish to invite the work of a nonmember and fail to get the approval of the committee, he was permitted to give up some of his own space to the stranger.

Gutzon was delegated to publish this statement of the principles of the organization:

We have joined together for the purpose of holding exhibitions of our own work and the best procurable examples of contemporary art, without relation to school, size, medium or nationality.

We shall make our exhibitions as interesting as they will be representative of American and European Art activities.

We have no canons but honesty and ability to express one's self. We do not believe that any artist has ever discovered or will discover the only way to create beauty.

Unfortunately, at its first exhibit the association was split on the very rock that was to have been its bulwark—the representative quality of the work. This was the exhibition, at the Armory, made famous by the "Nude Descending a Staircase," in which neither

the nude nor the staircase made much difference. The painting
was an orgy of color and distortion.

Gutzon had no quarrel with that. He lived by Voltaire's principle: "Sir, I absolutely deny the truth of your statement, but I
shall defend to the death your right to make it." What hurt and
angered him was that, by election, he was responsible for the
exhibit, and that the committee had rejected work which he had
approved and had accepted work that he had not even seen. Their
excuse was, "We don't care about the constitution. We are trying
to get up an exhibition." Sadly the sculptor resigned saying that
no other course remained to him.

He came home to Stamford profoundly dejected. After a silent
dinner he remarked: "I wish I had a million dollars in cash."

"What in the world for?" Mrs. Borglum inquired.

"I'd shut all those struggling young painters in a room and
throw it at them," he replied. "It would keep them while they
were hunting up something to do besides art."

He told of some of the studios he had visited while organizing
the new association and of the hard time some of the students
were having. Nearly all successful artists have been through such
trials but not many of them remember.

The National Sculpture Society had elected Gutzon to membership in 1903 shortly after his return from Europe. Here, too, he
found among the younger set a feeling of revolt against the older
members. He suggested changes in the constitution that enlisted
strong support from some of the members. However, President
J. Q. A. Ward took exception to this threat to his power and refused to let the report of the committee favoring changes come
to a hearing. Promptly the sculptor denounced such tactics as
"unfair and discourteous," which did not add to their friendship.
Most of the reforms were later adopted.

With the National Arts Club his relations were more pleasant.
When the club had to move to other quarters he helped make
the selection of the Gramercy Park site and was given full

charge of the food department which had fallen deeply into debt. Under his personal management the dining room soon showed a profit—a most difficult thing to achieve in any art club.

Borglum belonged to the Salmagundi Club, to the Fencers, (where he used to take lessons from a Cuban fencing master in the studio) and to numerous flying clubs. His lifelong memberships in the Players of New York and the Metropolitan of Washington gave him constant pleasure and satisfaction.

He taught one year at the Art Students' League in New York and returned the fees he received for teaching as prizes to his pupils, several of whom are now outstanding sculptors. At the time of the San Francisco earthquake and fire in 1906, he joined with other New York artists in donating works to a public auction for the relief of artists caught in the disaster.

Through his old friend Jacob Schiff of Kuhn, Loeb and Company, he got the fund through to California in record time. Another of his old friends, Arthur Matthews, San Francisco painter, was the custodian of the money. He did so good a job of spending it that a considerable sum was left over. The balance lay in a bank for forty years until it was turned over to a new committee by the State Banking Commission in 1946. The chairman of the committee was William B. Faville, the architect, another good friend. But by that time both Arthur and Gutzon were gone.

The sculptor became involved in so many outside matters that one wonders how he could have found time for them. His answer was that life and art are inseparable.

He wrote for a magazine in 1908 that the three elements absolutely joined for the production of great art are sincerity, individuality and reverence. He said:

Of reverence, I doubt if there is enough in all the United States to build one great temple. I doubt if there are men enough in all this land with unselfishness enough and love enough to build one great and beautiful shrine for commerce or industry, for liberty or art, for religion—from the bottom up, perfectly good, like an altar upon which the most sacred thing in our lives shall be offered to all the rest who follow.

Gutzon was a poet, but he seems also to have been an observing realist. He continued:

Art applied to utilitarian purpose is, proportionately, a larger interest in our lives than what have come to be termed "Fine Arts." I see no difference between them myself. I find in my study of art that the real artist is nine tenths of the time a craftsman. It is only in that small one tenth of his time that he rises to the elevated position of prophet and master.

The question of art education in general involves what I call "betrayal by democracy," though perhaps I speak with the prejudice of personal experience, being one of nine children who had no college degree. When democracy came into the American world the great mass of the people felt that the only advantage aristocracy had was "higher education." The world has taken that up in as blind a way as it takes up so many other things. While higher education goes on apace, machinery has to step in to supply the instant need of many things that before were made by hand, and all kinds of work that we used in the building of our homes has deteriorated.

In man's essential world the water color has changed to the lithograph, the drawing to the Kodak, and so on down through life. Man no longer sees. His eyes no longer search the form, line and color of any piece of work. His fingers no longer test the art and finish found on old master crafts.

I never look at a spoon or a knife or a fork, a table or a chair, but I wish to correct and improve it. I think our spoons are badly made. The prongs of our forks are too long and the blades of our knives are too long and badly shaped. It amazes me that such utilitarian articles are not designed for the purposes that they are intended to serve.

Some years ago I was sketching in California. A man wandered by and watched me a little while. "Why do you do that?" he asked. And when I wanted to know what he meant he told me. "I mean painting," he said. "Why do you do it at all?"

With reference to art, that is the most astute question I have ever heard asked. *Why do we do it at all?* I hope that those of you who care anything about art will never forget it. That question ought to be put to you in all you do in art, and it ought to guide you in your work. . . . *Why do you do it?*

On the subject of art schools he wrote bitterly:

I have said, that the higher education we were promised has failed, for it has taken away from the great body of the people their only opportunity to express themselves. That is why I am hammering on the value of craftsmanship for the real leaders in fine arts. We have taken from the race that great body of workmen from whom artists should come, and in order to supply a place for the man of an artistic temperament we have built art schools—institutions which, so far as I have been able to find any record, had no existence at all in the time of Phidias or during the great period of the Renaissance. We are teaching art as a fine art —a subject that cannot ever be taught at all.

He urged reforms in art education—reforms that have since come about. On this subject he wrote:

The art schools of this country turn out young men and women by the thousands every year, and mostly they aren't worth fifty cents a day to any artist or sculptor. It is a very sad fact.

The economic independence of every human being who feels that he or she wants to study art is something that we should not lose a moment to assure. I think the sweetness of life is not so much affected by any other dozen causes as by the present inability of the race to express its emotions in a creative way. If sociologists and humanitarians could help this great body of youths to put their little heartaches into some beautiful, individual expression by creating some article in daily use, this pent-up tension, everywhere at the breaking point, would be used up at its source, as are springs of living water. And their work, their contentment and their power would be felt in every home.

The message seems important because so patently the truth. Gutzon Borglum was certainly a master craftsman, from the design of tools to the art that was his profession. It is significant that while he always preached a doctrine of change and modernity and was soundly berated by the academicians, he never produced anything cabalistic. Down deep in him was the understanding of what people were thinking about and what they could understand.

They understood him best, perhaps, when he was denouncing something. He had a keen eye, a vibrant voice, and, undoubtedly, a fine vocabulary with which to do the denouncing.

CHAPTER EIGHT

VARIETY OF LIFE IN A STUDIO

GUTZON's first studio in New York was originally a barn that extended across the rear of some ancient brownstone-front houses in Thirty-eighth Street near Third Avenue. He transformed it into one large room with a high skylight and a narrow balcony across the end opposite the entrance. Under this, behind the spiral stairway, was a dressing room, then a door leading to a little fountain and a storage place for clay and coal, and finally an inglenook with built-in seats on both sides of the fireplace and shelves above them for books and bric-a-brac.

To enter the studio you passed through a green door opening from Thirty-eighth Street, along the old driveway bordered by geraniums to the proper entrance which led into a small anteroom. On the street door was a sign gruffly announcing that visitors were received "By appointment only." But it was easy to get to the anteroom; and no matter how hard a secretary might try to carry out orders, Gutzon would certainly call out a welcome to anybody who owned a voice he recognized. His studio was only a step from Grand Central Station; so many of his friends dropped in just to watch him work. And because he had decided to love all mankind and knew that many of these people had come from a long distance, he would never let them be turned away.

There was always something going on in this place until the day he moved to Stamford—politics, social reform, park improvements, drama, and sometimes sculpture. And in the background was a phalanx of New York's clever people, studio helpers, secretaries, models, friends and acquaintances. They flowed in and out at all hours of the day and night, and there seemed never to be any end to them.

Among his early helpers were Marian Bell, daughter of the inventor of the telephone, and her friend Alice Hill of Washington. Gutzon probably enjoyed making the pair of them sweep up the studio and mix clay. Once he made them dye untold yards of muslin until their hands were completely discolored. Art was difficult, he told them, because it was made up of so many different, disagreeable things. But, somehow, they liked his instructions, and they looked on the studio as a second home. Alice was married there to Frank Harris, a musician and inventor of an electronic pickup system to transmit music over the telephone. It was demonstrated successfully before an audience in the American Museum of Natural History in New York.

Other helpers developed into sculptors with independent studios of their own. Among them were George Lober of New York; Merrill ("Bud") Gage of Santa Monica, California; "Bob" Garrison of Denver and New York; M. F. Malin of Salt Lake City; and William Tolentino of the Philippine Islands. Tolentino had been recommended by Mrs. Woodrow Wilson.

Malvina Hoffman, though never a studio helper, was a familiar practitioner in it and often a guest of the Borglums. Gutzon gave her occasional technical advice, beginning with her first attempt at carving. She had modeled a head of her father on the end of a piece of lead pipe with no proper armature, and was copying it in marble. Another New York sculptress, Ethel Hood, whom he met later, impressed him so much that he invited her to work with him in the Black Hills, but by that time she was too busy in the East.

Perhaps the most indispensable worker and helper was Robert ("Bob") A. Baillie of Closter, New Jersey. Gutzon repeatedly called him "the best marble carver in the United States." He started in the Thirty-eighth Street studio to work on the carving of figures for the Cathedral of St. John the Divine, and remained there steadily for ten years. When Gutzon began to be called away more and more from New York on distant commissions Baillie's work for other sculptors increased, and in time he was one of the most sought-after assistants in New York.

The models, too, were interesting, but only a few are remembered now. There was a man with a white beard who had posed for many sculptors, including Mr. Barnard. There was Lord Methuen's former valet who had lost the weekly payroll while returning from the bank. Best of all was sweet, gentle Julia Percy, who posed for some of Gutzon's best marbles.

She married a sculptor who had worked in the studio and went with him to California. Unfortunately the marriage was not happy and ended in divorce. Long afterward, in 1947, she wrote a few recollections of her life in the studio:

During my youth while working as a model for Mr. Borglum, his talks to students talented enough to be invited to the studio were always of a constructive nature. He gave advice as to their outlook on life and conduct of living. The younger ones were told that they could set an example in their schools and be a help at home. His reverence and respect for womanhood were well known by all who were acquainted with him.

Talent and sincerity were what he looked for. He had no use for plagiarists—"cribbers," he called them—especially in the field of architecture. He had a keen sense of humor and many a laugh we all had at the way he would tell of an amusing incident he had seen. One of his sayings when referring to someone who lacked initiative was, "You can't pick up custard with a hook." He also could tell a man's character by a look at his clothes. If worn for any length of time, he said, they seem to take on the lines of the body.

When making a statue or a portrait bust in marble, he would first model it in clay from life. Then a plaster cast from the clay figure was made by the studio help. The stone cutter used the plaster figures to measure from and, with the aid of a pointing machine (with three points), he would cut the stone to within an inch of the finished surface in some parts. Then Mr. Borglum would take over, working with mallet and chisel direct from the model upon the marble. If a defect in the marble showed up (which in my experience occurred only in the cream-colored Maryland marble), he would cut deeper and set the whole figure back or change the pose slightly to escape the flaw.

To do the finishing he used fine tools and sandpaper, every now and then wetting the marble with a sponge to help bring out the lifelike effect he was striving for. His high ideals inspired me to do my best to express in the pose the spirit of the idea he was portraying in the marble. I consider it an honor and a great privilege to have worked for him.

An entertaining character who worked in the studio and slept there was a Japanese called "Humbo" by the others; and there was another student from Japan, scholarly Takamura, who was admitted by an introduction from Daniel Chester French and a somewhat exceptional letter written by himself. This notice had begun:

If you will not take me, I must greatly disappoint myself. I must have no work, no study, no hope, no pleasure. My coming to this country must end by all in vain. Please, please let me have your favor, just like Mr. Honpo. I do not care much of money. I shall be quite satisfied with only a little, if you could. I will do anything you order. Pray accept my request, sympathising with a lonely little soul from a far country over the sea.

Other models included young Lieutenant Phil Sheridan, who spent many hours posing for the equestrian statue of his father in Washington. Among the horses were Smoke, a Virginia hunter, and Halool, a thoroughbred Arab imported by Walter Davenport, the cartoonist. These horses wandered about the studio on the days they were needed, and were perfectly gentle. They were kept at a riding academy in the park where Gutzon occasionally rode bareback with a group of army men.

Edith Wynne Matthison, the actress and a dear friend, posed for the heroic-sized figure called "Rabboni" in Rock Creek Cemetery at Washington. That figure is in startling contrast to the beautiful, brooding figure of the Adams Memorial by Augustus Saint-Gaudens in the same place. The "Rabboni" expresses joy and hope, while the other is complete negation. Still others who came to pose were the Mortimer Schiff children of whom the sculptor made a portrait relief to accompany the portrait of the Jacob Schiff children made in the previous generation by Saint-Gaudens.

One of the sculptor's most revered friends was John S. Clark, much older than himself, who came all too seldom from Boston. He was engaged in writing a life of John Fiske, the historian, and took a great interest in the sculptor's work. He liked most of all the marble figures of "Conception," "Motherhood" and "Martyr," which he spoke of as a trilogy. In a letter written in 1907 Clark makes this interesting comparison of literary and sculptural work:

I daily realize that I am engaged in a task not unlike several you have in hand. I have really to create an imaginary portrait of a great man with mere words. My task is to create so distinct an image that it can be realized by the imagination as a truthful representation of the real man. In the process of work I have to employ many of your methods for producing effects, and I can see more clearly than ever before how widely different is genuine artistic work from imitative work of literal reproduction.

Whether you come to Boston or not, know this—that you stand in my heart as one of my dearest friends and that there is no success or honor that comes to you that does not warm the "cockles of my heart" to a ruddy glow.

In those early days in New York, before Gutzon became involved in many big public memorials, he had more time to express his creative fancies or "pipe dreams" in marble. A larger than life-size nude figure of a woman which he called "Conception" or "Inspiration" caused some stir and was considered too daring in certain circles. To him it represented the holiness of creation, and his small marble called "Wonderment of Motherhood" was produced in the same reverent, humble spirit.

A second marble figure symbolic of motherhood represented a woman on her knees, holding up her infant child in her arms as if offering it on an altar. This was a step toward his marble "Atlas," a female figure on her knees, about four feet high, holding a globe representing the world in her arms, lifting it up to God instead of balancing it on her back as in the old mythology. Of his "Conception," which with other of his works was exhibited at Columbia University, George Luks, the painter, said:

Here in all the sublimity of majesty we see the symbolism of life, the symbolism of love, affection, devotion and piety. Like the chrysalis that liberates the butterfly, we see the soul that hovers above this classic piece of marble. We seem to feel the same thrill as we watch the distended lips that drink the breath of life. We wonder. There is something in this appealing countenance that strikes us with peculiar awe. We see a soul rising above passion. We feel the same admiration that we do for a flower that forces itself up through the muddy soil into a new life and light—a sort of emancipation. We see the early morning sun break through the skies of splendor, the unfolding of the rose, the *Wille zum Guten,* the revelation.

The group called "I Have Piped and Ye Have Not Danced" was produced in the studio at about this time, but never during his life got out of the plaster stage because Gutzon could never afford a large enough piece of marble when he had the time to carve it. The thought of it had been in his mind a long time. The initial idea, he said, had come to him at a concert where Ysaye, the violinist, had been playing. The way the women stood up at the end of the concert, arranging their furs and chattering about where they were going next made him feel that the music had passed completely over them, leaving no impression. He exhibited the female figure alone as a pastel sketch in Boston in 1901, where it elicited the following description of the group from Lillian Whiting, poet and art critic:

It is the ideal figure of a girl, her hands thrown up and clasped to the right, the head turned a little to one side, and the countenance bearing the most inscrutable expression. She has been piping to Pan, who lies at her feet unmoved, unrecognizing, until she drops the pipes and the melody ceases. Then he is aroused and turns to see why the music is heard no more. It is one of the most typical interpretations of life. The artist paints his ideal vision. The poet offers his dream. The musician sings his song. And the world goes on, careless, unheeding. At last, saddened and spent for want of that sympathy which should have made life all joy and ecstasy, the painter turns his canvas to the wall. The poet drops his pen. The song of the singer is heard no more, and the world turns to ask the meaning of this silence.

Since Borglum's death the figure has been carved in marble and is in California.

In the meantime a very large "pipe dream," something made for his own pleasure, the sculptor said, was gradually taking shape in his New York studio. His love for horses and the exceptional opportunity for studying their movements at the Baldwin ranch in California were still bright in his mind. They always were. He said once that he never saw a horse anywhere that he didn't study it and learn something new.

In his studies for the Grant competition he had become acquainted with army equipment, and he later began a group of artillery horses with their trappings. Because such externals were bothersome to his composition, he abandoned them and concentrated on horses alone, adding the figure of an Indian for interest. He was familiar with the ways of those expert riders—how a man could decoy horses out of a corral and by riding around and around them until they followed his mount could lead a dash into the open. That was the moment chosen by the sculptor for his group—five wild horses in full gallop.

The group was cast in bronze by the Gorham Company and exhibited in their window on Fifth Avenue. Not only because the action of those horses was very lifelike but because the plan was wholly American in both subject and design, it attracted instant attention and was purchased by James Stillman and presented to the Metropolitan Museum. It happened that Sir Purdon Clarke, an Englishman, was director of that institution at the time.

For a long time it stood in the entrance hall and was almost the first thing that caught the eye of the visitor. Near it was Rodin's "Age of Bronze," a slight figure which was one of Gutzon's favorites. School children, who were taken on regular tours through the museum, used to vote the horses as their favorite exhibit. The name "Mares of Diomedes" was given to the group by some classical scholar who recalled the story of Hercules and the wild horses of King Diomedes. The sculptor never cared much for the name; it harked back too loudly to outworn mythology.

More and more Gutzon's sense of the bigness of America, of her value to the world, of the importance of her heroes, was growing upon him. He had bought a large block of marble and one day began to carve the head of Abraham Lincoln—his first experiment in colossal sculpture. He worked on it for weeks until it became a perfect likeness of the man, but still he worked while watchers feared that one more stroke of the chisel might ruin the whole work. And then a miracle happened. Suddenly a real character seemed to look out from the carved features. The face became inhabited.

A colored woman, whose duty it was to sweep the studio and to whom that huge block of marble had always been a nuisance because she couldn't push it around, at last raised her eyes from the floor and exclaimed in astonishment: "How's Mista Bo'glum know ol' Abe was in dat rock?"

The head was taken over to Gorham's and exhibited in their window. Robert Lincoln, son of Abraham Lincoln, happened along and he also exclaimed in astonishment, "I never expected to see Father again." Later he wrote that he considered it the best likeness of his father that he had ever seen. Truman Bartlett, who had made a study of all the known portraits of Lincoln, went farther, saying there had not yet been sculptured a head of Lincoln that could compare with it.

It was the centenary of Lincoln's birth, and Gutzon, as a matter of sentiment, asked President Theodore Roosevelt if he would let the head stand in the President's room at the White House during Lincoln's birthday. Roosevelt welcomed it and after it had gone back to New York wrote to inquire what had become of it. He said he wished it could be kept in Washington permanently.

The letter was brought to the attention of Eugene Meyer, Jr., who bought the colossal head and presented it to the nation. Congress, in accepting the gift, specified that it should be placed in the rotunda of the Capitol, never to be removed. As a demand for replicas began to be heard, the superintendent of the Capitol grounds allowed the sculptor to make a copy of it in plaster. Bronze duplicates of it are now at Lincoln's tomb in Springfield, Illinois, in the Hall of Fame in New York, in the University of Southern California and in the collection of the Chicago Historical Society. The sculptor made another head for himself, which is now at the Detroit Museum of Art.

The carving of this head in marble, done as a labor of love, had far-reaching consequences. It brought to Gutzon friends and admirers. It led, undoubtedly, to his making the seated figure of Lincoln in front of the courthouse in Newark and finally to the carvings at Stone Mountain and Mount Rushmore.

CHAPTER NINE

THE BIRTH OF A MYTH

THE BUILDING of the Cathedral of St. John the Divine at Morningside Heights, New York, might have been done for Gutzon Borglum alone. At any rate, it had his close and abiding interest for a number of years.

"It is a fine example not only of medieval art but of the spirit of the early churchmen," he said. "It is something out of another age untouched by pretentiousness and vanity."

So he was immensely pleased in 1905 when he was asked to make the statues for the structure and to supervise the carving on the Belmont chapel, the first section of the cathedral to be finished. It was a definite honor that must have been coveted by most of the sculptors in New York, and out of sheer enthusiasm for the work he agreed to make models of a hundred saints and angels. The fee wasn't anything that could be called remunerative in itself, and Borglum was presently to learn that medievalist sculptors had about as many troubles as moderns.

It was in this pious undertaking that he laid the groundwork for the first of the stories about his alleged evil temper. He was profoundly disturbed by this development because, he argued, he didn't have any evil temper at all. He could have admitted, however, that he was saltily vigorous in defense of what he decided was right. But anyway, the longevity of what he titled an unfounded legend frequently puzzled him.

He knew from the beginning that he had a large order. In addition to the topmost figures on the outside of the chapel there were larger, more detailed ones of the Virgin, the boy Christ, two saints and two angels. About the inside were any number of historic church dignitaries, bishops and saints. And there was a concourse of other symbolic figures in the King and St. Columbia chapels. Altogether there were twenty life-size statues outside and about seventy-five smaller ones inside. It has been pointed out by one shrewd observer that the chances for disagreement between the sculptor and the architects and committee members were virtually unlimited.

Heins and Lafarge, the original architects, had listened to discussions ten years before any of the building was started. They had listened to the reports of sundry committees who never came to them with anything but grief. And, if they were like other men, they must have become fairly callous and a little deaf to each new sound of woe.

G. L. Heins, State Architect and a member of the firm that had designed St. John's, seemed to have some doubts about Borglum. It is not quite clear whether he thought the sculptor too headstrong or too argumentative. Gutzon wrote to him a singularly polite letter at the beginning of his commission, outlining the Borglum theories of ecclesiastical art. And by that nobody could have been offended.

"There it will stand to praise or damn us," Gutzon said, "not so much concerned whether we have been wise or not, but whether we have been sincere or not." Heins replied to that but, unfortunately, his letter has been mislaid. One gathers the purport from the sculptor's answer. Gutzon wrote:

I agree with you about making the figures as archaic as possible. Still, if a little of the unstudied natural charm that was creeping into sculpture about the time of Donatello should appear in the figures of Christ, the Virgin and the two saints, I think that the gain in real beauty would be a great advantage.

It will be interesting to hit upon a character of interpretation in the sculpture of this great church that will be at once religious in the best sense, profiting even by the mannerisms of the Middle Ages, yet clearly a distinct product of the larger, modern view.

The sculpture should be what I feel you are making your architecture, no slavish interpretation of what has preceded, but an intelligent adaptation of what has proved best, not forgetting the large human view that our western civilization, in its best moments, holds in all matters religious.

That seems to have ended the architect's worries, although the sculptor appears to have had plenty left. Shortly thereafter a visiting English architect, E. W. Hudson, wrote this in the journal of the Royal Institute of British Architects:

Mr. Borglum's work shows a marked originality, tending even to impressionism. His determination not to sink his individuality has brought upon him the criticism of a passing generation of contemporaries working in Gothic, whose sympathies are with the archaeological exactitude of the Revival, and who strive to get as near as possible to the effects of a past age. On this account Mr. Borglum will probably have to wait awhile for full appreciation, as M. Rodin himself has had to wait. He seems, however, indifferent to praise or blame, and appears determined to retain his individuality, although it has involved the refusal of commissions for collaborating with architects whose buildings in American cities require as the *summum bonum* exact compliance with conventional precedent.

This critique seems a little out of step in view of Gutzon's declaration that the figures on the cathedral should be "made as archaic as possible." But he never took notice of it. He went on for months with his work, vigorous and pleased with all that went on about him.

When he raised his voice, however, all of New York heard him. He had discovered that John Barr, the contractor, was sending his models to a Hoboken stoneyard to be finished by machinery under contract. This, of course, had not been written in the bond. The machine treatment may have made the pieces look more archaic, but it also made them look cheaper. Some of them looked less like saints than gargoyles, and Gutzon was angrily indignant.

For once the art committee gave him a quick hearing, and presently he was allowed to exercise general supervision over the contractor's work and accept it or reject it as he saw fit. But that wasn't the end of the controversy. The contractor, it seems, wasn't so much interested in the shape of an angel as he was in the price of rock. He began to change the position of arms and legs and wings to suit the contours of his blocks of stone. Borglum declared that these revised figures were caricatures, and he condemned them. The contractor wouldn't listen to him. The committee gave him no satisfaction; so this time he carried his complaint to the press.

Borglum seems to have been his own best public-relations agent. He demanded that the carving of the stone should be done on the cathedral grounds under his own eye. Inasmuch as this was strictly in keeping with the medieval tradition in church building, he had one faction of the cathedral's congregation backing him to start off with. The art critics generally thought his point well taken, and thousands of people who knew nothing at all about sculpture wondered what was the use of models if they weren't to be followed.

Borglum won his point. A working studio was established on the cathedral grounds, and there Gutzon supervised the carving. He shared honors with his assistant sculptors, Price and Gregory, who had come over from England. Their names are signed to the work they shared in. Only the contractor thought that the sculptor was hard to get along with.

Many of the statues which Gutzon had condemned were recut and properly placed. The seventy-odd interior figures were one of the largest collections of images of religious leaders ever gathered under one roof since the beginning of the Christian era. They were also the largest collection ever carved by one artist. And as revised, they began to look somewhat respectable. Every detail of miter, chasuble and coat of arms was perfect. There had been much correspondence to determine the finger on which the pontifical ring should be placed.

By this time Gutzon had worked amicably with the cathedral authorities for two years. His early arguments about machine-cut statues were forgotten. And then came an incident which made people conscious of him again. A bit of newspaper confusion gave him a reputation for bad temper that he carried for the rest of his life.

It began in the meditations of Dr. John Peters, canon of the cathedral, in a bourn far from newspapers and street-corner arguments. Dr. Peters, all of a sudden, had become a little uncertain about the sex of angels. He wasn't at all controversial about the matter, but he thought that he should convey what he had learned to Gutzon Borglum. So, in an innocent way, he did. In a letter to Borglum he wrote:

Dr. Huntington calls my attention to something that in the execution of the statues I had quite overlooked. He points out that the Angel of the Incarnation is named in the Bible as the Archangel Gabriel.

Now Gabriel is a masculine name, and, in point of fact, unless I am mistaken, the archangels are thought of as masculine— Michael, Gabriel, Raphael, etc. I am perfectly aware that in art one meets frequently a feminine angel type bearing the lily of the Incarnation, but is that really correct? Should not the heads of both these angels and the figures in general be made if not distinctly masculine, at least not distinctly feminine?

There you have all the correspondence on one side of this important controversy. Gutzon's reply is appended because it is all that was said on the other side. He wrote this to Dr. Peters:

My Dear Dr. Peters, I have your letter referring to the feminine character of the angels. I fully recognize the correctness of your criticism from the standpoint of the Bible, though art and tradition have practically ignored this. I shall change them as you suggest.

One might have thought that Gutzon's quick acquiescence would have ended the "controversy" over the angels. But things seem to have been different in the rarefied atmosphere of the cathedral grounds. Severe trouble was on its way the moment Dr. Peters dropped his letter into the mailbox.

Gutzon wasn't much concerned with the sex of the angels. The model of the Angel Gabriel was still in soft clay. It was a simple matter to remove the offending face and model one with sterner features. Gutzon kept the original face, had it cast in silver and used a photograph of it as a Christmas card. It brought to the Borglum home a signed photograph of Bishop Potter. Everything was sweetness and light until a reporter noticed that Gabriel's countenance had quit being pretty and amiable and was now a little hard . . . and analytical and dour. The discovery pleased him and he made a quick departure for his office.

The next morning his story appeared under a headline that didn't seem to fit it:

BORGLUM SMASHES ANGELS IN A HUFF

Other newspapers took up the cry and soon the subscribers were filling the press with their personal, and no doubt authoritative, opinions on the intriguing subject: Were angels men or women?

Gutzon wasn't much concerned with this argument. He didn't think it concerned him. And, save for the fact that the first story had pictured him smashing up things in a rage, he was probably right. It seemed good fun, but twenty years later, during the Stone Mountain disagreement, a reporter dug up the original story to prove that Gutzon's temper was ungovernable and always had been. The Atlanta *Constitution,* trying to ferret out the truth, telegraphed the cathedral and got a reply from Dr. Peters: "Angels still stand serene in their places where Borglum put them," he said. "We never had any trouble with the sculptor."

The story of how Borglum smashed the inoffensive angels went on, however, for years and years—and it still goes on. The evil that men do, somehow, never lives as long as some of the evil that they never thought of doing. Borglum, however, did think that destruction might have been a good idea.

The last time he heard reports that he had gone berserk in his studio on the grounds of the Cathedral of St. John the Divine, he sadly shook his head. "I didn't think of it soon enough," he said.

CHAPTER TEN

PUBLIC MEMORIALS

IT ISN'T REMARKABLE that Borglum had virtually all the work he could do in the early 1900s. Nobody in New York seems to have been talking about anyone else. He was no mute and long-suffering artist. He was somebody who knew how to answer back . . . and he did . . . and the press loved him.

Gutzon was not disturbed because many of his commissions came to him through people who knew nothing whatever about sculpture except that it was expensive.

"It's no matter," he would say. "If they knew anything about it, they'd probably be calling for somebody else." Nevertheless, it is true that the commissions came from people and localities as varied as those he had to do with in his own swirling life. There is, for instance, the story of the John Mackay statue in Nevada. It begins with the revival of his boyhood friendship with Bob Davis, and it is typical of how things came to him.

One day in 1908 in some puzzlement he answered a telephone call from *Munsey's Magazine* and heard the explosive voice of Editor Bob Davis, a voice he hadn't heard in nearly twenty years.

"I knew you in Los Angeles—remember?" the editor began. "I have something in your line I want to talk to you about. Can you have lunch with me?"

So they had a reunion at a hotel near the studio and a pleasant meal during which nothing at all was said about sculpture. Gutzon thought that Davis was going to ask him to write an article and had quickly decided to do it. Then suddenly Davis came to his subject:

"Borglum," he said, "would you like to make a statue of John Mackay?"

"Of course," Gutzon answered in astonishment. "Who wouldn't make a statue of a citizen like that?"

"Well," said Davis, "my brother Sam is in town. The state of Nevada has trusted him with a commission. The state has authorized and voted some money for the statue, but Clarence Mackay has taken over the responsibility of financing it. So if you will take the job——"

"Let us go and see Sam," Gutzon suggested. The next day, after a meeting with Mackay, he got the commission.

Gutzon was more than ordinarily pleased. He was doing a lot of work but nothing spectacular. He had known of Mackay since boyhood and felt that a statue to him would attract national interest.

John W. Mackay, lest people of our war-tossed world forget it, was an international personality for several reasons. He was, among other things, one of the Big Four of the Comstock Lode, a silver king and a builder of the first cable laid across the Atlantic. He had been a consistent fighter with a tough constitution and no feeling, ever, that he could fail to win.

Gutzon told Clarence Mackay that he would need all the photographs that might be available of the man and also all the data, news and rumor about him that might still be extant. Mackay saw the point. He not only gathered up all the information that his agents could find, but he visited the studio every morning on his way from Long Island to Broadway and spent a half hour reminiscing with the sculptor. Gutzon presently began to feel that he knew John W. Mackay pretty well.

The statue, inasmuch as it had to stand in the open, was sched-

uled to be eight or nine feet tall. Because of the static nature of
the material, Gutzon said, anything less than that would look
smaller than human. He made careful sketches to determine position, expression and general composition, and all of this took several months.

"I want to show my father as he was," Mackay said, "a workman in the mines out of which his wealth and his position in
life came."

Because of this the model showed the capitalist in the dress of
a miner—top boots, loose shirt open at the throat and shapeless
working trousers. The left hand was grasping a pick handle
against which the body leaned. The right hand was upturned,
holding a piece of quartz.

Clarence Mackay liked it. When it was done he asked Gutzon
to take it to Nevada and find a place to put it. "It is very difficult
work to make a statue," he said. "I think it is more difficult to find
the right spot to display it. And I think the man who is qualified
for one job is best qualified for the other."

Thus began a new and complicated adventure. Gutzon met
Sam Davis and went to Carson City, Nevada, carrying letters of
introduction to state officials. There they met Governor Sparks,
who looked interested but extremely puzzled.

Carson City was without parks, city squares or, for that matter,
any cultivated landscape. The governor scratched his head and
said, "Doesn't seem to be much place where you could put a statue
around here . . . unless you want to stick it out in the middle of
the street."

The local organizations—patriotic, political, business, social—
all had something of the governor's attitude but were guided, in
public action, by good old Western individualism. Each one suggested where Gutzon could put his statue, but no two could reach
an agreement. The sculptor labored with them for several weeks
and got very annoyed. He began to think that there was no reason
for locating the work in Carson City. The right place for it, he

STONE MOUNTAIN

WORKING PLATFORM NEAR SUMMIT OF STONE MOUNTAIN

MODEL, OF STONE MOUNTAIN GROUP

thought, was Virginia City, where Mackay had operated. But Virginia City was in worse shape than Carson.

He came one night to the home of Sam Davis, after a weary day with a government committee, and asked if he would object to communicating with Mr. Mackay about where to put his father's statue. Sam burst into laughter. "You're growing up," he said. "Go as far as you please."

Gutzon picked up the telephone and called Joseph Stubbs, president of the University of Nevada at Reno. He never could explain why he picked President Stubbs except that he had met him and found him to be just the sort of man to develop a university in that sort of town. At any rate, he called and asked, "Would it interest you to have a statue of John W. Mackay on the campus of your university?" And Stubbs said, "Certainly . . . or is this a joke?"

At Gutzon's suggestion the president sent a telegram to Clarence Mackay asking him if he would consider having the statue in Reno on the university campus. Next morning the sculptor received a telegraphic order to call on President Stubbs. A place for the memorial was located at the upper end of the campus facing the sun. It was behind a corrugated-iron shack which bore the label "School of Mines."

In a short time the statue was dedicated with proper ceremonies and a tremendous turnout of important people. Clarence Mackay, who brought his friends from New York in a private car, didn't like the School of Mines structure as a background for his father. So he telegraphed architect Stanford White in New York to come out and lay plans for a new one. The result was a new building which cost, before Mackay equipped it, $475,000. After that came a second and a third building which, with Mackay's endowments, cost somewhere over $1,500,000.

That, to all intents and purposes, was the beginning of a new life for the University of Nevada. The statue that led to it cost, complete and erected, $12,000.

And it led to other things, too. Clarence Mackay was obviously a satisfied customer. He wrote to Sam Davis that he was so pleased that he had tried to discharge some of his debt of gratitude by recommending the sculptor to the sponsors of the Sheridan Memorial to be erected in Washington. Gutzon was definitely gratified. His study of the Civil War in preparing the model for the Grant competition had made him familiar with its leaders. And he loved Sheridan's saltiness, activity and audacious courage.

He respected the general's reputed ability to swear and his genius for making his men understand tirades that must have sounded like jabberwocky.

"A great general!" declared Borglum. "And unusual!"

Unfortunately, the United States government had already placed the commission for this memorial and the field was now open to all because the original artist had not yet produced a model satisfactory to the committee. He had been at it thirteen years.

A second misfortune lay in the fact that this sculptor was J. Q. A. Ward, president of the National Sculpture Society, who had failed to see eye to eye with Gutzon on many subjects, chief of which was the controversy over reorganizing the society. In spite of this he and Gutzon had exchanged letters expressing sorrow that there had been any bad feeling. The last thing Borglum wanted to do was to give further offense to the distinguished leader of the New York sculptors . . . but he did make the memorial. Art was art, and he got it done on schedule.

Gutzon found it easy to open correspondence with the committee in charge of the memorial. He had long been acquainted with President Theodore Roosevelt, and he had met some of his military aides through their common love for horses. It was arranged to have Mrs. Sheridan and her son visit the Thirty-eighth Street studio. They came and reported that they liked what they had seen—the model for the Grant monument with its three horses, the dashing horses of the "Mares of Diomedes" group, the marble head of Lincoln.

There was still some delay about the granting of a new contract. Gutzon was interviewed. He sent photographs of his work to the committee. Presently, however, he was contemplating his old annoyance. The committee suggested a competition. Gutzon Borglum refused.

"I shall be happy to make a sketch model for the committee's consideration," he said, "but only after I have received a contract."

After much discussion the committee gave in. The contract was awarded, and Gutzon made the sketch model as he had agreed. The sketch was eventually cast in bronze and presented to the Officers' Club of Rio de Janeiro as a gift from the Officers' Club of Washington.

The uncovering of the general's life brought contacts with many of his old comrades in arms, including a close friend, General George Forsyth. Colonel Royal E. Whitman, an old Indian fighter who had ridden with Sheridan in the Civil War, wrote Gutzon dozens of letters covering all sorts of details. He even declared he could produce the actual accouterments of Sheridan's horse.

Sheridan's horse, as is well known, is preserved stuffed and mounted on Governor's Island. Borglum wasn't much interested in it. It was unthinkable to him that a dead horse could pose for the one that carried Sheridan on his wild ride to Winchester. Through Colonel Whitman he had bought a Virginia hunter named "Smoke" who had the run of the studio and was a tractable pet. In due course "Smoke" qualified as Sheridan's mount.

One remarkable thing about the memorial—an innovation that now has become almost commonplace in art—assured its success. Sheridan was presented not as the older man he lived to be, but in his prime and at a supreme moment in his career—the turn of the Federal retreat at Winchester. Gutzon pictured the moment when the general, returning from a conference with Lincoln, came galloping to meet his fleeing soldiers.

In the statue he has pulled up his horse and is waving the men back into the fight. There is fury in his eye and, as the sculptor felt, a historic phrase on his lips: "You will sleep in your tents tonight or you will sleep in hell!"

Gutzon modeled the horse and rider in clay, in the size that they would have in bronze, which was another important characteristic of his work. He never turned over a small model to others to have it enlarged by mechanical process, as was being done by some sculptors. He wanted his own modeling, the imprint of his thumb, to appear in the finished work. He wanted to get the spirit of the action and pose. If he were to expend creative effort on a sketch, he declared, he would have lost interest by the time he came to make an exact copy on a larger scale.

There has been considerable controversy over Sheridan's ride to Winchester. Some writers, like Joseph Hergesheimer, have maintained that the wild gallop was only a mild trot. General Crosby and General Forsyth, brother officers of Sheridan, favored the accepted version. So would any cavalry officer. No matter how he might have been riding at the start, he was certainly riding as fast as the horse could take him when he came up with his defeated command. An eyewitness of the ride, Private Frederick Bullis of the New York State volunteers, reported:

I was near enough to him to touch his horse when he got there. There were lumps of foam as big as my fists on the horse's face, and his nostrils were bleeding. Sheridan stood up in his stirrups and yelled "Face the other way! Face the other way!" He kept yelling it over and over. He was swinging his sword and swearing like a demon.

The monument was unveiled with much pomp and circumstance on November 25, 1908. Mrs. Sheridan herself pulled the

cord that held the draperies in place. There was a parade of the
armed forces that included every branch of the services. There
were speeches by notables and concerts by brass bands. There was
also a long account of the event in the Omaha *Bee*. The correspondent identified Gutzon Borglum as an Omaha boy, which,
indeed, he once had been.

The turbulent figure of Sheridan was acclaimed as one of the
greatest military statues in America. Critics noted the anatomical
perfection of the horse and the faithful picturing of the general
as a young man. But their praise was for the terrific action in
bronze sculpture—the captured fear and climax of battle. It is
hard to imagine that this memorial and the monument to President Lincoln in Newark were both the work of the same artist.
Lincoln, shown in a moment of deep dejection during the Civil
War when the news from the front was bad, is pathetic. He is
every man's friend just as he is every man's other self, face to face
with unhappiness, harried by disaster.

It was Lincoln's custom to visit the War Office late at night to
get the most recent dispatches, and the memorial in Newark
shows him after such a call. He is sitting on a bench, his tall hat
beside him, dispirited and alone. Borglum's idea for the statue was
inspired by a letter from Lincoln to a friend shortly after his election. "I could appreciate the feelings of Christ in the Garden of
Gethsemane. . . . I am now in my Garden of Gethsemane."

Borglum received the commission to make this statue as a result
of the exhibition of his marble head of Lincoln in the Capitol.
Amos Van Horn, Civil War veteran and citizen of Newark, had
bequeathed $150,000 for three public monuments, one to Wash-
ington, one to Lincoln and a third to the soldiers and sailors who
had fought in the War between the States. He appointed three
executors, chief of whom was Ralph E. Lum, a Newark lawyer
who knew nothing of Borglum or his work except the Lincoln
head. That seemed enough evidence. He gave the sculptor the

commission for the Lincoln Memorial and thereafter was always his steadfast friend.

The work was carried out under pleasant, amicable, understanding relations. There was no competition. The executors had virtually no suggestions. They knew that Gutzon Borglum was a competent sculptor, and they left the details of the production to him. He submitted a small model which they considered and accepted. After that he made a full-sized model in clay. The location chosen for the memorial was in front of the Newark courthouse where much grading and change was needed. The city lacked a thousand dollars of enough to pay for what was needed; so Gutzon advanced the money to Park Superintendent Carl Bannwort. The architect who drew the plans for the setting was an old friend, William Price. The architect, Bannwort and Gutzon contrived to give the statue a perfect environment, and Bannwort seemed surprised to see it finished. "It's the first time," he said, "that I ever heard of a sculptor ever giving back a part of his own pay."

Work was begun in 1909, and a year later the Gorham Company announced the arrival of the full-sized plaster model at their foundry in Providence, Rhode Island. The sculptor had asked that they cast the bronze in one piece, which cost forty per cent more and took more time. He thought it worth the extra expense because there would be no seams in the bronze and no danger of breakage due to extremes of heat and cold.

Gutzon was pleased with the work when it appeared in bronze. "Lincoln never left the Garden of Gethsemane," he said. "He went right from Springfield to the labor of war. And Lee had hardly surrendered when Lincoln was shot. It is a curious and charming picture when you realize that he wandered away constantly into this garden alone."

There was much favorable comment on the work after it was set in place. The sculptor himself thought that he had never made a finer thing. The appeal of the statue is evident in the actions of the children who cluster about it. All day in summer they come here to play. They sit in Lincoln's lap, clasp their arms about his neck, roll about his feet, completely pleased. They could not say why. They don't know much of who this man is supposed to be. They don't know much about Lincoln. But they know his sadness and they feel his gentleness and friendliness.

Former President Theodore Roosevelt was principal speaker when the monument was dedicated on Memorial Day, 1913. Wildly cheering throngs of men, women and children lined his way of march and gave him an inspiring tribute all the way from New York City, an experience which Gutzon declared was what gave Roosevelt the idea of running for President for a third term.

Nobody seems to have remembered what he said as he pledged the country's support to what Lincoln had stood for—Lincoln who sat with bowed head, worried and disconsolate, on a bench before him.

CHAPTER ELEVEN

STAMFORD AND POLITICS

In 1909 John Gutzon Borglum married Mary Williams Montgomery, to nobody's great surprise. Mary Montgomery was born in Turkey of missionary parents and had lived there twelve years. She was educated at Wellesley and received a Ph.D. degree from the University of Berlin. She could argue with Gutzon, sometimes successfully.

Their meeting, in a way, was accidental. On her way back to the United States after her Berlin studies, she had boarded a ship at Rotterdam. It turned out to be the same one that the sculptor barely caught at Cherbourg. He joined her party for shipboard games and poker, and they were quickly friends. He met her family and she became well acquainted with his sisters; and a family association went on for years.

Miss Montgomery taught French for a year in New Haven, then joined two other girls in a literary agency that did translations, research work and special articles until they married and broke up the partnership. She worked with Dr. Henry Smith Williams on *The Historians' History of the World* and there met Rupert Hughes, another friend of Gutzon's. She also worked with Dr. Isidore Singer as manager in the preparation of *The Jewish Encyclopedia*. Much of her life was spent in the vicinity of Thirty-eighth Street. After leaving Dr. Williams she did secretarial work, some of it for Gutzon, and became acquainted with many more of the Borglum friends. She learned a great deal about the operations of the Thirty-eighth Street studio.

So, in 1909 they were married at Short Beach, Connecticut, with a New Haven divine, Dr. T. T. Munger, and Miss Montgomery's two brothers officiating. The Borglums went for a honeymoon to some trout stream in Canada and thence to a place on the Gunnison River in Colorado. By that time Mrs. Borglum was certain that her life was going to be vastly different.

And so it was. In 1910 Gutzon announced that they would move to Stamford, Connecticut, where they would cultivate peace and associate with gentle, quiet people. Almost overnight he was making speeches for the common man and beating the drums for politics.

In Stamford he was promptly introduced to the famous Connecticut Town Meeting and was intensely interested because he had never heard of anything like it. He went home with staring eyes to write that he had just learned the part an individual could play, first in his home town, next in his state and finally in his native land. He rewrote a pair of sentiments from his diary: "A man's first love is his mother; his second, his sweetheart; his third, art; his fourth, *all.*" And he underlined this warning: "No individual's life is worth the immortality he seeks unless he articulates the voice of his tribe."

You may take that as typical of Gutzon. He had been in Stamford one or two nights and he belonged to it as much as the oldest inhabitant.

The moving from the old duplex apartment in New York to the country was a momentous undertaking. The two horses, Smoke and Halool, were taken to New Rochelle for the night by the faithful Banks. The next day Gutzon and a friend, like knights of old, rode on horseback to the new domain. The feat wasn't so startling to beholders as it might have been in New York. Horses in Stamford in 1910 were regularly in view and con-

tinuously in use. Gutzon himself became a familiar figure in the
countryside as he drove Smoke back and forth between the railroad station and home. Wife and furniture arrived in Stamford on
that first day by train and van.

Most of the stable equipment came from the old establishment
of Colonel Whitman in Washington. Much of it accompanied the
colonel, who arrived to spend the summer. The procession of visitors who came to luncheon, to dinner or to spend the week seems
appalling from this distance of time, and emphasizes the contrast
of that era when there was no difficulty about entertaining. Stamford grocery stores of the day were primitive. They made no delivery to the Borglum ménage six miles away; so hampers of food-
stuffs were shipped by express twice a week from New York.

The old farmhouse was completely rebuilt, partitions pulled
down and new rooms added. The house stood on a slope, and one
large living room was dug out of the bank after the master bed-
room, above, had been finished and was being lived in. The barn,
which had been close to the house, was hauled a thousand feet
and placed beside a brook. The brook was dammed to make a
pond. Gutzon took an active part in all the digging, trimming of
trees and laying out of roads.

Road building had always been one of Gutzon's hobbies, and
in later years he was to become associated with national highway-
building projects. On his place in Stamford he built a road, cutting the arc on the Wire Mill Road, which until that time had
passed close to the Marshall House, the new home. The town accepted the sculptor's changed road and thirty-five years later it
was still in use. After the passing of those years a local highway
engineer located and unearthed an old drainpipe, placed there by
Gutzon. "Well," he said, "Borglum was known throughout the
town as a good builder."

Filled with the old Town Meeting spirit, the sculptor quickly
organized the neighbors living along the main road leading into
Stamford as an association to beautify and improve their grounds

bordering on it. Next he managed to get lighting for the road from the town electric company and a similar gift for the Long Ridge Road, which was equally important.

By studying the town, county and state road-building and bonding regulations, he discovered that the town could borrow money against the stipulated return to it of the same amount from the state or county, thus securing funds for the building of improved roads at once. The matter was taken to the Town Meeting, of course, and it caused much debate. But eventually it passed, and both High Ridge and Long Ridge roads were benefited.

Then, presently, he had a new and interesting idea. He founded a bus company "so that," as he said, "the farm women might have a chance to come to town when their husbands are using the horses in the fields." He was very happy in the designing of bus bodies to be fitted onto Reo Truck chassis and in arranging a suitable pageant to celebrate the beginning of the service.

There is a lamentable lack of detail in available information about the bus company. One doesn't know if the farm wives were able to ride into town on it more frequently, or if Gutzon was able to pasture his horse. He got out of it after a while and turned his attention to new and more stirring projects. The general belief is that he operated it until it needed rewinding.

One of the amazing things about him is that his art work always seemed to survive his other projects. Soon after moving up from New York he built a temporary studio out of glass cold-bed frames and there began a monument for North Carolina of the first soldier killed on the Southern side in the War between the States. He also started a creative "pipe dream" in marble called "Orpheus and Eurydice." The boy who had been guiding the oxen for much of the heavy work on the place was asked to pose for Orpheus. His wife's remarks, as repeated by Bill the husband, were striking. When she was informed of his new and startling occupation she demanded, "Did you have to stand in your underwear?" "No," he said, "I just had to take everything off."

She prefaced her critique with a ladylike sniff. "Well," she said knowingly, "you must have been a sight. . . . Just a perfect sight!"

At this time a location for the permanent studio was chosen across the Rippowam River, nearly half a mile from the house. The corner rock was christened in champagne, accompanied by a stirring speech from Colonel Whitman. For years the only way of reaching the studio by carriage or automobile was through a cement-based ford, devised by Gutzon. There was a swing bridge for pedestrians. At the very outset of the work Gutzon had brought out his architect friend William Price of Rosedale, near Philadelphia, who had helped him with the Newark Lincoln and other work.

On the river, at some distance below the ford, a group of camp-fire girls used to have a summer camp under the guidance of Mrs. Lanier, whose husband was the son of Sidney Lanier, the poet. On Sunday mornings the sculptor used to give the girls talks on art and life which are still remembered.

The studio was built entirely of stone from huge, pinkish granite boulders which Gutzon had located within a few hundred feet of his location half buried in the soil. These were dug out, cut and scraped by a crew of Italian stonecutters who came from a neighboring town the first of every week and returned on Saturday, camping out in the woods near the work. The fireplace was unique. It was made to accommodate six- to eight-foot logs and was open to a height of ten feet from the floor, where sandstone blocks formed the mantel. The size of the building was forty by sixty feet, and the style was Tudor Gothic.

When it was time to lay the sills of the studio doors, before the roof with its heavy steel was up, Gutzon invited the officers of the Masonic Grand Lodge of both Connecticut and New York, together with members of his own Howard Lodge, to take part in the dedication. It was a grand affair although something merely on the rim of the arts. Gutzon was gradually increasing his interest in other matters. For one thing, he was being inducted into a knowledge of the working of an elected group in a community, chosen to govern the finances and public interests of the electors. This was his conception of the meaning of politics.

Another matter to which he had given attention was the often debated question of consolidation of the town and city governments of Stamford. He worked out a scheme which he placed before the town selectmen in 1912, whereby, in successive steps, the selectmen would be placed in charge of departments as commissioners thereof, and eventually the city government would be abolished. The selectmen-commissioners would take over its powers. Thus a joint-commission form of government would be acquired for both town and city.

He wrote to Frank Butterworth, a prominent Progressive of Connecticut:

I enclose herewith a scheme that was put before the selectmen of Stamford. . . . We cannot get rid of the town form of government in Connecticut, so it has occurred to me and a great many before me that we had better take the principle of town government with selectmen, which from the very fact that it is primitive is good, and develop that. My plan here is to bring everything in town and city under one government.

In all these dealings Gutzon had come into close touch with the political situation. It was common gossip that both town and city, more particularly the latter, were boss-ridden and that it did not make much difference whether a Republican or Democratic administration was in control. The same machine went on and on, and expenditures for services rendered were out of all proportion to values received.

The time was the dawn of the Progressive movement which aimed to do away with bossed and machine-controlled government, demanding honesty and efficiency in high places. A new national election, that of 1912, was in the offing. Gutzon's old friend, Theodore Roosevelt, was running for President on a third-party Progressive ticket. What was more natural than that the sculptor should enter this campaign with gusto. He became chairman of the Progressive Party of Stamford, and nearly wore himself out trying to arouse the progressive element in the citizenship of the whole state of Connecticut.

There was a strong element of drama in the campaign as waged in the city and town of Stamford. In the first place, the "Old Guard" was not going to allow a newcomer to meddle unchallenged with their ancient customs. One of the most respected members of the community wrote an indignant letter to the Stamford *Advocate,* the only local paper, protesting against the upstart sculptor who "had not been able to achieve fame in his own calling" and was trying to gain a little notoriety by attaching himself to Roosevelt's kite.

Gutzon addressed mass meetings from the Town Hall steps. He spoke on street corners and in front of the huge Yale and Towne Lock factory where men and women were going home from work. He got to be a ready speaker and learned to think on his feet. One incident was memorable. Some heckler had asked why Roosevelt had suddenly changed his mind on a certain question. "Don't you know," Gutzon shot back at him, "that Saint Paul lived to be fifty-two before he suddenly changed his whole way of life and became a Christian?"

People in Stamford still remember the picturesque and effective fight carried on by the Progressives under the leadership of the imaginative Gutzon. On one occasion a torchlight procession was arranged in which the Borglum donkey, "Shamrock," a large, gray, intelligent creature, appeared as a symbol of both the old parties, wearing on his rear end an elephant head, the trunk of which concealed his tail.

Two Stamford citizens, who were Gutzon's chief lieutenants in the fray and remained his friends ever after, were featured in the press of the day as "Handsome Harry" Abbot and "Young"

Arthur Crandall. The latter lived and worked with Borglum at one time and never got over his youthful reverence for Gutzon, which was not diminished by close contact. When he heard this book was being written he said: "Don't forget to mention his real humility," which was a side of the sculptor's nature revealed only to those who knew him best.

Joseph Alsop was state chairman of the Progressive Party of Connecticut, and Gutzon developed a deep friendship with him. Mr. Whittaker, editor of the Stamford *Advocate* for many years and a reactionary and autocratic individual, came to the Borglum farm one night about midnight to try to influence the sculptor to change his attitude. The mayor of the city, Charles P. Rowell, came out at dusk, wearing a big black hat and a long cape, like a villain in a play.

He would not come into the house, where someone might hear what he had to say, but asked Gutzon to come outside. They talked by the footbridge on the way to the studio. Mr. Rowell tried to make a deal, and when the sculptor refused he exclaimed with conscious drama, "Then it's a fight—a fight to the finish!"

"Yes," agreed Gutzon solemnly, "and a sword to the hilt!"

A few days after the election S. E. Vincent, the newly elected Progressive congressman, wrote to Gutzon.

With election over it is now time to figure up and take inventory of conditions. If I have a clear idea of how the Progressive party stands, that party has every reason to be proud of the results accomplished in a campaign of only ninety days, without funds or party machinery, with all the papers against our cause and some of them not overcareful about telling the whole truth.

Herbert Knox Smith, a Connecticut leader of the party, wrote on November 4: "I cannot let this fight close without sending you my heartfelt personal thanks for what you have done. It has certainly been fine, and I appreciate it more deeply than I can say. Best regards to you."

And the colonel wrote from Oyster Bay, November 12, 1912:

My Dear Borglum: In this great fight for elementary justice and decency, for fair play in the industrial no less than in the political world, and for honesty everywhere, there are many men to whom I feel peculiarly grateful, not only personally but because of what they have done for the people as a whole. You come high among these men; and in this very inadequate but far from perfunctory manner, I wish to express my profound acknowledgment.

Faithfully yours,
Theodore Roosevelt.

In his records Gutzon somehow fails to note that the Progressives, despite Roosevelt's defeat, did rather well in Connecticut. After all, what interested Gutzon was the fight.

CHAPTER TWELVE

CHICAGO CONVENTION

THE First World War started in August 1914, and was catalogued as somebody else's trouble by nearly everybody in the United States. Its effect on local politics was to start arguments about whether or not our government should spend money to rearm.

Anyway, the situation in 1914 was different than that of 1912. Woodrow Wilson, who had become President largely as a result of the Progressive-party movement in 1912, was being looked at askance by manufacturers, bankers, shippers and conservative politicians who thought that he was a mistake.

Borglum, still standing fast by the Progressive banner, figured that another election would see his party in power if enough people got interested in the prospect. At the moment, he pointed out to those who would listen to him, the policies of the federal government involved something besides a waste of money. Human lives were concerned. He declared that if England had been prepared, the Kaiser would never have invaded Belgium, and that he would certainly have stayed at home if the United States and England had been prepared and had showed they would support France. Theodore Roosevelt had always advocated preparedness. His words, "Speak softly and carry a big stick," were well known and often quoted.

In the crisis during the Congressional election of 1914 the sculptor did not advise Progressives to return to the Republican party. Instead he tried to persuade Republicans to nominate candidates whom Progressives could support. In Connecticut the Progressives held the balance of power. Gutzon did not believe that they should put a ticket of their own into the field. They should keep their identity, he felt, and place their power as a group behind the best candidates nominated by other parties.

At the same time, he believed that the Progressive element was stronger in the Republican than in the Democratic party. He advised adopting a liberal attitude toward Republicans to avoid a further breach with the parent organization. By following such a policy in the 1914 election, he hoped that by 1916 it would be possible to elect Theodore Roosevelt President. At all events, he considered a strong Congress essential in 1914.

After careful consideration Gutzon decided to support for Congress Ebenezer J. Hill of Fairfield County, a man who had previously been in Congress and had been defeated by the Progressives in the 1912 election. He chose Hill because of his stand on the nonpartisan tariff board, which he favored, and his open quarrel with boss rule.

The sculptor's stand for Hill was strongly opposed by Herbert Knox Smith of Connecticut and George W. Perkins of New York, national leader of the Progressive party. Gutzon and Perkins had an argument over the matter on Mr. Childs's yacht on Long Island Sound one night about midnight. Other Progressives were there, including Colonel Roosevelt, who appears to have been noncommittal on the subject of Progressives supporting Republicans. Gutzon always believed, however, that Roosevelt approved his action.

The sculptor was concerned only with what he believed to be right. He walked out of a meeting in March 1914 when Herbert Knox Smith had put through the state central committee a resolution that only enrolled Progressives could vote in the primaries.

Smith's methods were unfair, Gutzon declared, and he wrote an open letter accusing him of gag rule. Despite such difficulties, however, he did take time to prepare and deliver a resolution of welcome and allegiance to Roosevelt at a public rally held in Hartford in August 1914.

There is some evidence that to him politics had begun to look less like a fine tournament. To Isaac Ullman of New Haven he wrote: "I am pretty sick and discouraged with what is called politics. You know only too well what I mean—the sordid and selfish side of the little ones and their own personal advancement. The best we can do is to do our best, and I try to do that all the time. . . ."

Another disappointment to the sculptor in this campaign was the placing in the field, by the state central committee, of an independent Progressive ballot which he had consistently opposed. The fact that he was named candidate for one of the offices in no way placated him. He refused to let his name appear on the ticket, and he was bitter in giving his reasons.

In the 1916 campaign Gutzon again supported Mr. Hill, who had been elected two years before with about eighty-five per cent of the Progressives voting for him. But by that time the sculptor had become conscious of the political boss John T. King, who had appeared at the first Bridgeport meeting sponsoring Mr. Hill. The congressman entered into long correspondence with him explaining Mr. King's motivation.

A year later when Colonel Roosevelt met Mr. King in Stamford the sculptor wrote an open letter of protest to Roosevelt. The former President took the rebuke good-naturedly. When a reporter in 1918, during the aircraft investigation, asked Roosevelt if it was not true that Borglum was a traitor on account of his charges against the administration, Roosevelt snapped back, "What! Borglum a traitor? If he isn't a patriot there aren't any!"

"But Colonel," the newsman persisted, "didn't Borglum criticize even you?"

Roosevelt laughed. "Oh, that," he said. "Nothing! Borglum just didn't like the company I kept."

As for the national situation after 1914, the chief question was: "What will Theodore Roosevelt do in 1916?" It was discussed wherever men gathered. Come to think about it, 1916 is now some thirty-six years behind us, and to much of the populace the interesting characters of that season's presidential campaign are merely a confused collection of names.

Colonel Theodore Roosevelt, veteran of the Spanish-American War, governor of New York from 1898-1900, had been drafted to run for the Vice-Presidency of the United States in William McKinley's 1900 presidential campaign. He became President in September 1901, after McKinley was killed by the terrorist Leon Czolgosz, and was re-elected in 1904.

Roosevelt was a man of vision. He was popular and he was fearless. He was also an experienced and naturally shrewd politician. He began his service as President with an outcry against Big Business in politics. He dissolved the Northern Securities Company and other corporations for violation of the antitrust laws. In 1903 he instituted the Department of Commerce and Labor. Also in 1903 he promoted the Elkins Act which forbade railroad rebates to favored corporations. In 1906 he sponsored the Hepburn Act which regulated railroad fares. That same year he was behind the passage of the Pure Food and Drugs Act. And it was his influence that made possible the Reclamation Act and the employers' liability laws. He mediated the peace between Japan and Russia in 1905 and won the Nobel Peace Prize. By recognizing Panama he made possible the construction of the Panama Canal, which was started during his administration. He was a great showman and singularly active, and most Americans loved him whether they liked his political philosophy or not.

In 1908 he got the presidential nomination for his friend William Howard Taft, and Taft was elected. But there was some difficulty during the next four years. Roosevelt turned a bit sour on the President because he thought Taft wasn't liberal enough. A real political crisis came in 1912. Taft wanted the presidential nomination and he got it. Roosevelt, it seems, also wanted the presidential nomination. So he walked his delegates out of the Chicago convention and organized the Progressive party. Woodrow Wilson, the Democratic candidate, was elected.

The Progressives turned out to be a pretty strong organization, and they made some gains during the next four years. The split in Republican thought was still pretty wide when it came time to think about the 1916 campaign, and Theodore Roosevelt was still one of the biggest men in the country. There were some indications that in his promotion of harmony between the Progressives and the regular Republicans he might accept a nomination and run for a third term.

Gossip had touched on two other men who might be considered by the delegates—Charles Evans Hughes, who had been governor of New York for two terms, and Major General Leonard Wood, former Chief of Staff of the U. S. Army, commander of the Department of the East and close friend of Theodore Roosevelt. Hughes was an old-line Republican. Wood was a Progressive.

To the former President, Gutzon sent a five-page letter showing his fear for the disunity between the different groups and the certain disaster it could bring to the nation. He said:

You can be the next nominee for the Presidency of the U. S. if that is what you wish. But it will be wrung from the powerful grip of powerful forces, and I very much question the result that would follow such a conquest.

I think you should boldly and frankly name a man close to you, a man long known and tried by you, a man who would include you in his private councils. There is another advantage in this besides quieting the antagonism and putting the lie to a million or more irreconcilables. You would enter for good that position so enviable as the First American.

There was no doubt whatever that General Leonard Wood was
the man Gutzon had in mind when he made this appeal. He
had been on friendly terms with the general for years, and had
boundless respect for the abilities he had shown as a soldier and
as the chief administrator of Cuban affairs after the Spanish-
American War. He had never been more cheered than when a
newspaper reported that Colonel Roosevelt had himself proposed
General Wood as a nominee to be considered by the Chicago
convention. Promptly, in April 1916, he wrote to Roosevelt, "In
naming Leonard Wood, your lifelong friend, you have given the
conservatives and the irreconcilables the key to the threatened
deadlock, or, as some have boasted, 'deathlock.' You have said
the first thing that has been said to make impossible a bitter
struggle."

He had many friends who did not share his belief that Roosevelt would turn out to be altruistic at Chicago. It is interesting to
see how he clung to his faith in his hero despite all indication
that for once he might be wrong . . . and it is also a little pathetic.

Meanwhile, he went about the country on artistic commissions,
interviewing Progressive leaders on the way for the information
of George W. Perkins. He was on his way home from Atlanta
in May when he got a mysterious call to stop in Washington.
There he learned that Progressives had made overtures to the
Republicans asking that a representative acceptable to both
sides be chosen to act as a confidential go-between for the inside
leaders. An approach had been made to Colonel Roosevelt by
Congressman William B. McKinley of Illinois, who asked if
Borglum would be acceptable. The colonel had said that he
would. Gutzon was notified. And that is not the least fantastic
thing that happened at this fantastic convention.

Old Guard Republicans would not allow Roosevelt to be nominated, but they knew they couldn't win without his aid. They
were willing to accept Leonard Wood if Roosevelt wanted him,

and they were glad to have Borglum to carry such important messages.

The sculptor called on McKinley, then interviewed Colonel Roosevelt and General Wood. Their agreement, plainly stated, was that if Roosevelt could not be nominated, he would throw his influence to Wood. Others aware of this agreement were John A. Stewart of New York, and E. B. Johns, correspondent of the *Army and Navy Journal* in Washington.

Gutzon went to Chicago early in June and registered at the Union League Club. There he met Speaker Joe Cannon, Representative McKinley and other high-ranking Republicans with whom he kept in constant touch. Also, he visited Perkins and Governor Hiram Johnson and other Progressive leaders at Progressive headquarters. He was as widely and officially informed of the situation, he thought, as any man could hope to be. Everybody was friendly and straightforward. His great advantage, he felt, was that, as a well-known artist who had no political ties or aspirations, he was to be trusted. Well, maybe. . . .

Most of the lads he was meeting had never in all their lives trusted anybody. What Gutzon seems never to have realized is that he was squarely in the middle of what amounted to a species of civil war. The Republican party was definitely split—make no mistake about that—and its two factions, after giving the Presidency to the Democrats, had been doing well enough in other elections to survive. Neither side was as good as it said it was. Neither side could stand any losses. So the leaders of each side wore broad, confidential smiles in public, and in private they moved in the fashion of morose and wary conspirators. Each side feared the other with a real, practical fear, and each side looked on a messenger from the other as a self-seeking ferret who must be lulled by soft—and wrong—answers.

Excerpts from Gutzon's detailed report to General Wood give one coherent account of the convention, many details of which are still the subject of controversy after more than thirty years.

The sculptor shows himself to have been an able observer, though puzzled; and he seems to have overlooked one fairly evident feature—that Roosevelt in the midst of turmoil was serenely waiting for a miracle, well aware of his importance and convinced that in the failure of others he might well grow stronger. He certainly would have liked to be nominated . . . and who can say that he overestimated his chances?

In the beginning of his report to Major General Wood the sculptor said:

I had been in Chicago hardly twenty-four hours when I found out that the Progressives would not have anything to do with Republicans. They were playing a foolish game of waiting to be called on. They had even turned down the proposition of entering the convention on equal terms for the first few ballots and adjourning at will. Apparently they were afraid to run the risk, although they were boasting that they had as high as 400 votes. Where they could get half that number nobody knew but themselves.

On the subject of the Progressives' failure to join Republicans in presenting favorite sons in the early balloting, the sculptor wired Colonel Roosevelt on Thursday, June 8:

ONE OF THE MOST POWERFUL INDIANANS JUST SAID THAT IF YOU DECLARED NOW PUBLICLY FOR ANY CANDIDATE, THE REST MIGHT AS WELL GO HOME. HE ADDED THAT THIS POSITION CAN'T LAST. HAVE SEEN LEADERS OF OHIO, PENNSYLVANIA, NEW YORK, NEW JERSEY, INDIANA, ILLINOIS, NEBRASKA, CALIFORNIA, MASSACHUSETTS; ALSO HITCHCOCK, WHOM I KNEW PERSONALLY. BAD EFFECT CREATED BY PROGRESSIVES NOT DARING TO WORK ON FIRST BALLOTS WITH FAVORITE SONS. PROGRESSIVES PASSIVE TOWARD HUGHES. OLD GUARD SAY THAT UNDER NO CONSIDERATION WILL THEY ACCEPT HUGHES UNLESS FORCED.

Before this message he had sent two to the colonel on Wednesday, June 7: The first message read:

FAVORITE SONS SUCCEEDED IN PASSING RULE TO GIVE A MAN AS MUCH TIME AS DESIRED FOR NOMINATING SPEECHES. NUMBER OF FIVE-MINUTE SPEECHES UNLIMITED. THIS GIVES US TIME TO ARRANGE FORCES BEHIND WOOD IF YOU WANT HIM.

And the second read:

CRISIS REACHED. IF ANYTHING BUT PULLING DOWN TEMPLE ON OUR HEADS IS TO BE DONE WE MUST DO IT NOW. IMMEASURABLE CONSEQUENCES TO OUR COUNTRY AND VAST INEVITABLE ADJUSTMENTS FACING AMERICA HANG IN THE BALANCE. THEY WAIT FOR YOU. DELAY MEANS SUICIDE.

But there was no response from the big man in Oyster Bay.

On Wednesday and Thursday Gutzon received two telegrams from General Wood on Governor's Island. Both were hopeful. The first one read:

NO INDICATION ANY CHANGE IN ATTITUDE OF COLONEL. REMAIN IN TOUCH HERE FOR FEW DAYS.

And later:

SAW THE CHIEF YESTERDAY. POLICY AND ATTITUDE UNCHANGED.

The sculptor, putting all this together, continued his report to General Wood. Here is part of that revealing document:

Before three o'clock the next morning (Friday) I was awakened by 'phone call telling me that the favorite-son group had over 518 votes and that they did not need the colonel. That was the first definite rebuke, and my telegram of Thursday indicates my feeling at the time. I am of course bearing in mind what I learned months ago, and I cannot understand why Progressive leaders do not know it, or why the colonel did not know it—that he never had a chance in Chicago. When I found that he was not willing, or that his agents in Chicago were not willing to risk their ability on the floor of the convention against the favorite sons, I felt, and many felt, that they were simply playing poker with the threat of an independent Progressive convention back of them.

Thursday night I sat with a number of gentlemen at Union League Club. We went over the entire situation regarding the colonel's candidacy. There were in this group men representing three states that had favorite sons. Finally, after their declination to consider the colonel on any terms, I urged upon them your availability. I pointed out to them the colonel's friendship for you and his *absolute faithfulness* to the friendship, and I urged upon them the desirability of nominating you directly. They replied that they would be glad to do this and that in ordinary circumstances it would be done, but, because of their relation to the favorite-sons group, such a step would be considered disloyal and would endanger the whole situation.

They further said that your great value as a candidate was the colonel's loyalty to your lifelong friendship and that your nomination would secure the colonel's support of the old organization. After considerable debate I proposed sending a telegram to the colonel. This telegram was duly approved and Speaker Cannon remarked, "If the colonel answers that in the right spirit, we will know that he is sincere. And if he doesn't——" Mr. Cannon shrugged his shoulders. Here is the telegram:

"Colonel Roosevelt, Oyster Bay, New York, Thursday, June 8, 1916, 2 A.M.

"Please send me a line confirming your approval of Wood. Powerful members of Old Guard approve and ask your approval. They say he can be nominated. Address me, Union League Club."

I sent this telegram and, as you see, it contained my address and asked for a reply. I waited twelve hours, until about 2 o'clock in the afternoon. Having promised a reply to these Old Guard gentlemen, I was extremely anxious. I called the colonel on the phone and succeeded in getting him. The day was wet.

The wire was noisy and the connection bad. I told the colonel that I had wired him and was waiting for an answer. He replied, "Didn't you get my telegram?" I told him I had not. He then said he had answered my questions by telegram and told me that if there was anything else I wanted to know, to see his son Theodore. The connection was bad, the answer unsatisfactory.

I immediately tried to find Theodore, Jr., but could not locate him. I searched political headquarters in Chicago for the telegram the colonel said he had sent me. I went to the head office and had them search the wires, but could find no telegram. None had reached Chicago. I requested both companies to go back over the lines to Oyster Bay and locate the message. They did and reported in two hours that no message had been received at Oyster Bay or in New York for me from Colonel Roosevelt.

Following the failure to receive a telegram from the colonel that would support you, or any definite answer whatever on the subject, I sent another telegram warning him of the situation and the loss of time. And again I received no response. That there might be nothing lost by oversight on my part, I sent a copy of this telegram to you; also one to Mr. Perkins, together with a letter. Perkins, too, remained silent and continued to believe that Roosevelt would be nominated. At least he said so, and that no one else would be nominated or could be. Reports were being circulated bearing his name saying that you would not be nominated and that you could not be nominated. Perhaps I ought to add here that the only objection I have heard to your nomination came out of Mr. Perkins' headquarters.

Friday arrived. The convention was ready to ballot. We all waited on the result of the conference for which we had long worked and from which we believed some harmonious solution might come. It reported—failure. But we all still hoped. By that time we knew that the conference was not a party conference; that the Progressive party no longer had any authority, having lost what standing it possessed. The only conference now was between Oyster Bay and Republican leaders.

On the other hand, this Republican convention was the soundest, solidest body of men of that sort ever assembled in America. They were patient; they were independent; they knew the world of politics; they wanted the Progressives; they wanted the colonel to join with them in naming a President. They were even willing that he should try his strength with them openly. But 900 delegates absolutely declined to let him either force the convention or to destroy the party's chances of defeating Wilson.

About 2 A.M. Saturday all hope was really abandoned, and the most influential member of the Central States group said, "Well, no man can say I have not done everything, tried everything, and waited till the last minute to harmonize this situation. And here we are forced to move in the nomination none of us wants."

After two in the morning, quick and definite plans were made for the Saturday-morning session and wholly without consideration of Oyster Bay. What happened at Perkins' headquarters I do not know. But results came quickly and everybody soon knew that a great harmonious plan, each group compromising for the common interest, had failed, and the cause of its failure was at Oyster Bay.

The Central States had the key, and they had the moral courage to sacrifice personal advantage for the larger good. At 2 o'clock they took the bull by the horns and turned sharply to Hughes. Illinois and Indiana were from the beginning the brain and the power of that convention, and it was this powerful group that wished to work with the colonel and who favored you. When forced to follow another leader they showed their wisdom by selecting McCormick, a late Progressive, to announce the move of Illinois toward Hughes—which swung the whole convention into line behind them.

The reading of the colonel's message was unfortunate. It came too late. It was too long. In naming Lodge, it was as disappointing a thing as could be contributed by the colonel's worst enemy. It was met without applause of any sort. All Roosevelt interest died then and there.

Regarding your name at the Convention, it rose head and shoulders above the names of other candidates, and I heard nothing but praise of you, such as would most gratify a sincere man. Some fear of a military man was expressed, but I heard no one among the influential inner group of Republicans who did not always say, "Wood has a record. We can elect him if the colonel will work with us."

Several years later Gutzon learned, from inside sources not to be doubted, several items of information which threw light on the bewildering events of the last night of the convention. In relation to that urgent telegram to the colonel that was never answered, he learned that someone at Progressive headquarters had tapped the line to Oyster Bay; that Gutzon's message, which had been endorsed by Republican leaders who anxiously awaited the answer, was instantly followed by a message from Progressive headquarters saying that Borglum was all wrong, the author or victim of a "frame-up," and that the colonel would surely be nominated by acclamation on Saturday morning. It was presented that he, Roosevelt, should withdraw and nominate Senator Lodge, who would refuse by agreement, and the convention would then turn immediately to the colonel.

Another item was that Nicholas Murray Butler had likewise talked to Colonel Roosevelt on that fateful Saturday at early dawn and in answer to a query about Leonard Wood's chances had shaken his head. "Impossible," he said. "At this juncture in the international situation it would be suicide for us to nominate a military man." This was told to Gutzon by Herman Hagedorn.

All parties returned from the convention in a state of complete exhaustion. E. B. Johns wrote, "It was three or four days before I got back to normal, and I am still doing some mental swearing at the stupidity of Colonel Roosevelt and some of his advisors." For Gutzon it was one of the bitterest experiences of his life.

Wilson, it will be remembered, was elected by the vote of California after most of his newspaper support had conceded the victory to Hughes. It took three days to find out who had won.

CHAPTER THIRTEEN

AND DR. TRUDEAU

THREE WORKS that Gutzon Borglum completed around 1915 had nothing at all to do with war or politics. One was a tablet with a bas-relief sketch in honor of Robert Louis Stevenson, the second a touching memorial to Governor Altgeld of Illinois, and the third a simple and beautiful memorial to "The Beloved Physician," Dr. Edward Livingston Trudeau. The three are linked intangibly through the same fine quality of emotions that brought them into existence. The subjects of all three accomplished much in the world and were well loved.

Once in Stevenson's wanderings as a consumptive vainly questing health he stayed for a year at Lake Saranac in the Adirondacks in the care of the not-so-well-known Dr. Trudeau. Trudeau, also tubercular, had cured others but had started too late to cure himself. He was the central character of Stephen Chalmers' engaging book *The Beloved Physician*.

The idea of a memorial to Stevenson originated with Mr. Chalmers and was brought to the sculptor's attention by his friend Bob Davis. Gutzon was busy at the time working on two monuments in the South, and Davis caught up with him in Grand Central Station as he was boarding a train for Chicago. His interest was aroused, and from the train he wrote to Davis to say he would be delighted to do anything "to promote attention to this kind of men of genius." He further offered to make the bronze tablet, bas-relief of Stevenson and an inscription to be decided on by the committee for just what it would cost—somewhere around $200. The tablet would be placed on the cottage in Saranac where Stevenson had lived.

It was September 1915 before the sculptor could find time for a day at Saranac, where he looked over the ground, listened to all that was told him about Stevenson, was taken to see Dr. Trudeau and returned to New York on the night train. The work was finished and ready for unveiling in October of the same year, as the committee had hoped, "because it was the gorgeous month of the year." The only sad note was that Dr. Trudeau was not well enough to take a prominent part in the proceedings. He died the following month.

On receiving the preliminary photographs of the tablet, Mr. Chalmers wrote to Borglum:

I congratulate you on the tablet. You have done something in that bas-relief that Saint-Gaudens didn't do. You have brought out the spirit of the sick man who didn't believe in lying in bed, and the little uplift of his head is a perfect expression of "Come!" said I to my engine, "let's work anyway!" This thing requires no study. It hits you between the eyes first glance. I showed it to Mrs. Baker, who owned the cottage where the Stevensons lived, and the best compliment from that old lady is this: "Yes, it's just the way he looked when he was here."

A few months later Lord Guthrie, acknowledged leader of the Stevenson cult in Scotland, wrote:

Gutzon Borglum the sculptor, in his Saranac memorial bas-relief, has got beneath the surface and behind the mask as Saint-Gaudens, fine as his bas-relief is as a work of art, never did. I liked the first sight of Borglum's work, and it grows on me. It has charm, it has strength, and it has pathos. It is the invalid, but the invalid who can say, "O Pain, where is thy victory?" It is the fascinating personality of a man of genius who, with all his gaiety of manner, was yet, in the matter of essential principle, like flint.

Hundreds of people whom Dr. Trudeau had cured were anxious to erect a memorial to him, but were too poor to contribute substantial sums. They appealed to Gutzon, who again responded generously. He was deeply impressed by Dr. Trudeau's self-sacrificing work and by the devotion of the afflicted ones he sought to heal. He agreed to put up a bronze-and-marble memorial for the cost of materials—about $7,500. After studying the matter for some weeks he made a life-size clay model of the beloved physician seated out of doors, a rug over his knees, and invited the committee to come to his studio and pass on it. Mr. Chalmers wrote in the Saranac *News:*

By the end of the day something little short of miraculous had taken place, the sort of thing that may be called a miracle of genius. Before the figure was again shrouded in the wet clothes that keep the clay from cracking, it had become to us not a conventional photograph image but "The Beloved Physician" himself.

"Well," said the sculptor, stepping back with a smile, "are you satisfied?"

"Yes," said his visitor, but with hesitation.

"I know what you miss," said Mr. Borglum. "It's the artificial something you used to consider Dr. Trudeau's expression." As he spoke he was modeling a small piece of clay in his hands. Presently he placed over the strained eyes of the face the frame of a pince-nez. And at that instant the illusion was miraculously complete. It was as if the doctor would presently lean forward and say: "Have you read Osler's *Redemption of Man?* No? Oh, you must, you must!"

The figure was complete and ready for casting by the end of May 1917, but there were delays caused by the sculptor's enforced absence on other work and the beginning of the aircraft investi-

STONE MOUNTAIN, SHOWING SUPERIMPOSED CARVING OF CENTRAL GROUP

NORTH CAROLINA MEMORIAL AT GETTYSBURG

gation. Also there were vexatious problems of cutting, setting and preparing the site for the statue. All these were generously solved by Doctors Walter James and Lawrenson Brown and others of Trudeau's physician friends. Eventually the memorial was unveiled in August 1918. On the marble was carved Dr. Trudeau's favorite quotation:

> *Guerir quelquefois, soulager souvent, consoler toujours.*
> (Heal sometimes, soothe often, comfort always.)

Carl Snyder, the writer, at that time connected with *Harper's*, after driving to Saranac to examine the statue wrote this friendly word to the sculptor:

May I tell you that I have never seen a portrait that impressed me so deeply. This was equally true of my wife. She and I agreed that we never had seen a piece of sculpture that seemed so alive. It seems to tell the whole life story of an extraordinary man. And I am told you only saw him once!

Man! Man! Man! With the genius to do magnificent things like this, to create and to embody the living likeness of a great man, why, why, why do you waste your precious time on anything else?

One answer to the query, which he was often heard to give, was that he was never given half the work that he was capable of and wanted to do. In quick succession members of the Plymouth Church in Brooklyn wanted a monument to Henry Ward Beecher, the famous pulpit orator; the Wheeler family in Bridgeport wanted a memorial fountain in honor of the inventor of the sewing machine. For St. John's Church, near by, he was asked to make a reredos back of the altar. From North Carolina came a call from the Daughters of the Confederacy to build a memorial to Henry Wyatt, the first Southern soldier killed in the War between the States. From England came a committee to join with

Americans to plan monuments along the border between the
United States and Canada to celebrate the hundred years of peace
between the two nations.

All these were not enough to keep him busy. He wrote an incredible number of letters to committees that were planning public monuments, but he got very few commissions that way. Most
of his jobs came through friends or others who had seen his work
and liked it. Every commission brought a different set of characters and circumstances with it and threw different side lights
on the sculptor's personality. His commission to build a memorial
to Altgeld in Chicago was due to the crusading spirit which had
made him widely known as a champion of democracy in art as
well as in politics.

Governor Altgeld of Illinois had become widely and unfavor-
ably known as "the governor who pardoned the Haymarket
rioters" after they had been tried and condemned as bomb throw-
ers. Such was his reputation for a long time, during which he
remained silent. Then an unbiased study of his career brought
about a reversal of public opinion. It was presented that he was
wholly unselfish; that his life motive had been to help the under-
privileged; that, in the words of the poet Vachel Lindsay, "He set
himself tasks which took a lion's courage and a martyr's heart,"
and that to carry out his purpose "He threw his reputation and
his health into the furnace every hour."

So it happened in 1913, eleven years after Altgeld's death, the
Illinois legislature appropriated $25,000 for an Altgeld monu-
ment. A committee of five was appointed, including Louis F. Post
of the Department of Labor, with instructions to select a sculptor
after a public competition. Two competitions were held, bringing
over thirty models, none satisfactory. In a letter to the committee the landscape artist, Walter B. Griffin, wrote:

This particular task should be committed to a sculptor who has
attained in his art that fundamental character, the American

ideal, which Altgeld served in his own field and exemplified in his career. There appears to be in our time at least one sculptor, Gutzon Borglum, who is recognized as bearing to the plastic arts a relation like Whitman's to literature. It would be a pity not to avail ourselves of the opportunity to bring together such a man and the work he is so eminently fitted for.

Following this suggestion the committee awarded the commission to Gutzon, who received it with intense satisfaction as a recognition of what he stood for in public life as well as a testimonial to his ability as an artist. When the news came out the Chicago *Tribune* published this comment:

A powerful illustration of how not to do it is the history of the competition for the Altgeld monument. The commission has now been awarded to Gutzon Borglum without his being required to furnish any preliminary sketch, design or idea. That is, the committee has done what it should have done in the first place—selected a sculptor and left him free to do the work.

General competitions are so unjust to the competitors and so unproductive of good results as to be forbidden by the American Institute of Architects. The best architects never enter them, and the better sculptors have learned to follow their example.

When the contract was signed in April 1914 the sculptor began to work on two different models. Before they were done he wrote to his friend Felix Frankfurter saying that he had been reading up on Altgeld's life and ending his letter with this statement: "That man has become a perfect giant to me. He was a kind of hero when I was a kid, but he lived out his governorship and died before I got back from Europe. So he comes along almost like a new star to me."

Of the two small models submitted, the one selected by the committee represented Altgeld standing on a slight eminence, his right hand extended as if quelling a disturbance, his left stretched over a man, woman and child beside him. The pedestal was low, so that the governor seemed to be near his audience, his

expression was noble, almost defiant in his determination to protect his charges. The committee unanimously accepted the full-
size model of this statue except for slight changes which the sculptor approved. The figure was cast in bronze and erected in Lincoln
Park for unveiling on Labor Day, 1915.

Then a thing occurred which to the sculptor was incompre-
hensible. The model had been on exhibition in the Chicago Art
Institute for a whole year with no voice raised against it. Then
various municipal art commissions suddenly declared they didn't
approve of it and would not permit it to be unveiled. The reason,
they said, was that it was not big enough and that the laborer's
family seemed to occupy a servile position. To this the chairman
of the purchasing committee, Daniel Cruice, made a quick and
indignant reply:

I take exception to the criticisms which have attempted to show
an insult to labor. I do not believe that labor is making a fight on
the statue. Altgeld's enemies in life are the enemies of his memory. They do not wish the perpetuation of the principles for
which he stood. Consequently they are doing all in their power to
destroy any reminder that such a man lived.

When the sculptor declared in characteristic fashion that he
forgot more about art overnight than ordinary art commissions
learn in a lifetime the Brooklyn *Eagle,* always quick to record a
Borglum controversy, declared editorially:

The controversy between Gutzon Borglum and the Municipal
Art Commission of Chicago over the statue of the late John P.
Altgeld adds to the gaiety of nations. The Art Commission criti-
cizes the conception of the work—Altgeld raising a protecting
hand over a man, a woman and a child, typifying the working
classes. It likewise objects to the proportions of the Borglum design. And the artist answers in his characteristic temper.
It was the fate of John P. Altgeld to be a storm center in his
life. Now he becomes a post-mortem center. Large elements of

the Chicago electorate still doubt the historic proportions of the Governor who pardoned the Haymarket bomb men. It is not to be wondered at if the proportions of the Borglum Altgeld annoy them. Nor is it surprising that the design, representing the Governor as the laboring people's defender, gives offense to them. It is a safe wager that this element in the electorate is represented by the Municipal Art Commission.

The issue is really not an art issue at all. In essence it is historic and political, or rather sociological. Altgeld's keenness as a thinker and debater no one who ever heard him doubts. That he showed moral courage in that historic pardon, most of his enemies will concede. Our guess is that Borglum will succeed in immortalizing him as the friend of labor, though many obstacles may first have to be overcome.

The surprising denouement was furnished by William H. (Big Bill) Thompson. He was then mayor and had made an appointment to discuss the matter with the Art Commission. They were waiting for him at the Art Institute where his messenger rather bluntly announced to them that the Commission was no longer in existence nor had any authority, its term of office having expired. "The statue looks good to me," said the mayor, "and the committee doesn't."

So the memorial was unveiled as scheduled on Labor Day, 1915, before an immense crowd including thousands of labor-union men and women. Governor Edward F. Dunne presided, and William Jennings Bryan delivered the speech of the day. The sculptor made a puzzled comment:

I have been not a little surprised that in America, the foster mother of mankind, there exist no memorials of consequence dealing with the struggles and pathos of life. It is a matter of amazement and regret that Chicago, a city whose life has been crowned through sacrifice and struggle as it has been sweetened by suffering, should show antagonism to a memorial which develops or suggests a humane situation where one human being befriends another.

There is something stern and vital behind this. But censorship, be it ever so official, will not arrest one beat in the natural heart of mankind, nor stop the natural expression of what is true, of what is good. And that which is true and good is, at least, a full sister of that which is beautiful. Millet's "Angelus" and his "Man With a Hoe" would be subjects of supreme beauty and pathos in sculpture, admirably composed for public parks. How much more human and akin would be this interpretation of life than the cheap allegories or conventional vagaries which the unthinking call art.

General Daniel Butterfield was a Union hero who distinguished himself at "Little Round Top" in the battle of Gettysburg. His wife outlived him and at her death bequeathed a fortune, part of which she specified should be spent on a monument for her husband. She left instructions for the unknown sculptor who might be chosen by her executors. He was to visit the battlefield, familiarize himself with Little Round Top and, so far as possible, incorporate the contour of that famous site in his design for the monument. He was also to study certain photographs of the general, one of which represented him standing with folded arms and wearing a cocked hat, "as in the bas-relief at Utica."

In the contract all that was said about the figure was that it was to be over eight feet high, in the dress uniform of a major general, supported by a foundation of natural work representing Round Top. It was specified that the sculptor was to make a model forty inches high and that when that was approved he would proceed with a full-size model "which shall be submitted to the executors for their approval and acceptance and shall be in accordance with the will of Julia L. Butterfield."

All that appears plain enough, but there was a catch which would presently cause the sculptor no end of tribulation. To him it seemed that in financial reward it was the best commission he had ever received, the only one from which he might expect a reasonable profit. For a single figure, with side panels at the base, he was to receive $54,000, a generous allowance. The chairman of the executive committee, Colonel E. M. Ehlers, a Dane by birth, showed him one photograph of the general in full-dress uniform, arms folded, wearing an imposing military hat with a plume. Another photograph showed him hatless, with his hands at his side. But this, said Colonel Ehlers, should be ignored because Mrs. Butterfield preferred the other.

Following his instructions in good faith the sculptor made a forty-inch model, using the selected photograph as a guide for the pose. One of the executors, Mr. Hagar, criticized the nose and mustache of the model and the sculptor changed these features to his satisfaction. All four executors then approved the model and signed the voucher for the payment due at this stage of the work. When the full-size model was accepted only three executors were present, but again the voucher for payment was signed by all four. The model was then cast in plaster and sent to the Gorham Company to be put into bronze.

Gutzon was delegated to find a place for the memorial, preferably in Central Park, New York City. He was told that the park was out of the question but was offered a site near Riverside Drive, opposite Grant's Tomb, where the statue was placed in January 1917. The secretary of the executors, Dr. May, in formal acknowledgment that the work was completed, added this friendly, personal word:

I am sure that it will ever remain a monument to your art. Could Mrs. Butterfield see it, it would have her complete approval and gratify her pride in leaving a memorial so creditable to her husband and to the city. It is located, as I can tell you, only a short distance from the home of her birth and girlhood.

And then the unbelievable happened. The three executors with whom most of the sculptor's contacts had been made all died within a very short time of one another. Everything was left in the hands of the fourth, Albert Hagar, who announced that he had never liked the statue, that the "bas-relief in Utica" mentioned in the will showed the general without a hat, with his arms down, and that he didn't think the figure was big enough. He wanted the whole thing done over and refused any further payment unless this was done. The worst feature of this arbitrary decision was that many beneficiaries of Mrs. Butterfield's will could not be paid until the status of the monument was settled. Hagar's sudden reversal was no doubt sincere but it made inconvenience and trouble for many.

The Gorham Company offered to handle the suit which had to be brought against Hagar. The case dragged into the time when the sculptor had the aircraft investigation on his hands. Meanwhile the contractors who had done the granite work sued Gutzon for the payment of their bill. Gorham had not been paid for the casting, the architects were clamoring for their money and Stamford taxes were in arrears. The suit was carried on at Cold Spring, near Poughkeepsie, so far away that the sculptor lost a whole day every time he appeared as a witness.

Of course the Gorham Company won the suit eventually, but payments were not made until 1920. By that time the sculptor had assigned what little would have been left over for him to other debtors, so it is doubtful if he ever received a penny for all his work on this big contract. It was said by people who should know that some of the Butterfield heirs went to the poorhouse while waiting for their inheritance. Gutzon blamed himself for having accepted the commission in the first place. When later the location of the statue had to be changed on account of the Rockefeller church construction he declared he wouldn't mind if they dropped it into the Hudson River.

The Vance memorial for North Carolina, of which a copy stands in Statuary Hall in the nation's capital, was made during this period. It remains where it was put in the first place.

CHAPTER FOURTEEN

AIRCRAFT INVESTIGATION

The American Congress appropriated over one thousand million dollars that were expended for aviation during the nineteen months of war. When the armistice was signed, not a single American-made fighting or combat plane had reached the front. No American-made fighting or combat plane was ever produced. America depended upon her allies to furnish a few obsolete fighting planes with which our armies were equipped. Our contribution to wartime aircraft consisted of two hundred and thirteen "utterly dangerous" observation planes that reached the front with others on the way. That is the record. (Report of aircraft investigation under House resolution of June 4, 1919.)

Mr. Borglum is the man who started the entire aircraft investigation at the outset and performed a great public service. (Congressman James A. Frear, Wisconsin, speech to House of Representatives, *Congressional Record,* March 1, 1920.)

YOU MAY HAVE GATHERED from the record thus far that Gutzon Borglum was a bit unused to doing things the way other people did them. There was only one of him, and there were so many of the rest of the population that maybe one shouldn't be disturbed by this technique. He had a genius' variety of talent; so it probably isn't remarkable that his art studio should have been filled with frightening projects for roads, transportation, parks, breakwaters, engineering, airplane models, philosophy, abstract science and the saving of the world. He believed he could do anything—so he did it. All of this is fairly obvious on his history sheet. But, for all that, his investigation of the aircraft industry in 1918 remains today one of the most incredible things that ever happened to America.

We start our study of this attempt of one man to produce some honesty in a $1,000,000,000 delusion with the knowledge that Borglum was not only a fairly competent theoretical engineer, but also a practical mechanic who had been following closely the growth of air power. And that is fortunate, because few other matters in the aircraft investigation are that obvious or sensible. In November 1917, after the United States had been eight months in World War I, he got a look at an airplane factory in Dayton, Ohio. He was shocked, as he admitted, almost into a state of speechlessness. He had a brief visit with a man in a high position in the direction of aircraft production, listened to him, and, instead of going home, made a quick trip to Washington. Next morning he was at the White House, demanding to see President Wilson.

And here is the first amazing part of his procedure. He had seen that the United States wasn't producing airplanes and he felt that something ought to be done about it. But he didn't look for anybody to help him prepare the case for presentation to somebody who might be able to correct the situation. It never occurred to him that he needed any. The man best able to get quick action was, undoubtedly, the President of the United States.

Gutzon Borglum knew Woodrow Wilson and Woodrow Wilson knew Gutzon Borglum, but the pair took a dim view of each other, as well they might. Borglum, in his Progressive-party campaign, had been loudly critical of the Wilson administration. Wilson, who was a scholar, appreciated Borglum's art. But, as the record shows, he didn't think enough of his politics to consider him a crusader for the democratic ideal.

And yet Borglum was appointed, with authority direct from the President, to conduct his investigation from an office in the War Department. He ran the boys into corners for several months, and he stirred up senators and congressmen and Department heads and cabinet officers. That in the end his inquiry failed to put anybody in jail or get back any of the $1,000,000,000 is not surprising. What is incredible about the whole affair is that he was allowed to start at all.

There isn't much doubt about our dismal performance in building airplanes in 1917-1918. The propagandized public was a long time finding out that the chief trouble with our planes was their continued nonexistence. But we did get to hear about the "dangerous" De Haviland Fours, of which we sent 213 to France. This plane was widely celebrated across the country as "The Flaming Coffin." It had a large gas tank mounted in the most vulnerable position, and a pilot was seldom able to get away from one after it was hit.

Soldier after soldier from the front came before the Frear committee to tell of seeing his comrades shot down in these planes. Yet reports of such catastrophes, as the Frear report scathingly pointed out, did not prevent Secretary of War Newton D. Baker and Aircraft Director John D. Ryan from continuing the manufacture of DH 4s.

After the war the taxpayers began to find out what they had purchased for $1,000,000,000. Captain Eddie Rickenbacker, ace flyer and national hero, told them when he came home to testify before an investigating committee. "Why did the army continue to use French planes?" he was asked. This was his reply:

The answer is simple. We hadn't any others except the two hundred and thirteen "flaming coffins." The American air forces were in dire need of machines of all kinds. We were thankful to get any kind that would fly. The French had already discarded the Nieuport for the steadier, stronger Spad, and our government was thus able to buy from the French a certain number of these out-of-date Nieuports for American pilots—or got on without. Consequently our American pilots in France were compelled to venture out in Nieuports against more experienced pilots in more modern machinery. None of us in France could understand what prevented our great country from furnishing machines equal to the best in the world. Many a gallant life was lost to American aviation in those early months of 1918, the responsibility for which must lie heavily on some guilty consciences.

There had been a lot of inquiry before the House began its investigation. And when Congress had finished there was a widespread display of indignation with the aid of aeronautic associations, farmers' associations and two New York daily newspapers. For a while the scandals they dug up overshadowed what had caused the wrath of Borglum. He had worked in wartime and in a closed circle, and what he found out was reported to the President and the few others who had a right to hear. He was satisfied with that arrangement, for he had no faith in the efficiency of official inquiries. On this subject he said:

There is a radical defect in a system that occasions such investigations. A political inquiry of this nature must inevitably arouse enmity and opposition in the most powerful quarters. The credit, nay, the very existence, of the government in power is at stake. An inquiry may seem to start something, but what it starts is an avalanche that will surely crush its initiators and the truth they seek to discover. Thus they will remain buried under the debris and obscured by the dust.

When Gutzon Borglum first took his demand for an aircraft investigation to the White House he was politely, if somewhat shortly, received by Joseph Tumulty, the President's secretary. Mr. Wilson was frightfully busy on account of the war, Mr. Tumulty mentioned, but he would undoubtedly be able to read a note explaining the purposes of Mr. Borglum's visit. Mr. Borglum left the note and went home to Stamford.

There in due time he received a short letter from Mr. Tumulty saying that the President wished Mr. Borglum to get in touch with Mr. Howard Coffin of the Aeronautics Board. Mr. Borglum thought this humorous inasmuch as Mr. Coffin was principally interested in automobile production, which was what Borglum found wrong with the Aeronautics Board. So he wrote something of the sort to the President's secretary on November 22, 1917. He finished it somewhat tartly:

The program of the Aeronautics Board was invented by Automobile Production men before they had picked up their representation on that board, or even before the appropriations had been passed. They are now engaged in a grandiose project, incapable of fulfillment, which cannot but bring scandal and disaster, and which, in turn, can harm your administration.

President Wilson was disturbed and sent a reply on December 5, asking Borglum to point out specifically the weaknesses in the aircraft organization as it then stood. Borglum replied at once and suggested that the Aeronautics Board should be really two boards, one of design and one of production, and that the military board should have nothing to do but order what sort of planes it needed. When he had posted this suggestion he went back to Dayton to take another look at the plant he had first seen, and he loitered on his way home at the Curtiss factory in Buffalo. That was a better-looking establishment, but it seemed disorganized and full of idle men, and it wasn't producing any airplanes.

Then, on Christmas Day, 1917, he wrote to Wilson the letter that, no matter what you may think of it, put his aircraft investigation in business. He said:

Since writing you, I have visited two other factories and attended several aeronautics conferences. This so disturbs me that I must write further with the hope that Congressional investigation of the aeronautics bodies may be avoided while there is yet time to correct conditions from within and so avoid the ship-and-ordnance scandals.

If the opportunity arrives, I will tell you of conditions which strike at the root of honest, disinterested public service; of irregularities, graft, self-interest and collateral profiting in the very heart of our production department. But public knowledge of actual aeronautic conditions would be a military disaster to American arms, as well as an unwarranted blow at our Government.

Therefore I suggest:

Immediate selection of three competent, fearless and incorruptible men, whose loyalty to you is above question. Give them authority, without publicity, to go quickly over the present plan and accomplishment in our aircraft and report on:

Engines, planes and propellers.

Contracts placed where, system employed selecting contractors.

Supply sources, by whom held.

Relation of members of production board to supply controls, also to contractors.

Test experiments. Why are our planes inferior to all foreign planes and vastly poorer than German planes?

What use is being made of data constantly being sent here covering Germany's planes.

Such inquiry should not audit accounts. A larger principle is at stake.

For this report you need a highly trained engineer, an expert production man and a man who knows the art of machine flying and the history and possibilities of machines.

1. Your engineer should be an internal-combustion engine man who knows that an airplane engine is not merely a refined truck engine. He should know propellers. This latter item has almost been forgotten. No reliable propeller exists that can safely be standardized.

2. Your production manager should be trained as a specialist on organization.

3. The third position I should like to fill personally. There are no principles related to flying heavier-than-air machines that I am not thoroughly familiar with. I feel as Da Vinci did when seeking a commission. He wrote: "As for that art, I know all that is known." The open-mindedness of this carries its own forgiveness. I observe accurately, avoid prejudices, have no fears that I know of. I know I'm a good organizer, one who can handle and keep the confidence of men. I am not only anxious but prepared to serve

you and the great service which you, for America, have undertaken. I could put into your hands in the briefest possible time a report on existing conditions and war needs, and avoid scandal. Investigations during wartime should be periodic and automatic. This would rob them of abnormal interest and make them policy affecting functions.

Somebody slipped the letter out and published it. The automobile industry was noisily indignant and Borglum was much annoyed. But those results somehow seem natural in the circumstances. What must continue to confuse students of political procedure for some time is the fact that it brought a quick appointment. On the second of January President Wilson had written a letter. The Secretary of War would be pleased to give Mr. Borglum full authority. Stanley King of the Secretary's personal staff would be at Mr. Borglum's disposal for advice or assistance. Mr. Borglum would be put in touch with General George Squier, whom he already knew, and he was to have the assistance of any experts he might think required. He was to report directly to President Wilson.

Why this appointment should have come through is one of the things that surpasses all understanding. It is quite likely that Wilson suspected what was wrong with aircraft production and thought an investigation by a recognized Republican not connected with politics might stir up some action without hurting the administration. That is one thought. It also comes to anyone who has watched political maneuvering that a good way to get rid of an investigator who was getting troublesome would be to put him where he couldn't talk for publication.

Anyway, the sculptor went to Washington, notified the White House and the War Department of his arrival, called on the Secretary of State and was assigned to a room on the second floor of the War Department offices. Borglum felt that he would have every possible aid. The Secretary's office door was just across the hall.

Gutzon went to work at once. He asked Mr. King to get him a report on how many war planes had been ordered and how many delivered up to January 1, 1918. The War Department's answer was quickly brought and easily digested: "Training planes contracted for, 7,500; delivered, 1,444. Service planes contracted for, 12,500; 4,000 to be built by Dayton Wright. Service planes delivered to January 1, 1918, none."

Borglum called that same day on Josephus Daniels, Secretary of the Navy, who telephoned instructions to the Intelligence Bureau of the Navy. Naval records were laid open to the sculptor and he went through them personally, making what notes seemed relevant. Three days later when he went to the War Department he was informed that they had none of the records he requested— nor any memory of any. He was virtually compelled to pick up a copy of the Aeronautics Committee report from the office of the chairman, who apparently did not even know of its existence. He was blocked in an effort to get Intelligence reports on spy activities in Buffalo. Secret Service men were assigned to follow him wherever he went. One of his aides in the War Department warned two of his witnesses not to talk to him. He was informed of the looting of a bank in Dayton, Ohio, by an agile group which substituted Aeronautics Board agreements and checks for tangible assets. He was invited to join the Aeronautics Board, but he didn't accept. He discovered that his office telephone was tapped and that his mail was being systematically examined. He opened an outside office as headquarters for his own aides, investigators and stenographers.

By the end of February he knew that we hadn't planes of any kind and that we hadn't engines of any kind and that, nearing the second year of war, we had less than 130,000 soldiers at the front and that they were using shoes, socks and other equipment provided by France and England.

Borglum went to talk about this to Secretary Baker. Baker, slumped in his chair with his feet on his desk, puffed his pipe and listened with indifference. Not until the condition of aircraft manufacture was reached did he show any animation. Then he shifted his feet and said casually, "Why, Borglum, you don't think we are actually getting into this war, do you?"

"My God!" said Borglum. "Do you mean to tell me that all this is just a gesture?"

Baker nodded and puffed contentedly.

Borglum couldn't contain himself. "Do you mean to tell me," he said, "that all America has to do is hint that she is going into war, loan Europe a lot of money, send over a regiment or two and that this is going to bluff Germany into retirement?"

"I mean," Baker said, "that there won't be any real war as far as we are concerned." And so closed an astonishing interview.

Hurriedly and in anger Borglum made his second report to the President. He hadn't been too successful with his first report; there had been leaks concerning its contents. His second report, which he delivered himself on February 9, was in the hands of Secretary Baker on February 11. Baker made light of it after it had become public property.

Who released the report was never learned, but shortly the newspapers had it and were charging that America, after spending hundreds of millions of dollars for aircraft, had produced nothing but brag and bluster; that we were in a war with no planes and no engines of our own. White House and War Office press departments began to make counter charges, ridiculing the report and charging Borglum with falsehood.

Washington seethed for a couple of weeks. Some unknown person called the Dayton factory to fill two freight trains with airplane parts and to paint on the boxcars in big letters, "Planes for Europe," "Right of Way," "Our Boys Need These Planes," and similar legends. Newspaper reporters and government agents were posted between Dayton and Hoboken to see these trains pass with their painted signs. From them the news flashed to all parts of the country, and Borglum was a liar by official count.

Borglum had his own agents scattered over the route and he knew that not a single plane had left Dayton for anywhere. He was just getting part of the pay for his appointment. Verification of the reports of his own investigators was made two or three days later by General Goethals, whom he met at breakfast at the Metropolitan Club. General Goethals was then Quartermaster General and well acquainted with what was shipped out of Dayton. Borglum wrote in his journal:

About this time Senator Thomas of Colorado turned bitterly upon me and introduced a resolution "inquiring into the charges that Gutzon Borglum had so recklessly made." A small committee, composed of himself as chairman, Senator Reed of Missouri, Senator Frelinghuysen of New Jersey and Senator Wadsworth of New York was appointed. Its duty was to visit the factories against which Borglum had cast aspersions.

This committee proceeded via New Jersey up the Hudson to the great Curtiss plant, on to Detroit and down to Dayton. At Elizabeth, New Jersey, they reported that the speed and anxiety of the workmen to get parts of planes into cars and on their way to Hoboken was "little short of phenomenal." The officer in charge was courteous to the senators but begged them to keep out of the way, saying that the boys in Europe needed planes and there must be no delay—all of which impressed the senators so much that they thanked him and left. Then they proceeded north to the Curtiss plant at Buffalo—a plant having 14,000 men on the payroll and producing only ten to twelve planes a day. (In Toronto a factory employing 2,800 people was producing twelve fighting planes and twenty-four training planes a day.) There was present the same kind of apparently furious activity which the senators had witnessed at Elizabeth.

The committee then went on to Dayton Field, where, after watching a schooling of the officers and a workout of the young men, they turned to leave. As they were walking away, the officer of the day approached Senator Reed and said, "Aren't we going to be heard?" Without waiting for a reply he said, "I'm through. You can strip my buttons off, but I'll have no more damned humbug. I am killing two boys a day. We dig two graves every morning before breakfast, just to be ready for their deaths. You may do what you like with me. I am through."

As a result, so the senator himself told me, the committee determined to return secretly to the factories they had just visited. There the men who had brusquely pushed the committee aside in their anxiety to ship planes to Europe were disgorging the airplane parts they had so carefully boxed. Thomas, who had been very rude to me, wrote the report and presented it to a Senate that had less than a dozen members in their seats. He complained feelingly of the lack of interest, the lack of patriotism in a matter which had impugned the honor and the integrity of our War Department. To one of his committee he said afterward, "I wish there were some way I could apologize to Mr. Borglum and tell him how mistaken I have been."

There was a little more to come before Gutzon could be through with his aircraft investigation. His inquiry had brought reliable evidence of the theft of securities worth more than a million dollars from a Western bank through the connivance of some members of the Aeronautics Board. This matter he took to Gilbert Hitchcock of Nebraska, chairman of the Senate Military Affairs Committee, whom he had known for many years. With his own authority from the President he took it for granted that he would not have to tell the names of the people involved until after subpoenas for them had been issued. Hitchcock agreed. The next day he declared he couldn't do it, and the day after that he made a speech in the Senate declaring that he had had a long conference with Mr. Borglum, had seen all the aircraft evidence and that there was nothing to it.

Monday morning Borglum saw Hitchcock and was in the middle of his attack when Senators Joseph Frelinghuysen, James Reed, John Thomas and James W. Wadsworth, the military committee, came into the room. Somewhat informally, as everything in Washington seems to have been done in those days, they sat down and listened to Borglum's demand for blank subpoenas. Senator Reed nodded, stood up, and said, "Mr. Chairman, owing to the high character of this witness, I move that the subpoenas he asks be given. If he gets the evidence he says exists, I will move from the floor of the Senate the hanging of those men."

Borglum thanked him. "Senator Reed," he said, "I have not told you the half of it, and I can't. I beg of you to give me the subpoenas and assist me in getting the evidence." Frelinghuysen and Wadsworth seconded the motion.

The subpoenas voted by the committee were never issued, however. The chairman, in whose hands the matter was left, never seemed to find time. He retired to private life after the next election.

Borglum's last interview with Hitchcock relative to the subpoenas was just about the last of his aircraft investigation. President Wilson telegraphed that Gutzon had "misunderstood" his letter of January 2, and that he wished the inquiry stopped. When the sculptor was slow in stopping, the President made his order of dismissal public. Borglum published a letter in which he asked: "What is it, Mr. President, in this country that you are afraid of? What is it in this America that the President of the United States dare not face?"

Charles Evans Hughes conducted the next investigation. He worked from May until October in 1918. The New York *Times* of November 1, 1918, printed his report. Gutzon said of it that it reminded him of the story of an Irishman who was sent to locate a bucket lost in the bottom of a well. He climbed down and he climbed back with great difficulty. Then he returned to his office and reported: "Sure, it's there."

And that, in truth, was the result of the aircraft investigation. There were other inquiries and other suggestions, but nobody went to jail. Nobody seems to have been seriously discommoded. There weren't any airplanes that anybody could lay a hand on. And the $1,000,000,000 just disappeared.

Gutzon Borglum was much disturbed about this. He could get

angry thinking of it to the day of his death. But it always seemed
to a casual friend that he was puzzled by the wrong side of airplane production. What he should have contemplated as the
scintillant miracle of all the days he was to live was the fact that
he was allowed to make the investigation at all.

It is a little late after all these years to try to figure out how a
billion dollars could disappear without leaving a trace on somebody. Borglum used to get indignant about the matter ten or
twelve years afterward, but the targets of his wrath were always
anonymous. He had some shrewd suspicions, but left at the bottom of the well was the evidence which in this situation would
have been necessary to convict anyone of wrongdoing.

To give the fiasco a fair estimate, it seems likely that we were
very young then. Up to the time when war was declared we had
left the building of our planes to rugged individuals who whittled
out the parts for them with jackknives and put them together in
moldering barns and sheds. When we had to get an air force aloft
we did the best we could, which wasn't very good. We didn't trust
our cow-barn airplane manufacturers. Largely, they weren't where
we could find them anyway. They had gone into the air corps
themselves.

So the searchers for planes took a chance on some people who
apparently knew something about a gasoline motor and how to
make forms out of tin—that is to say, of course, the automobile
makers. These lads muddled through and nobody got any airplanes. They produced pieces in large numbers and blithely
shipped them away to places where they were supposed to be
assembled into airplanes. But, apparently, nobody had thought
to provide an assembler.

It is one thought about this—a thought that would have meant
nothing to Gutzon Borglum—that nobody about the airplane
production, if it can be called that, got rich . . . not so far as can

be determined. Nobody seems to have had the remotest idea of what he was doing, and it takes at least a billion dollars to keep thousands of men in jobs where they have nothing to do but nothing.

CHAPTER FIFTEEN

FLIGHT, PATIENCE AND
SHERIDAN'S HORSE

NONE of his sundry war activities seems to have had much of an effect on Gutzon Borglum's handiwork. His figure of James McConnell, in the monument to him on the University of Virginia campus at Charlottesville, is one of the first memorials to the First World War to be erected, and it is surely one of the finest. It was because of his intense interest in aeronautics that he knew about McConnell and got this commission. And his creative skill had certainly been enriched by new experiences.

The McConnell figure was a labor of love and, considering the nature of the subject, could hardly have been otherwise. Its start is told in a prospectus of the project signed by Edwin A. Alderman, president of the university:

On March 19, 1917, James Rogers McConnell met his death fighting for France. He had been flying for France for over a year, and it was meet and fitting that he should encounter death in the upper air, battling with her enemies. The story of his life, since the beginning of the Great War, is a beautiful and heroic story. Out of pure idealism and devotion to the idea of freedom as established in France, he gave his service to the French Republic, first as an ambulance driver and then as one of the pioneer aviators of the famous Lafayette Escadrille.

McConnell was a loyal son of the University of Virginia. He has enriched her traditions and bound about her brow some of his glory. His fellow students and his teachers take a solemn pride in his great devotion to freedom and right, and think of him as a new and secret tie binding us to the land of Lafayette and the home of Thomas Jefferson. They desire to place here some simple memorial of beauty and distinction that will recall to future generations of youth the beauty of heroic death, the virtues of duty, valor and self-sacrifice, and will keep green the memory of one who counted it a gladness to give his life for a lofty end.

Gutzon's sympathy for a boy of McConnell's character, and his acquaintance with others in the Lafayette Escadrille, gave him a particular incentive to do this memorial. The commission came to him through a very dear friend, W. W. Fuller of North Carolina and New York. Borglum had also a deep admiration for Dr. Alderman. The sculptor's conception of the statue was new and extraordinary.

The form he chose was a male figure, standing tiptoe on a globe representing the earth, in the act of taking flight. Vast wings were strapped to his arms, almost concealing them, and to the calves of his legs were bound something like greaves, showing that the youth was a mortal in armor and not the mythological figure that a first glimpse would suggest. President Alderman's letters were numerous and helpful. He was much concerned about the wings. In a letter to Mr. Fuller he wrote:

Will one tire of their mass? Are they needed in such mass to subtly suggest battle flight? Is there not some symbolism less realistic and obstructive that would turn the trick? This thing cannot be *near* great. It must either be *great* or miss greatness altogether. Hence my anxiety. . . . I have faith in Borglum and admire the calm, fine way he receives the layman's counsel. But this work is not a mere statue. It is a daring spiritual expression. It must not offend any canon of form or grace.

Sometimes in writing I weary of seeking the hidden, difficult, aptest phrase and content myself from sheer ennui with a lesser form. He cannot do that, for my expression is ephemeral—his is eternal and unlimited. . . .

It is significant, in view of later comments on his irascibility, that the sculptor welcomed such criticism as this. Because of the positioning of the memorial—in clear space, free from buildings and silhouetted against the sky—he made some changes in the figure. The wings were made lighter, the feathers outlined more distinctly, and some of the feathers were separated to admit light between them.

Characteristically, there seems to have been no discussion of price or of compensation to the sculptor until the first model was completed. At that time he wrote that the cost would be $12,000, owing to the increased cost of bronze. Then he moved on to some work in Cuba. There was delay in getting the marble from Tennessee in time for the unveiling. Because of this the braces and rivets attaching the figure to its round base were not in place when the draperies were lifted. Dr. Alderman went through his speech in grave apprehension that the whole exhibit would fall on his head. But it all came right in the end—through sheer luck, perhaps.

Mr. Fuller wrote that a friend of his, "a learned physician and a just and judicious man," had looked at the memorial from an unusual point of view.

This friend reported:

I am sure it is a great work of art, but I studied it mostly from the position of the anatomist. The lines are perfect. What a grand specimen of the human architecture, as if just from the hands of his Maker! A model of human architecture! I noticed particularly the different prominent muscles, tense and drawn in preparation for flight—how anatomically correct they were in location and function. . . . I shall never forget. . . .

The aviator's father was deeply touched by the figure. He wrote to Gutzon:

I attended the unveiling of the memorial to my son at the University of Virginia. I want to congratulate you on this wonderful reproduction. It is magnificently beautiful . . . expressive and highly inspiring. I know of nothing in America that equals this splendid work. I believe that not only the University of Virginia but all America will regard this aviator as a triumph of art and will cherish it as a priceless possession.

Then there came a committee which had thought about building a memorial to a former governor, Charles Brantley Aycock, in Raleigh, North Carolina. From Josephus Daniels came a letter enthusiastically outlining this project. Gutzon read it without much interest. The committee had decided to hold a competition but wished Borglum to submit a model before they made a decision.

Gutzon replied that because Daniels asked it, he would be glad to lay aside his ideas about competitions, but that he simply did not have the time to put in the work of several days on a model that might or might not be satisfactory. "Committees do not realize," he said, "that the making of a model is about one third of the entire work. Neither do they realize that in at least nine cases out of ten, no model is carried out as first presented. Not only the committee but the artist himself develops it."

So the committee abandoned the competition, invited the sculptor to come to Raleigh for a conference and gave him the commission the day after his arrival. He telegraphed home, "Returning this afternoon. Have contract eighteen thousand." The family received the news with decent restraint. They knew Gutzon. He was always sanguine. A contract was always the same to him as money in the bank.

The Aycock memorial was conceived by its promoters as the monument to an ideal rather than to a man. Aycock, governor of North Carolina from 1901 to 1905, had established two reforms of importance. The first was to make suffrage dependent on education. The second placed education within the reach of all, rich or poor, black or white. And the sculptor soon realized that he was going to have some trouble telling about this in a statue.

Most of his correspondence was with Dr. Clarence Poe, son-in-law of Governor Aycock and editor of a widely circulated paper, *The Progressive Farmer*. He was a man of exceptional gifts, but sculpture worried him. His first worry was because Gutzon was working on a life-size model without having made a plaster cast of the small-sketch model. Gutzon wrote him a long treatise on models in which he said:

I don't mind making three or four. The man must be on his feet. Except for that every action of the body is changeable. . . . In the work I do in my studio I keep my small model in clay and do not cast it in plaster in order not to be bound by it. If it is in plaster it cannot be changed. . . . I am anxious to keep it as flexible as possible, and to keep in mind that the big figure is the sole thing and the permanent thing. . . .

There was more correspondence and eventually Gutzon invited the committee to come and look at the life-size model. In the fall of the year the party arrived—Colonel P. M. Pearsall, Mrs. Charles Aycock, the widow, and Judge Frank Daniels, Josephus' brother. After suggesting some slight changes they expressed complete satisfaction and went home. The sculptor was on the point of casting the statue in plaster when he got a telegram from Dr. Poe, who had been unavoidably detained. Poe, who had learned his lesson about models, begged Gutzon to delay the casting till he could get to Stamford. Nobody had told him what work it is to keep a heroic-size clay figure moist for an indefinite time. For the next three weeks Gutzon had little else to occupy his time.

Dr. Poe and a new committee were more critical than the first group had been. Dr. Poe shook his head and announced that for one thing the model was underweight. Aycock, he said, had weighed at least fifty pounds more than the sculptor allowed. The rest of the committee agreed.

Gutzon had acquired patience. It was not serious, he said. He would adjust the governor's proportions. Sleeping quarters were engaged at a hotel for the committee. And for three days Dr. Poe and his friends sat around the studio while Borglum added to the governor's girth. For this work Judge Daniels was a voluntary model. In the end everybody was pleased. Dr. Poe declared that "The result is a *distinguished success.*"

The memorial was unveiled on March 15, 1924, a year later. Dr. Alderman and Josephus Daniels made the chief speeches. Thousands of the governor's old friends attended, together with a crowd of school children. It was a grand affair.

The Sheridan equestrian statue, which stands at the beginning of Sheridan Road in Chicago, came out of this same period and was one of the sculptor's favorites. The technical perfection of it gratified him. He used to say of the horse, rearing with his front feet off the ground, that he could see the play of the muscles under the skin—and that is very likely true.

The work was accomplished under external difficulties. In the first place the construction of an armature for so huge a group was no small undertaking. It was built of heavy timbers, boards and lath and looked something like the pictures of the Trojan Horse. It wasn't as commodious, perhaps, but several able-bodied men could work inside it—and did. A new studio was under construction with the sculptor supervising all details. And outweighing all physical handicaps was the mental strain of his work on Stone Mountain, where things were rapidly approaching a crisis.

However, for his creative work there was always one tranquil spot in his brain that no outside disturbance could enter. He believed in changing his models frequently, stopping only when he could see what he thought to be right. Jesse Tucker, the Stone

Mountain engineer, recalls that this was one feature of his sculpture in which he would permit no compromise.

At one stage of the Sheridan memorial, Tucker pointed out, the sculptor was seriously handicapped by lack of funds. Everybody in the studio knew that he would receive a substantial sum as soon as the group was finished and ready for casting. And one evening it looked as though this happy moment had arrived.

Gutzon walked around the model, seriously studying it. He stopped and picked up an ax. "Tucker," he said, "I believe I can improve that horse." And without further discussion he began to hack down part of the armature and added two weeks to the work.

This habit was well known to his assistants. Once his colored attendant, Banks, reported on the progress of a statue: "Guess the boss is about through. He's started pulling it to pieces."

The personal contacts he made during the production of the Sheridan monument were particularly pleasing to Gutzon. "Big Bill" Thompson, storm center of political controversy, was mayor of Chicago at the time. They became warm friends. Stamford political leaders declined an invitation to meet the mayor when he was due to look at the models, but Thompson knew nothing about that. He arrived at the studio accompanied by nine carloads of New York politicians.

Michael J. Faherty, Chicago's commissioner of public works, was the mayor's first deputy in the memorial project. He had a summer home near Hartford and would drop in at the studio at unexpected moments on his frequent trips back and forth from Chicago. His chief interest was in the development of the over-size model of horse and rider that nearly filled the studio.

To save the expense of casting bronze in the United States the contract was given to Vignali Brothers of Florence. There was an endless interchange of letters and cables. Telephone wires had to be removed and replaced to permit the trucking of the bronze casts to Genoa because some of them were too high. This was the fault of the foundry and added expense for Gutzon. On its trip from New York to Chicago the group encountered patches of the same difficulty and had to be rerouted on a wild course to avoid low underpasses. Faherty, who was anxiously watching all this, finally reported, "Winchester and Sheridan still twenty miles away."

Sheridan eventually arrived for the unveiling. A special "Sheridan Day" had been declared. And there was a big military display with speeches by the governor, the mayor and other dignitaries. All went as scheduled, after which Faherty found time to write of his own troubles. To Borglum he wrote:

Surprises turn up as usual in reference to expense. The governor has ordered the soldiers to turn out, but the officers have no money; and the Sheridan Monument Association is called upon to pay $2,500 to defray their expenses. The total receipts from the State and others will amount to about $43,000, and the expenses will be about $53,000. However, the job is done and meets with satisfaction, for which I have to thank you and your wife.

Gutzon felt that he had never had a more pleasant association.

CHAPTER SIXTEEN

WARS OF AMERICA MEMORIAL

THE Wars of America group in Newark, New Jersey, is the story of a nation told in figures from life and not by allegorical or classic symbols. It is one of the largest bronze memorials in the world, composed of forty-two human and two equestrian figures, all of heroic size. It is the first monument in America to depict mass action. It took three years in the molding, another three years to put it into bronze and ten years of preliminary thought and study.

The same patriotic Amos Van Horn who had left money for the Lincoln memorial had also provided for a monument to George Washington, which was created by the sculptor J. Massey Rhind, and for a third memorial to the soldiers and sailors of all our wars, to the men who had given their lives in making and maintaining the republic. Since Mr. Van Horn's death, World War I had been added to the list. Almost before the Lincoln was finished, Ralph Lum asked Gutzon to begin thinking about the military monument, but the sum of a hundred thousand dollars bequeathed for the purpose was not immediately available and he had to wait. Of his idea to portray mass action the sculptor wrote:

We do things in the mass, not as individuals. Mass action is the keynote of our civilization. Why should it not inspire our monuments? What opportunities there have been in our history for the inspiration of great sculpture animated by that mass spirit. What I should like to see, for instance, is a monument to Lincoln that would include his cabinet. The more one grows, the more his close associates grow with him. And there are the colonial settlements, the founders of the republic and the Western pioneers still waiting to be memorialized in mass action.

The sculptor began his first designs in more or less the conventional way. He adopted the shaft or the upright column, which is often used as a symbol of civilization, and surrounded that shaft with figures, struggling, rising above material difficulties. In making this model he discovered that it failed completely to express the natural impulses of the human being under stress, either attacking or defending himself against an enemy. All war monuments, he decided, should be planned to depict emotions when threatened by loss of a way of life which was at once familiar and sacred to every family, tribe or nation.

When that idea became clear the problem of a memorial to men who had sacrificed their lives for home and country became one of human anxiety and confusion out of which order, organization and direction gradually developed. This went hand in hand with the thought that the wars of America were defensive wars, that America was not a crusader in a militant sense. The war with England, for example, was a declaration of independence, in no way a struggle for dominion beyond America's own boundaries. And the First World War was, in the sculptor's own words, "probably the most remarkable example of utter disinterestedness in conquest." Monuments that are built for war, he concluded, generally treat battle and fighting as part of the process of civilization, while in fact civilization develops its lines of peace on confidence and in ways that are antagonistic to war. Of how the plan slowly developed in his mind he said:

My first sketch, following abandonment of the shaft idea, represented a confused group of men who were attempting to organize

"THE TRAIL DRIVERS"

This group is in Breckenridge Park, San Antonio, Texas.

THE BORGLUMS' DAUGHTER
Mary Ellis Borglum is now Mrs. David Vhay.

themselves and move toward leadership, with Washington and Lincoln symbolically present. But symbolism, though necessary in a group of this kind, had great disadvantages in that it introduced an unnecessary idea of unreality in the passing of great individuals, which appeared to me to be hurtful in a work of art. It seemed that Lincoln and Washington standing together as historic characters introduced a thought that was hurtful to the life and reality of the group. It might give a mystical character that would detract from its vitality.

Finally in the last sketch I introduced two horses because the horse is not only a companion to man but is his closest companion in times of danger, as a carrier, a weapon, or a friend. Artistically and sculpturally his excitement and nervous tension can be used either realistically or symbolically in a group to add life and strength and to suggest a fear that we would not want to show in a human figure. I felt also that in a group of so many figures an upward movement was preferable to keeping them flat on the ground. When I elevated the center of the base of the monument the change instantly increased the sense of struggle and effect.

The defensive character of American wars is suggested in the first part of the work, consisting of a group of four figures. I have drawn the figures of men who will resist anything they think unjust. I have clothed these men in the uniforms of three wars, over a century apart, and strangely enough there is no incongruity of effect.

Although these figures represent mass resistance in the Colonial and Civil War and World War periods, only one man in the group has drawn a weapon. I have shown here four men who form the front and bulwark of a group of forty-odd characters, representing an entire nation mobilizing under pressure of war, and only one man among them displays an implement that could injure another. I have chosen the sword because it is symbolic of authority.

Immediately back of this group I have represented the only organized mass action indicating battle. There are five or six figures, infantry and marines, charging forward with their rifles, six guns in the hands of as many men, and they represent the entire armament of this national monument.

Just at this point, as an allegro of the symphony, I have introduced the two horses to accent the power and movement of an irresistible forward plunge, with plain indication of the loss of control that always appears under great stress. In these horses I have shown a different character to indicate their separate response to the movement.

From this point backward the composition indicates organization, preparedness, equipment and such confusion as extends behind the battle line to the recruiting source and into the home, indicating, I feel, that America's battles are all for the *defense* of her homes.

Nine different models were made, and the development of the composition covered considerably over two years of time. The entire composition was modeled full size, as it appears in bronze, without having been "pointed out" as is usually the custom. About forty tons of clay were used. Every bit of it was handled four or five times. The large group itself required about three years of incessant labor.

The characters of the group are known people of our time. They are portraits which it is not necessary to indicate. For example, the aviator was a personal friend of mine, John Purroy Mitchell, former mayor of New York, whom I included because of his patriotism and because he, like so many other gallant airmen, was a sacrifice, I have been told, not to battle but to criminal mismanagement behind the battle line.

This group in bronze is the first accomplished part of a plan I have had in mind for over thirty years—to develop monumental art into a living, active, historical record of moods, lives and characters of the men and women who are responsible for our national development.

In the enlargement of the idea and the making of various models Ralph Lum, whom the sculptor had come to know in the making of the Lincoln memorial, played an important part. The mutual trust and regard established between the lawyer and the sculptor was a dominating factor in producing the memorial. Such a relationship between sponsor and creator is unique in the annals of public memorials in America. A like relationship is not a matter of record anywhere else unless, perhaps, between Pericles and Phidias.

On February 11, 1921, ten years after the completion of the Newark Lincoln memorial, Mr. Lum, acting for the three executors, awarded the commission to Gutzon Borglum and authorized him to go to work. When photographs of the model were published wagers were laid among artists that it would be impossible for any sculptor to keep his creative impulse fixed on one subject long enough to produce an art work of such proportions. They did not know that monotony or dulled interest was an impossibility to an artist who regarded variety not as the spice of life but as its bread and butter. Always he had two or three productions on hand as well as an enormous correspondence, a lecture to art students, a promised magazine article and a political campaign in which a "progressive" candidate must be elected lest the heavens fall.

He was doing the Sheridan memorial for Chicago, which nearly filled his Stamford studio, when he received the Wars of America commission. Characteristically, he immediately began to clear a place in the woods near his home and to dig out the ground for a foundation. The foundation he built of stones covered with cement, a support stout enough to be unshaken by any number of tons of clay or marble. On this he built a bigger studio with walls of stone, while at the same time he laid out the armature for the big group in the middle. Under his personal supervision large rocks for the base of the walls were dragged by horses and tackle from the bed of the near-by river.

The location of so huge a monument demanded much thought and preparation. Eventually the City of Newark cheerfully spent another hundred thousand dollars for the setting of the group. Regarding this matter the sculptor wrote to Carl Bannwort, of the Newark Parks Department:

Now that the monument matter is settled, won't you get hold of Caparn, your landscape architect, and let us have a conference about where it will be placed? If you and he will come over and lunch with me, we can talk this park proposition over in detail.

You have a chance to have the best memorial in the United States and I don't want any slip through my failing to be beforehand. You are always in such a hurry yourself, anyway, you will be rebuking me if I don't keep one or two steps ahead of you.

A little later Mr. Bannwort replied:

This is a subject I hardly dare mention. The mere whisper of it may cause as great a stir in the large area of your cerebellum as when a brick is tossed into the pond and visibly agitates every molecule of water.

When we move the bandstand and other excrescences from Military Park, the memorial site, to make room for the monument, we must have a tool shed. Is there no way of putting a door at the northern end of your plinth and using some of the space under the bronze group for this utilitarian purpose? For fear that a whole load of bricks will be heaved by you with deadly aim, I say no more at present.

The modeling was "going splendidly," as the sculptor wrote, when Mr. Lum brought up a subject of prime importance, which of itself involved a whole volume of correspondence. This was the casting in bronze of the huge memorial. Mr. Lum wrote:

I am wondering if you could within the next week secure some estimate for the casting from some reliable concern. I have no thought of your giving the contract to anyone at present, for I think the prices are apt to decline further; but I would like to get some definite estimate. The way many sculptors and other people are constantly putting it up to me—that the casting can never be completed and the work delivered for anything like your contract price—would unsettle my nerves were I not so sure of you and your ability to put through anything you undertake. But I would feel relieved to see some cost estimates just the same.

In answer to Mr. Lum, whose chief concern now was that the sculptor was putting so much into the memorial that he could expect no profit for himself, Gutzon sent a list of bronzes he had produced, with a careful comparison of size, weight and cost. His conclusion was that the forty-two figures of the Wars of America were equal to about sixteen single figures and that the contract price of $100,000 would "see him through." As a matter of safety, he added, he was corresponding with European bronze casters who might do the work for much less than would be charged in this country.

He was dismayed when the American estimates came in—from the Gorham Company, $123,000; from Roman Bronze, $87,000; from Henry Bonnard, $78,857. This meant that every bit of the available money would be spent for the bronze casting alone, which is usually less than half the cost of a monument. It was an immense relief when from the Vignali Brothers of Florence, Italy, came an estimate of 475,000 lire, which at that time, October 1921, was worth about $20,000. A contract was signed to the effect that the monument would be shipped from New York in eight sections (plaster casts) and that the first bronze section was to be returned not later than February 1, 1922, and the other seven sections before the end of the same year.

And then the misfortune that had dogged the sculptor if ever he went into a business deal was again at his heels. He had an Italian friend in the United States who said he was going abroad and for the honor of being a part of so noble a work would gladly make all the business arrangements with the Vignali firm. Into the contract the friend inserted two wholly unexpected clauses— that the sculptor was to be penalized for every day's delay in getting the plaster casts to Florence, and that the friend was to receive a ten-per-cent commission on such a penalty as well as on the contract with the sculptor himself. It was later learned that the friend sued Vignali for refusing to inflict the penalty on the sculptor. Vignali, being familiar with the optimism of art, had never expected Gutzon to deliver the models on time.

There was a weary imbroglio. The sculptor sent his assistant, Hugo Villa, to superintend the whole bronze-casting business.

Hugo reported in 1925 that the first group of figures which had been shipped in 1922 were only partly cast; that later groups to arrive had been cast and were scattered all over the foundry; that the contract made by the sculptor's friend was a pretty bad one.

In Newark, meanwhile, all the burden of explanation fell upon Ralph Lum, a man of exemplary patience, who was being constantly asked by artists, reporters and expectant citizens what had become of the memorial. In answer to one of his many letters Gutzon wrote in 1922:

The new studio I had to improvise for this memorial has been a great physical burden, while the sheer labor of creating such a group has been terrible. However, that is all overcome now, and I have simply to take up figure by figure and group by group, with some concentrated work of course, but it will be like revamping a manuscript you have written.

Now about finishing the group of horses by the first of this month, as you hope. This is quite possible in point of time and labor, but it would be bad and harmful. You will be surprised to hear me say I'm a little sorry the main figures are gone to be cast so I cannot work more on them. I do not need to tell you I shall do nothing that will hurt the final result, but I ought to say that I work so rapidly no allowance is made for my slowing up. This work is a colossal undertaking. A true, clear perspective of it as a whole must be maintained throughout its making. Handling a mountain of material is of itself a man's job continuously. For that I calculated, but the housing and the danger of freezing and the responsibility of caring for so much I did not consider as I now would.

If a sculptor should undertake to do one figure a month, complete—twelve figures a year—it would be undertaking the unheard of in art. Yet as the work stands today, I've done much more than that. In the next sixty days I shall have done nineteen human figures and two horses. I have spent at least half my working time, by necessity, to properly house and protect the work. These nineteen or twenty figures are all separate and amount to about two thirds of the whole. I don't believe anything like it was ever done before. I certainly could not repeat it and should not want to. As to its value, you know better than anyone else that the group is worth half a million if it is worth a cent.

In a previous letter the sculptor had written in a different mood: "The work is going splendidly, but I am terribly tired—more constantly tired than at any time in my life—and it's not because I have reached the age of one hundred." Answering both letters, Mr. Lum wrote:

I can realize, as you know, better than anyone else all that you say, except the single fact of your having grown so terrifically fatigued by the labor of our great work. I can't think of you as tired. Somehow I don't associate it with you. Can't you just go away from it all for a week or two and then get the labor of the rear group out of the way and get it shipped and boxed? I am leaving for abroad next week, and of course I realize now that we can't possibly unveil this fall. But I know I will have to move out of town if everything isn't in readiness by early spring. That you should have a million dollars and ten years' time for this work I know full well.

Gutzon was still at his wit's end. The first group of four figures had not been shipped until September 1922, and by contract all the forty-two figures in eight groups were to be returned before the end of December. There had been delays in getting clay into wax, delays which eventually made the unveiling four years late. For these delays the dimensions of the group and the sculptor's determination that only his best work should be fixed in bronze were responsible.

The Stone Mountain project, started in 1915 before the Wars of America project had been authorized, had now been suddenly revived and the sponsors were demanding Gutzon's return to Atlanta. Still the sculptor's work was virtually done when again, as the Italians say, "The devil put his tail in the business." The total expense of shipping the crates of plaster casts to Florence had been about $2,000, as done by an American shipper, Caldwell and

Company. Now came a bill for twice that amount for returning bronzes which occupied less space. The shipment was handled by an Italian who added extra fees for trucking from Florence to Leghorn and "deck charges." Finally there was a peremptory demand from Gutzon's friend for $2,000 as his commission.

In paying other bills that he thought to be legitimate the sculptor had already used all available funds while he himself worked for nothing because, as he wrote to Mr. Lum in 1926, "This monument must be put up if I have to keep on paying for it to the end of my life and mortgage all I possess." Confronted now by demands that he thought unjust but could not carry to court, he borrowed money to pay them and gave several of his small marbles as security.

Troubles never come singly, says an old proverb. Gutzon was at Stone Mountain, absorbed in another work, when word came that all the bronze casts had at last arrived in Newark, where no one had the slightest idea of what to do with them. By keeping the wires hot the sculptor located his old friend Bob Baillie, who dropped his own work and hurried to Newark. There presently he was joined by Villa. At the hands of these two, and by what the sculptor gratefully accepted as an act of Providence, the great work moved swiftly to its climax. Several years later Mr. Vignali asked the sculptor if he had found a case of champagne in the neck of one of the horses. Gutzon said he hoped that the welders made a party with it.

The unveiling at Military Park on Memorial Day, 1927, was thrilling enough to efface all memory of the years of waiting. The mayor of Newark, Thomas L. Raymond, had formally proclaimed a public festival; he eulogized, among other things, "the excessive generosity and spirit of self-sacrifice of the sculptor Gutzon Borglum, who has given without limit of his genius, his time and effort." Because the memorial was national, not local, invitations had been sent to the President of the United

States and his Cabinet, to all governors, to senators, congressmen and persons of distinction in national life, scores of whom responded and were present in festival spirit with tens of thousands of New Jersey citizens.

The orator of the day was Secretary of the Navy Wilbur. Over the inspiring scene floated silvery captive balloons. At a bugle signal they rose, lifting the flags which had been concealed in the monument, and out flew forty-eight pairs of carrier pigeons to speed the message of good will to every state in the union. The sculptor's contribution had been to scatter poppies over the green around the memorial as an expression of his own feeling for the soldiers and sailors who had given their lives for the United States. When it was his turn to speak he said:

It would be impossible for me to express the pleasure I feel and the gratitude to God that I am able today to deliver to you and through you to Newark and to America this memorial monument to the people who have founded and protected a new freedom of the world.

The design in its dramatic sense is conceived as a moment of crisis when the life of the state is threatened and depicts America's manner of meeting such a crisis. It is a memorial to soldiers and sailors. It is a monument to the fortitude of the American people. It is located here because here Washington stood. Here he many times assembled his troops. Here Lafayette was received by your forefathers, and the building of this monument was prophesied. Here Jackson met your citizens, as did Lincoln, Theodore Roosevelt and the other great leaders. All these staunch souls foregathered here on the very ground whereon this design is set, to discuss their course or part or, if necessary, pay sacrifice to national service.

The design itself represents a great spearhead, consistent with the character of Military Park. Upon the field of this spearhead we have placed a great Tudor sword, its blade the pool, its hilt the monument representing the American nation at a crisis, answering the call to arms.

As news of the unveiling spread through the country, with descriptions of the impressive ceremony in the newspapers, a flood of congratulatory letters came in, some from old friends, some from strangers, many from distinguished sources. All criticism of the sculptor who had undertaken two big jobs at once was now forgotten. He was assured that such a work of art was well worth waiting for. One of the letters was from Robert Baillie, most valued by the sculptor because of its human quality and because the writer had worked in the studio and understood him and what he had been trying to do. Baillie wrote:

Mrs. Baillie and myself want to say how much we thought of the group and the unveiling ceremony. It was simply glorious in spite of the rain. I liked what you said, and Mr. Lum's acceptance was well worded; but what appealed to me most was the message from the governor of Georgia. I think that was the most sincere tribute to your efforts that I have heard at any time, and well it may be so since they now know what they have lost. You certainly have made a warm spot in the hearts of Newark's citizens and one that will not be forgotten by them. I am sure that you have had many letters of congratulations but none, I can assure you, more sincere than ours.

And Ralph Lum added: "You know how much the association with you has meant to me, and my joy that it has all worked out so beautifully is an abiding and comfortable one."

CHAPTER SEVENTEEN

STONE MOUNTAIN

You PROBABLY have heard the story of Stone Mountain, Georgia, as who, alive, hasn't. Stone Mountain is an isolated mass of granite that rises abruptly from a plain near Atlanta, and on its precipitous face Gutzon Borglum once started to carve the pageant of the Confederate Army. The idea had its inception somewhere around 1910 or 1911. Borglum was asked to look at the project in 1915; began his preliminary work on it shortly before the First World War; carving was started in June 1923; the head of Robert E. Lee, a gigantic sculpture, was unveiled in January 1924; the figures of Stonewall Jackson and Jefferson Davis were roughed out during the summer of 1924; on February 18, 1925, there were words between the sculptor and a representative of the Stone Mountain Confederate Memorial Association; by midsummer the models were broken, Borglum had left Georgia, and what was probably the world's first attempt at mountain carving was abandoned.

The years have produced a variety of stories about what happened at Stone Mountain, most of them untrue, and there is little use now in summing them up. But the wreckage on the mountain was an evident fact, as was the finish of one of sculpture's most astounding efforts. From what remained of the carving it was easy to envision the Confederacy's last glorious march

—the ride of the great leaders with horse, foot and artillery across the vast granite wall toward what had looked like immortality. But there wasn't going to be any immortality.

Borglum's plan for the depiction of the army had kept pace with his far-reaching mind. He hadn't overlooked a detail: In the front would be the leaders. Behind them the men, a horde of gray-uniformed men, riding their horses or dragging their guns or staggering afoot from the brink of the great cliff top, entering this last great parade from out of the sky. He had made no count of the figures. Apparently there was to be no end to them . . . and no matter. There was a tall precipice in front of him—thousands and thousands of square yards.

All that was gone now, not only the first of the striking carvings, but the hope for the memorial's completion. Gutzon Borglum waited for a long time for the aid he felt must come—for the miraculous intervention that would bring the stone soldiers back to the mountain. But nothing came of half a dozen efforts to put the hard-rock men back at work. Gutzon Borglum died, and nobody in Atlanta talks about Stone Mountain any more. Borglum, they figure, is the only man who ever knew how to carve a mountain, and they are at least partly right. He is certainly the only man who ever did it.

On February 27, 1927, Lynn Haines, who obviously knew something about this dramatic episode, introduced Gutzon Borglum to the Penguin Club in Washington. What he said may not have been too reserved, but anyone who knew anything about the Georgia project would have admitted its truth. Haines declared:

Borglum had an impossible dream for Stone Mountain. Its inception was beyond belief. Its execution was unimaginable. Every phase of it presented problems which his smart friends considered insurmountable. He ignored human limitations and took up the job. He created a national state of mind that accepted and approved his impossible project. Then he financed the memorial. He calmly accomplished what it was said could not be done in engineering. He had to have and therefore produced entirely new and hitherto unknown devices in photography, and in mechanics and in his own art. He proceeded to carry out his idea on a scale so colossal as to make it the most miraculous thing ever shaped by human hands. . . . I have been at Stone Mountain several times with Mr. Borglum. It is rightly described as "the largest upthrust of unbroken granite in the world." It stands alone.

We have all wondered about Mr. Borglum in that work. He was so high that he was merely a small black spot moving across the mountain in the wind. He was giving shape to statues some two hundred feet tall and giving them the grace and detail that you would find in figures in his studio.

They said it could not be done. . . . So Gutzon Borglum did it.

And then Lynn Haines told the story of Stone Mountain. Or rather he told an important part of it. He neglected to call attention to the fact that what one man can *do* another man can *undo*.

In 1910 the Civil War was still one of the South's active and bitter memories. There were still plenty of people alive who could tell from personal experience of the pillaging of homes, the burning of Atlanta, the devastation of the Southern countryside by Federal troops.

The women of the South had banded together as The United Daughters of the Confederacy to alleviate as well as they could the misery caused by the war and to cherish the memory of their heroes. Gutzon had been commissioned by a branch of the U.D.C. to carve a memorial to the first Southern soldier killed in battle; so he came to meet many of the remarkable membership, including the national president, Mrs. C. Helen Plane of Atlanta.

Mrs. Plane was a singularly able woman. Although nearly eighty years old when Gutzon first saw her, she was still vigorous and highly opinionated. She was a person for whom the War between the States had never ended.

She was living in Mississippi in the first part of 1861 when her husband, a surgeon, had been killed. With her old colored nurse for company she had toured the battlefield in a one-horse wagon looking for his body. She had found it and taken it home for burial.

Years afterward, when she and the sculptor had become friends, she asked him if he had noticed that she didn't shake hands with him when they first met . . . and she explained. "I was afraid," she said, "that you might in some way have been responsible for my husband's death."

For many years there had been talk in Atlanta about using the flat granite front of Stone Mountain to present some sort of Confederate Memorial. The U.D.C. approved the idea and Mrs. Plane gave impetus to it. Her plan had little more form than anybody else's, except that she had seen the head of Lincoln, by Borglum, in the national capital. She said that she would like to have the same man carve a head of Lee on Stone Mountain's great bare wall.

She interviewed the owner of the mountain, Sam Venable, who promised her a spot twenty feet square near the base of the cliff on which to carve the memorial to Lee. And armed with this promise, she wrote to Borglum.

Gutzon did not know anything about Stone Mountain, but he was interested in Lee. So, in the summer of 1915, he came to Atlanta to meet Mrs. Plane and her committee. The women met him at the railroad station, drove him to Stone Mountain, and pointed out the spot donated by Venable. He looked at it in puzzled silence.

"Well," snapped Helen Plane, "what do you think of it?"

"Ladies," gasped the sculptor, "I don't know what to think. But it seems to me that a twenty-foot head of Lee on the side of that mountain would look like a stamp on a barn door."

The stunned women wanted to take him back to Atlanta where they had arranged a luncheon and a reception, but he begged off. He wanted to study the mountain, he said, to see if something could be done with it. So the U.D.C. committee left him in the rambling old summer home of the Venables at the lower end of the mountain and trooped off without him.

On that day a friendship and mutual understanding sprang up between Samuel Venable and Gutzon Borglum that was to last as long as they lived. The Venable family at the time included Mother Venable, who had been Cornelia Hoyt and had lived in Atlanta during the Civil War; her son Sam, already in his fifties, a whimsical bachelor and head of the family; his two sisters, Leila and Elizabeth; their husbands, Dr. James N. Ellis and Frank Mason; and the two Mason children, Sam and Leila. They all lived together in a huge house built of Stone Mountain granite in Atlanta, spending their summers at the home near the cliff which they called "Mount Rest." Sam Venable had been in the granite business with his brother Will who had died leaving two daughters, both married and living in their own homes—Mrs. Robert Thornton Roper and Mrs. Coribel Kellogg Orme.

With the Venables at "Mount Rest" Gutzon passed three pleasant days. He got up in the early morning to see whether or not the sun's first rays touched the cliff. He watched the light traveling all day and studied the angles and shadows of its fall. On the night of the third day he watched the mountain with a wisp of pale moon hovering over it. He seemed to see a gray-uniformed host stealing quietly over the upper edge of the great wall, moving northward across its face.

That evening he pointed out to Sam Venable what he had seen. Near the top and sweeping downward, the Confederate armies. Above, the artillery, appearing at the summit as if coming from beyond. Dropping down and over to the left across the cliff, a procession of men, guns, horses. Left of these, the cavalry in full forward motion. And in the center, where the wall bulged outward, was a colossal group of the principal chieftains of the Confederacy—Lee, Stonewall Jackson and President Jefferson Davis. Swinging away to the left were column upon column of Confederate infantry.

Sam listened and smoked vigorously. Then, after a long study he made his comment. "I suppose," he said, "it will take an awful lot of rock."

Gutzon didn't smile. "A strip at least two hundred feet wide," he said. "The whole of the steep side, clear to the top for the central group alone."

"That all?" asked Venable sarcastically.

"No, I'll need the sky, too. Can't have any buildings or chimneys sticking up from behind."

Sam laughed. "All right," he said, "you can have it."

The next day Gutzon went back to Atlanta and told Mrs. Plane and her committee of his additions to their dream. "We haven't got enough money!" declared the practical Mrs. Plane. But Borglum talked to them. Enough people North and South would be willing to help, he said. He would go through the country and solicit funds. People would come from all over the world to pay tribute to these heroes, he said, to pay tribute to the ones who had died for the right as they had been given to see the right. It would be a shrine for Americans who had fought, without hope, without money, without arms, for the things they believed in. It would be the greatest memorial ever conceived. That's what Gutzon Borglum believed, and what he said, and the women agreed with him.

There was to be a national convention of the U.D.C. in San Francisco in October 1915 and Mrs. Plane and Mrs. Walter Lamar, president of the Georgia Division, called on Gutzon to attend and tell the delegates about what he intended to do and why. Gutzon went, marched the warriors down the mountainside as he had for Sam Venable, and produced the same results. It was the speech of his life.

The imagination of Gutzon Borglum was just as valuable in his speechmaking as in his sculpture. That the national organization of the United Daughters of the Confederacy should rally in support of his prodigious memorial is not surprising. The interest and support that the press stirred up in the North and East and West as well as in the South was something of a sensation.

In the spring of 1916 the sculptor took his family, Mrs. Borglum and little Lincoln, to Atlanta to live. There Mary Ellis, partly named for Dr. Ellis of the Venable family who saved her life, was born.

Sam Venable and his two nieces consented to deed the necessary portions of the cliff face to the Atlanta chapter of the U.D.C. The deeds were formally presented on May 20, 1916. At that time a stone marker was unveiled and a ceremony of dedicating the mountain for a memorial to the Confederacy was performed with Mrs. Plane and a number of Atlanta citizens assisting.

In December of that year the businessmen of the community were invited to a meeting at Decatur, county seat of the county in which Stone Mountain is located. Some routine business was being transacted when the sculptor came in and sat in a chair with the audience. He quickly heard the conversation of two men directly in front of him.

"What's this meeting being held for?" whispered one of them.

The other sniffed. "Oh," he said, "some damn fool artist from New York has a notion he can carve up Stone Mountain, and they want him to tell us about it."

When Gutzon rose to speak he addressed all his argument to this second man who turned out to be Forrest Adair, one of the prominent citizens of Atlanta.

At the end of the speech Mr. Adair came forward and apologized. "I'll admit I was skeptical," he said, "but now I really think it can be done and that you're the one who can do it." He was a firm supporter of the memorial plan ever after.

Gutzon's success with the businessmen that day was general. But although he could make mountain carving seem easy to a skeptical opponent, he had more trouble convincing himself. The difficulties began to haunt him day and night. A mural painter facing a vast canvas has a uniform surface on which to

lay out his design and balance its parts. Stone Mountain, however, had an irregular, uneven surface, with a huge overhanging
bulge which must be harmoniously utilized unless the sculptor
wished to convert the side of the mountain into a flat wall before
starting his design.

How was he ever going to locate his sketch on the mountain?
How could he be at once near enough to outline his figures and
at the same time be far enough away to get a proper perspective
of the whole and establish right proportions?

How was he to get his workers to their working stations without utter exhaustion? How were they to work at ease, unham-
pered by constant dread of a sudden fall? How were they ever
going to be able to remove enormous amounts of stone without
growing old and gray in the process?

His friends begged him not to become involved in so hazardous and fantastic an undertaking. His younger brother Solon,
whom he had summoned to the spot in 1915 when the monument was first contemplated, gave the only encouraging suggestion. He said: "You have an advantage here over most sculptors.
All you have to do is remove what stone you don't want."

Helen Plane and her group had collected about two thousand
dollars for their monument to Lee. For the time being Gutzon decided to use that sum for a scaffold and for steps leading down
over the side of the cliff to permit an examination of the rock and
to make preliminary drawings.

A man by the name of Jesse Tucker happened to be working on
the Venable home, and the sculptor became acquainted with him.
Gutzon discovered that he had unusual intelligence, ingenuity
and resourcefulness—qualities indispensable in this entirely new
and different kind of work. He engaged him to construct a flight
of steps going down over the face of the mountain from the top.

This was a hazardous undertaking. At its northern end Stone
Mountain slopes gradually to the ground level. Horse-drawn

vehicles as well as automobiles can reach a point three fifths of the way up with difficulty. The steep side, the side chosen for the carving, is precipitous. The slope starts treacherously easy for some feet from the top and then swiftly changes to a sheer drop of hundreds of feet to the plains of Georgia. A red line shows where the danger begins. Many stories are told of those who have disregarded the line and plunged to their deaths. At one or two points there is a narrow ledge, which occasionally catches a goat or a child who is more lucky.

Mr. Tucker depended largely on Negro labor and was singularly successful in working with it. He is a man who naturally inspires confidence and, by going ahead and showing the men just where and how to step, he soon had them crossing the red line and drilling holes in the rock. Into these holes steel bars were cemented. The woodwork of the stairway was attached to the bars. The first stairway was 480 feet long and ended on a platform ten feet wide with a barrier twenty feet high on the outside.

Conspicuous among Tucker's Negroes was one called Homer, by whom the Borglums were adopted. He could take a piece of timber four by eight inches and eighteen feet long, lift it from the wagon, put it on his shoulders, carry it to the top of the cliff and down the stairs without dropping it or pausing for breath.

Jesse Tucker proved to be a helpful organizer and superintendent and a faithful friend. He played an important part in all that followed. Over thirty years after this first meeting, the Borglum family was driving through the Florida town in which he lives. Answering a phone call, he came over with his whole family. He refreshed Mrs. Borglum's memory with many details of work that she had forgotten. He made one memorable remark: "Men didn't work *for* Mr. Borglum. They worked *with* him." That, possibly, is an explanation of how he was able to carve mountains.

The immediate problem which faced the sculptor was how to

get men to their work in the middle of a steep cliff 800 feet high. The quarry men who had been taking granite from Stone Mountain for years had never thought of taking any from the steep side. How then were men who had to be able to handle drills freely and easily without fear on intricate work to get to their places. Engineers were consulted. All advised against tackling such an insurmountable problem.

Finally, at the suggestion of the inventor Lester Barlow, The Brown Hoist Machinery Company of Cleveland, Barlow's firm, sent two of its best engineers to Stone Mountain. They went into the matter in great detail. They evolved a grandiose plan for a steel mechanism 550 feet high, with sliding platforms and elevators to carry the workers to their stations. The cost of this structure was set at $200,000, not too much, probably, but far beyond the reach of the sponsors of the project.

The sculptor, however, was undaunted. He devised a strong leather harness with a seat attached, to be buckled around the waist, in which a man could sit and push himself around by his feet, leaving his hands free to use drills or paintbrush. The harness was attached to a steel cable fastened at the other end to a winch or wheel hoist, which could be operated by one man turning the wheel so the worker could be pulled up or let down as was necessary. The winches were firmly anchored to the stone.

By this device the sculptor could and did go all over the face of the cliff, exploring the surface imperfections. Tucker got a bad jolt doing it in the dark. Even Governor Trinkle of Virginia proved—to the terror of his wife watching from below—that he too could go adventuring over the rock. By adding more platforms on which carvers could stand securely and on which stepladders could be placed to increase their reach, it was found that men could soon learn to carve as comfortably as in a studio on the ground.

The sculptor had gone back to Stamford to work on sketches and models for the carving when the First World War intervened. The government needed all the engineers in the country. Jesse Tucker joined the army and went overseas. Gutzon took up the aircraft investigation. The project of Stone Mountain came to a stop. Work on it was to be delayed for some eight years.

CHAPTER EIGHTEEN

THE IMPERISHABLE MONUMENT

THE SCULPTOR came out of the war and the aircraft investigations heavily in debt. Fortunately he received some large commissions for carving public memorials, but the sponsors of these projects wanted to have his exclusive attention. There was the customary trouble of the setting for one finished piece, and the creation of another, the Wars of America group, was a matter that seemed impossible to finish. As a result Stone Mountain, which seems to have become his most important interest, was a long time hearing from him.

Jesse Tucker, back from the wars, paid a visit to the old workings and made an earnest report. "The stairs and scaffolding need immediate repairs if they are to stay where we put them," Captain Tucker said. "In fact, I should earnestly ask you to come down here if you don't want to lose everything you accomplished before the war."

There wasn't much more money available. People digging down in their pockets to support a world war didn't have much change for a memorial to the Confederacy. That had waited until now; it could wait further. But lack of cash did not delay Gutzon after he had heard from Tucker. There never had been any cash anyway.

When Borglum arrived at Stone Mountain in the summer of

1921 he was filled with new enthusiasms, new ideas that had come to him during the war years and during his struggles with head-strong committeemen who couldn't decide what they wanted. The sculptor looked at the granite mountain and took a deep breath. After all, this was home. This was one place in America where he could never have harsh words with anybody. Here were people who thought as he did—people willing to sacrifice any-thing they had, to glorify the spirit of those who had gone.

Something more than a tremendous picture of the Confederate Army was to be left here, Gutzon decided. He needed a studio in this area; so he would build one at the foot of the mountain—a huge one made of permanent materials. And when the project was finished this building could be converted into a vast art school of a sort much needed in the South. The students, he de-clared, would be able to learn about sculpture by looking at it, by being a part of a great work as they did in medieval Italy.

He designed a great hall to be cut into the rock below the marching statues. This was to be a memorial to the women of the South and a depository for their records. In addition to that he was planning an open-air amphitheater at the base of the mountain. He gave this some tests. Marie Tiffany of the Metro-politan Opera Company came down to sing for a select few and demonstrated the perfect acoustics of the place. This will be a shrine to gladden the soul, said Gutzon. And it looked as if it might be.

For a year the sculptor was forced to commute between Stam-ford and Atlanta. But with Tucker looking after the work on the cliff it began to progress. Sam Venable and Forrest Adair took up the assignment of raising more money.

Borglum decided to scaffold the entire area necessary for block-ing and carving the central group, nearly an acre of perpendicular granite wall. This arrangement would have a higher initial cost but would make it easier and quicker to work the rock. An en-tirely new approach to the project was built from below, 700 feet of steps up to a solid platform. The platform was hung on the mountainside 550 feet above the base, and on it were the blacksmith shops, drill-sharpening apparatus, hoists, power plants, supply rooms and machine shops. Air compressors were installed with air lines and feeders 1,700 feet from the base. A cable hoist was erected and the mountain electrified.

The cost of bringing electricity to the mountain was estimated by the Georgia Power Company at $15,000, but it never came to that. Preston Arkright, president of the company, was interested in Gutzon's plan to carve a mountain. He reduced the bill eighty per cent and presently canceled it altogether.

Once the way was provided for the men to get to their working stations, Gutzon faced the problem of getting something arranged for them to work on. He had next to place his design on the great wall of rock in exactly the right place and proper proportion to the scale of the mountain. The size of the figures was so great and the surface of the wall such that the ordinary scale model which sculptors use was not satisfactory. It was absolutely impossible to get any sense of correct proportion from a steel cage let down over the face of the mountain on cables.

Large drawings were hung over the cliff without success. Then Gutzon began experimenting with a lamp projector which could throw photographs of his models on the mountain face. Up to that time the largest projection machine had a range of only 300 feet. The manufacturers of such machines, whom Gutzon consulted, declared that a lamp powerful enough to project a picture 800 feet would produce such intense heat that the lens would be broken and the slide melted.

Finally Gutzon went to E. S. Porter of the Precision Machine Company of New York who promised to build a projector according to his requirements. After months of experiment the lamp was ready for trying out on the photographic slides of Lee and his generals taken from Gutzon's sketches. The test was made in Stamford; the lamp placed on a terrace near the house and the biggest sheets he could find stretched across the meadow several hundred feet away. The Connecticut Power Company ran the electricity through a special wire.

While the sculptor was fussing with the slide to get the proper focus, his little girl began jumping up and down and pointing her little finger. She exclaimed: "Oh, Daddy, look! Horses riding through the field." And sure enough! There were horses carrying Generals Lee and Jackson riding like ghosts upon the slightly misty atmosphere, far ahead of the sheets hung there to catch them.

The lamp was taken down to Stone Mountain where another difficulty was encountered. The carving was at an elevation of 350 feet. That meant that the light beam carrying the design traveled upward at an angle of a little more than fifty degrees, which meant great distortion. The sculptor discovered that by tipping the slide at a corresponding angle, this distortion could be overcome.

Consequently he first photographed the model on the level. Then he photographed the photograph tipped forward at an angle equal to overcoming the distortion in reverse. Thus a distorted slide was made to meet precisely the conditions on the mountain where the design was to be placed. As a result the picture appeared at that high elevation as it would directly in front of the lens. The picture was then traced on the mountainside in white to guide the blocking-out process of the carvers.

The lamp, weighing about a ton, was bolted to a concrete foundation to avoid the slightest movement. It would be swung to any angle, up and down, right and left. A slide three inches high produced a picture 200 feet high. The enlargement was so great that a pin scratch on the slide measured nine inches in width on the mountain. The head of Lee's horse was thirty feet from tip of ear to end of lip; the stirrup was nine feet long. A man standing on Lee's shoulder needed a nine-foot stepladder to carve the ear.

In these dimensions absolute precision was of the utmost importance. A telephone for communication between the operator and workers on the mountain was installed so that with micrometer adjustments, the same picture could be superimposed night after night on the incomplete tracings. In addition to locating the design on the mountain the lamp made possible infinite changes in the original plan. Even a complete change in the composition of a dozen horses or a hundred soldiers could be projected on the mountain and the effect of the change shown at once.

The picture as it appeared on the mountain shown at night was as clear as the scene in a movie. In fact, one night when the photograph was being shown a passer-by stopped in great excitement, thinking that the figures had already been carved, so life-like was the illusion. The projection machine, Gutzon estimated, saved him at least two or three years' labor in placing his sketch upon the mountain.

A third problem, equally important and seemingly insolvable, was what could be done to remove the stone with the rapidity and facility that a sculptor enjoys when he works on a marble bust in his studio? This thought occurred to Gutzon before he even measured the acreage he intended to use for his carving. How could he whip these enormous dimensions and reduce a mountain to a handful? He related this experience in an article later produced in the Dupont trade magazine. He said:

When I first put drill to that eight-hundred-foot-high block, directing the hands of men I could hardly see at a distance of fifteen hundred feet, I was still impressed by the thought that without some effective substitute for the thousands of enslaved craftsmen of the Egyptian days, our undertaking would never come to an end. I spent weeks experimenting with the ways and means of blocking out masses of unnecessary stone and trying by plug and feather and wedge drills to split them off. All these efforts proved childish and inadequate. After months of failures and careful calculation of costs I began to see that the work would be next to interminable with the labor we could afford and by the known means at our disposal.

I had thought of explosives but, knowing little about them, had vetoed their use. The general idea is that high explosives can be used only to destroy. As I thought this subject over, much as I am writing it, another thought came to me: Why not *control* explosive force? Firearms control it. Why not develop some means by which we could blow off just what material we wanted to be rid of, in precisely the quantities we wished to remove, and at the same time preserve the stone left in place, intact and without injury? That problem I pondered over for months without discussing it with anybody.

Just at that time a Belgian engineer, who was passing through Georgia, visited me at Stone Mountain. I told him what our difficulties were, quite apart from the safety problem of carrying men to such a height apparently unprotected, to work on the side of the mountain. The removal of stone was costing too much and was too slow. The old methods were detaining the development of the design.

"Why don't you use dynamite?" he calmly asked.

"I've been thinking of it," I said, "and I am on the point of making experiments. But it's close work."

He then told me that he had recently enlarged a tunnel through a ledge of granite only a few inches, and that by arranging his drilling and adjusting the charges of dynamite, he was literally able to cut off six or eight inches of the main ledge as cleanly as if it had been channeled.

Of course anybody who knows anything about granite knows that it splits easily in some directions and in others is stubborn and cranky. I spoke of this and he said he had found means of overcoming that trouble.

"Where I cross the grain of the granite," he said, "I put my drill holes closer together. While I drilled my holes to the same depth I did not place my dynamite at the bottom of each one, but scattered the charge, zigzagged it up and down the wall. Then I measured my charge carefully, kept it so light that the six-inch shell often only cracked the stone loose and sometimes a hand bar would be required to release it."

If ever I had that gentleman's name and address I have lost it, but that night in the lamp room I projected the photographs of my models of Lee, Jackson and Davis on Stone Mountain, which was a little over eleven hundred feet from our location. The slide was small enough so that I could hold it in the hollow of my hand, but the picture projected without distortion over nearly an acre. We studied it together. It was this traveling engineer who gave me the assurance and impetus that resulted in the practical use of dynamite in the carving of gigantic figures, in dimensions to harmonize with the colossal thought and life of our day.

I spoke of this experience to a great friend of the mountain memorial idea—the late Coleman Dupont—and, following his suggestion, I communicated with the Dupont powder people at Wilmington, requesting that one of their experts be sent to Stone Mountain to instruct me and my assistants in the use of explosives. They responded very graciously and sent a man who, I believe, was on special duty in Florida. So it was that the amazing, almost fantastic idea of carving with dynamite came into being.

A charming letter from the Belgian engineer has recently come to light, written after the visit referred to above. His name was Jean Vanophem, and he appears to have been summoned back to Belgium. He did not have time to visit Stone Mountain again.

Mr. Tucker remembers that the Dupont man was recalled after a few days at Tucker's own request, because he insisted on using too large a charge—one or two sticks of half-pound strength —whereas Mr. Tucker had found out that a half ounce was a successful charge. Mr. Tucker, after much experimenting, trained one of his crew in the use of dynamite so that the man, Cliff Davis, became such an expert in this artistic form of blasting that he was known as "Dynamite Davis." Cliff could place a row of charges, draw a line on the rock under them and make bets that the result of the explosion would not be more than three inches from the line.

It soon became apparent that the women of the Atlanta chapter of the United Daughters of the Confederacy alone could never raise funds for the tremendous undertaking, estimates for which ranged from two to three and a half million dollars.

The first voluntary contribution had been $5,000 from J. S. Cobb, a North Carolinian as was his friend W. W. Fuller, both of whom were connected with the American Tobacco Company. Forrest Adair, one of the first and most loyal supporters of the memorial, succeeded in raising a few thousand dollars for the most pressing necessities—lumber, compressor, electric motor, etc. Venable and Gutzon both advanced large sums for materials, the sculptor going even more deeply into debt. His Stamford property was heavily mortgaged. It was characteristic of him not to ask pay for services until creditors were making such insistent demands that he was obliged to take action of some kind. This led to misunderstandings. Unfriendly persons called him mercenary. He resented the charge and was called irascible. And, bitterly denying it, he proved that he was.

It was decided to invite some of the bankers and businessmen of Atlanta, as well as other prominent Southerners interested in the Confederate cause, to serve on the executive board of the Stone Mountain Confederate Memorial Association. Neither the name nor the constitution of the original organization was changed in any way, and the United Daughters of the Confederacy continued to comprise the main body of the membership, annual dues for which were fixed at five dollars. It was distinctly understood that the men were to help only in financing the design and plan created by Gutzon Borglum and adopted by the Atlanta chapter. It was not a question of a civic committee engaging a sculptor to carry out a design made by someone else.

Mrs. C. Helen Plane was made president-emeritus. W. W. Fuller was made nonresident honorary president and vice-chairman of the executive committee. Four members of the U.D.C. were made vice-presidents, and four others served on the board in different capacities.

Hollins N. Randolph of Atlanta was made president of the association. R. Rivers, familiarly known as "Petie" (not to be confused with a later governor of Georgia named Rivers), was head of the executive committee. Rogers Winter was made publicity director. These three with their lawyer, Reuben Arnold, were the most active in controlling the policy of the memorial association. David Webb became executive secretary and furnished many constructive ideas for raising the necessary cash. So did the sculptor. The remaining members of the executive committee were Sam H. Venable, Robert Harvey, Eugene Black, W. A. Sutton, Thomas W. Connally and Mrs. Sam Inman, a woman of wealth and social prominence.

In March of 1923 the real financing of the memorial began. A working organization was perfected, and Atlanta was asked to set a precedent for the United States as a whole. The city responded and tentatively pledged $100,000, payable in five years. Fulton County pledged a like amount. Individual subscriptions totaled approximately $40,000.

Dave Webb suggested the idea of memorial tablets to be placed in the U.D.C. Hall, at the base of the mountain, to carry the names of relatives who had served in the Confederate Army. Each contributor of $1,000 or more to this fund for carving the memorial was to have the privilege of designating a name for one of the tablets. A family or group contributing a thousand dollars could designate the name of one man for a tablet. Each bronze tablet was to show the name, rank, company and regiment of the soldier or officer so immortalized. This was known as the Founders' Roll and became very popular and lucrative. In setting forth the purpose of the tablets an announcement was published with the following eloquent preamble by Rogers Winter:

As old as human nature is the yearning to memorialize the buried dead, to perpetuate the tradition of illustrious heroes, but never has mankind in all the centuries succeeded in erecting an imperishable monument. Stonehenge is a jumble of granite slabs. The Colossus of Rhodes collapsed two hundred years before Christ and lay in ruins for a thousand years. The Parthenon of Greece, whose marble figures were the most perfect sculpture ever produced, has been virtually dismantled by vandals and art collectors. The pyramids of Egypt are slowly crumbling. Those marvelous temples which adorned the Nile when Egyptian civilization was in its glory are but mounds of debris. The Roman Colosseum is a skeleton of pagan grandeur.

But now, in the Providence of God, it becomes our privilege to create here in the heart of the South, in memory of Southern heroes, the one supreme imperishable monument of human history.

The sculptor made all the designs for this hall, working on them for weeks and delivering the blueprints of them to the committee in July 1923. It was to be cut in solid rock to a depth of sixty-seven feet; in width it was to be 265 feet. It was divided into three rooms: Georgia Hall in the center, with Venable Hall on the right and U.D.C. Hall on the left. There was to be room for 2,890 memorial tablets.

The first work of carving anything at all on Stone Mountain was started on June 18, 1923. The first figure to be carved was, of course, that of Robert E. Lee. The sculptor had made a heroic-size model of the head, seven feet high, in his Stamford studio, and a plaster model of this was brought to the mountain. Much blocking out and roughing off of the surface had to be done before the actual surface of the final figure was reached. The whole area had been gone over carefully and marked out with the aid of the projection lamp.

The sculptor appointed Mr. Tucker superintendent, giving him complete charge of the work. He was assisted by Hugo Villa, an Italian sculptor from Milan, who had crossed the Atlantic years before with a commission to erect a monument in Mexico. A revolution had put an end to the project. Villa had worked his way up to New York and went to Gutzon's studio, where he soon became a permanent fixture as sculptor's assistant. The best in the world, Gutzon called him.

With these two men in charge and on the spot, the "Master," as Villa called his chief, felt that he could safely go back and forth to Stamford or wherever else the business of the Southern memorial called him. He was greatly in demand to speak at U.D.C. gatherings and women's clubs all over the United States, and the Memorial Association expected him to attend such meetings. It also expected him to be on hand to show off the work on the mountain whenever there was a convention of Elks or Rotarians or Sunday-school workers, and there was a continual procession of such events in Atlanta.

In July 1923 the sculptor wrote to Mr. Rivers, reporting a meeting he had attended with Hollins Randolph in Cleveland and their visit to the factory where some of the new machinery for the mountain work was being completed. In the same letter he mentioned that Mr. Tucker had reported to him several times that Mr. Rivers had cautioned him to go slowly with the work on account of lack of funds. Gutzon warned Mr. Rivers that no real carving could be done without the preliminary work Tucker was doing, repeating that the carving was the most important thing and the only thing that would get subscriptions. He deplored the fact that he himself had to be concerned with the money-raising, and cautioned Mr. Rivers against spending more money in the office than was being spent on the mountain, which he had learned was also a fact.

The goal set for the finishing of Lee's head was January 19, the general's birthday. The sculptor left Stamford for Atlanta more and more frequently as the work neared the final surface. It was his practice to do the finishing himself. He never finished a model perfectly and handed it over to someone else to copy or enlarge, as is common practice among sculptors. Especially in enlargements, he believed that better, more individual results could be obtained if he himself modeled the figures in their full size. If he had al-

WOODROW WILSON MEMORIAL AT POZNAN

Mrs. Wilson is at the center.

TORSO AND LEG OF DANCER

ready expended much of his creative interest on finishing a small model, the final figure, he felt, would lack spontaneity and vigor.

In mountain carving this practice was absolutely necessary, owing to the unpredictable character of the stone surface. Blemishes are often found in a block of quarried marble when the sculptor starts to carve into it. It requires little imagination to realize the imperfections that are bound to appear on a cliff exposed to all the elements for thousands of years. As an example, when the Jackson head was being carved a crack suddenly appeared on the bridge of the nose. In previous cases such cracks were not deep, but in this instance the blemish persisted even after the position of the head had been pushed back four times. One more move and the whole design would have had to be changed.

The crack was slight and might have been left, except for the danger of water getting into it and freezing. After fifty years or so it might have become a serious defect. Jackson's face in the original model was looking at Lee. The sculptor decided to turn it to look in the direction toward which Jackson's arm seemed to be pointing. Thus that crack was lost in the six-foot hole of the eye socket, and the nose occupied an area of solid stone.

Only the sculptor made the change possible. He stood over the carvers directing the work. A man trained only to copy a model would have been helpless and hopeless in a situation like this.

During the final six weeks of working on Lee's head, when it appeared that the carving could not be finished otherwise, the men worked all day and all night, in shifts of eight hours each. Gutzon worked with them and was there virtually all the time. Frequently he worked the whole night through.

It was cold on the mountain in the winter, and a canvas was stretched over the work to break the wind. Huge pots of burning coals were placed on the platform and slung along the surface of the rock. The stoneworkers, for the first time in the lives of many of them, were dressed in heavy clothes. They wore what they could keep tied to them and swathed their feet in bulky wrappings of burlap and blankets. But the work was still cold and miserable, and only the calm presence of Borglum gave them any indication that it was ever going to be finished.

Borglum, however, was tired but satisfied. He had never carved a mountain before and in all truth he must have had his moments of misgiving. But Lee's face, as it began to emerge human and understandable from the stone in those last weeks, must have answered all his queries. Nobody would ever tell him again that he didn't know how to carve mountains. Here was the proof. He knew.

CHAPTER NINETEEN

THE EMERGENCE OF LEE

THERE have been few days in the history of Atlanta so festive as the one set for the dedication of the Confederate memorial. And, possibly, there will never be another. The progress of the carving against unspeakable odds had been such that visitors were pouring in from all over the United States. There were artists, engineers, dynamite salesmen, machinery designers, Civil War veterans, politicians and unaffiliated patriots.

When three governors—Brandon of Alabama, Neff of Texas and Trinkle of Virginia—had appeared two days before the unveiling, Gutzon decided that it would be proper to give them a luncheon on Lee's shoulder. It would give them some idea of the size, he thought.

So, with the aid of Hetty McCurdy, who ran "The Golden Glow," a Stone Mountain tearoom, Mrs. Borglum arranged the luncheon. The stoneworkers hung out a pulley, and hot fried chicken, hot biscuits, hot coffee and other things were served with very little trouble. Twenty leading citizens of Atlanta sat down with the governors on Lee's shoulder. One of the governors turned pale when he descended the 400-foot stairway, and sat down to rest several times. At every move he seemed to be stepping off into the infinite.

Three more governors—Morrison of North Carolina, McLeod of South Carolina and Walker of Georgia—were present when Lee's head was presented to the world, besides former governors, representatives of governors, two representatives of the President of the United States, and a long list of distinguished individuals appearing for the Daughters and Sons of the Confederacy and for Georgia and other states. The event was accompanied by all the pageantry and oratory that the South knows so well how to produce. There were pieces about it, too, in the *Stone Mountain Magazine,* published by the Confederate Memorial Association. Said one of these bits:

The dream of the world's greatest memorial began to come true Saturday afternoon at 3 o'clock. With a stately dignity that held something of a caress, a bright, broad national emblem was lifted and gathered as a flowing coronet on the majestic brow of Robert E. Lee, looking now and forever from the sheer wall of Stone Mountain. . . .

And nobody knew—or had even a remote inkling—how wrong that was.

Mrs. Helen Plane, the Old South's daughter, who had hoped for this great memorial, stood by the sculptor's side and leaned on his arm as she gave the signal for the unveiling. Under the gray sky of a typical January afternoon the flag swept aside and the calm, sad eyes of Lee looked down upon ten thousand of his people. The crowd stood hushed in awe and admiration.

Since before noon a pilgrimage had been under way from Atlanta and surrounding communities toward Stone Mountain. There were no good roads hereabouts—not in that day—so presently there was a crush of vehicles parked on the approaches for nearly a mile from the mountain. They never reached the unveiling. Hundreds upon hundreds of automobiles were in fields along the highway, and in ditches and on crossroads. The occupants of some of them walked on miles and miles to the ceremony. Others were stopped in their tracks when the first trickle of cars back to Atlanta began at 3:30.

Ten thousand people stood bareheaded and silent as the statue of Lee was unveiled. Another ten thousand were in the group that could not see, blocked in the crush of traffic miles from the mountain.

Hollins Randolph, president of the Memorial Association, stood on the platform briefly to introduce Dr. David Marx, who delivered the invocation. Mrs. Plane, in a costume of the sixties, was carried onto the rostrum by the sculptor. With bared head he stood motionless as she waved her hand.

Up on the mountain platform, a thousand yards away in an air-drawn line, tiny figures moved beneath the two vast American flags that hung like a curtain. Mrs. Plane's hand was scarcely raised before boulders of granite began to slip from resting places under the flags and flash down the sheer drop of the precipice—five seconds in their fall from the flags to the base of the mountain, then two more seconds before the dull thunder of their impact rolled across the valley.

The flags parted and rose, and between them, to the thunder of cascading granite, the head of Lee appeared—a majestic head that even in its colossal size and distance seemed vibrant and lifelike. The silence of the spectators was long. Then suddenly out of the stillness spoke a voice clear though quavering—an old man's voice: "It's General Lee! It's the general!"

Borglum turned wonderingly toward the source of this unscheduled salute. It was a bent old man who spoke—an old man in a gray uniform. His day seemed to be done. Not many had heard his outcry—not more than a hundred or so who happened to be standing near him—but his voice had brought the awakening of the throng. Applause—cheers, screams and the shrill rebel yell—crashed across the valley and came echoing back again, an amorphous sound like the din of a hurricane. Lee had been well acclaimed.

Gutzon, holding the trembling arm of Mrs. Plane who seemed to have undergone a tremendous emotional shock, suddenly realized what the people were cheering for: the head of Lee. And he gazed up at it openmouthed, conscious that he was looking at it for the first time.

Gutzon Borglum had worked on this massive carving for weeks on end, day and night. He knew every dimension of it, every curve. Its magnitude was no surprise to him, because standing on the upper lip of the statue he had been unable to reach the upper eyelid. He had swung across the face in a bosun's chair, drilled holes along the nose, placed his dynamite sticks and exploded them. But he had had no time to travel down the face of the mountain and into the distance to look at it.

It was a pleasing sight that day. The monument looked logical, perfect in scale on the great wall of granite. The day was mild and gray, and the light was fading; but for all that, there were lifting shadows in the face. Each part of it stood out in its proper place. And for the first time in months Gutzon was really happy.

After a time the cheering thousands were quiet again. They moved in silence to the road, slowly, sedately, like people emerging from a solemn religious service. They got into their cars and just as silently and just as unhurriedly moved out toward Atlanta. Then in an hour or two it was dark—a thick, impenetrable dark.

Gutzon escorted Mrs. Plane to her car and she shook his hand. "I am ninety-four years old," she said. "I have waited a long time for this day and I have never, never in my life seen anything like it."

The unveiling of Lee was merely a beginning for the Confederate memorial. Work on the mountain was resumed immediately.

The bust of Stonewall Jackson was the next subject, and that promised little trouble. Gutzon had made a model of the head in his Stamford studio and had brought a seven-foot enlargement of it to Georgia. While the rough work was proceeding on the mountain, a local studio was completed. Modeling stuff was moved in and Borglum's horse "Smoke" was brought down from Connecticut to pose for the mount of Lee.

Then the arguments began.

There had been no doubt about whose face would be the first to be carved out of Stone Mountain. Jackson was an easy second choice. But after that nearly everybody in Georgia had a departed Confederate relative who should rightfully be memorialized in the first group. In the original plan Borglum had made room for five figures in this group. Lee, Jackson and Davis were certain of their places. Forrest and Longstreet had many supporters for the last two places. Then somebody suggested that seven men be given this immortal recognition, and trouble renewed itself. The committee squabbled. The state legislature rattled with sonorous debate. Church societies and high-school debaters aired their views, and Gutzon Borglum made a fine assortment of models.

The models were a disconcerting problem because modeling clay in the vicinity of Atlanta was difficult to get and expensive to import. For his preliminary work the sculptor modeled in plaster which turned out to be a pure makeshift, because it is not pliable and cannot be used for fine work. Wax was better for small figures but out of the question for the stupendous casts used on the mountain.

In addition to these causes of delay, funds began to get short. Borglum found the money situation an imposing study. The executive committee seemed to be getting plenty of financial aid, but this money didn't seem to be coming in quickly enough. There were always enough funds to support the office and hire the stenographers and get the printing done. But there was never enough of a residue to push the work on the mountain as fast as the sculptor wanted it pushed.

Gutzon was hard-eyed about this situation. Some of the com-

mittee members declared that he was an irascible old obstruction-
ist—that he didn't understand their difficulties nor give them
credit for the work they were doing.

To this Gutzon's reply, generally delivered to them in a harsh
tone, was that the only thing of real importance about a carving
on a mountain was the carving. If the fund raisers couldn't raise
enough funds to pay the hard-rock men, he declared, then there
wasn't much use in their raising any funds. During the first eight
years of getting ready for the work on Stone Mountain—which
started in 1915—Gutzon said that he had advanced $20,000 for
labor, materials and machinery. He had kept no account of the
expense of traveling around the country in support of the enterprise, he said. Nor had he kept any record of what he had put out
for experimentation with new tools, his sketches, studies, drawings and models.

He observed more violently that for the first few months of the
newly organized association he had worked without a definite
agreement. A contract was finally drawn by which the sculptor
agreed to carve the central group for $250,000, he to furnish labor,
power, machinery, explosives and other materials and his own
salary. A portion of an old labor-and-lumber bill was paid to him
on account of his advances during the preceding years. Other payments were postponed for future settlement. For the time being
the association was supposed to pay all expenses at the mountain,
together with a certain monthly stipend for the sculptor. These
payments were always in arrears.

"And why is this?" the sculptor demanded witheringly.

"But, Mr. Borglum," answered the treasurer, "we just haven't
the money. We're sure to have it next week."

Out of nowhere came the plan to persuade the United States to
issue fifty-cent pieces carrying the picture of Stone Mountain Memorial to be turned over to the committee for resale at a dollar.
This looked like a wonderful solution to all money problems and,

to tell the truth, that's what it was. There was some argument about who had first disclosed the idea. Dave Webb was warmly mentioned by some of those close to the subject. But in the end, Henry Stilwell Edwards got official credit for it and is said to have received $30,000 as a reward from the Stone Mountain Memorial Association. Mr. Edwards was certainly a well-known writer, and even without his fifty-cent-piece idea his support seemed to be worth paying for.

Once the plan had been accepted and Edwards properly acclaimed, there seemed to be some difficulties. It was a difficult matter, some Atlantans pointed out, to ask the government to memorialize the valor of soldiers who had so recently been at war with that government. Nobody on the committee had friends in high places or, for that matter, knew much about where to go for help. Gutzon Borglum had come into the Stone Mountain situation as a sculptor whose almost impossible task was the carving of a granite precipice, but he had friends in Washington from the President down. So the executive committee approached him, and all the labor of fostering the memorial coin fell on his shoulders.

It is common knowledge that many things annoyed Gutzon during his vigorous lifetime and that he spoke of them sometimes loudly and witheringly. A careless hard-rock man on Stone Mountain had once observed of him with reasonable fairness, "He's a pretty good stonecarver—but he ain't no sweet talker." And there had been little cause for him to improve his ways since the committee began to think about finance.

The idea of the resalable half dollar appealed to him. It would get funds—plenty of funds. But, he pointed out, the promotion of it wasn't his job. And he was cold and hard about it. He would undertake the work, he said, because he was ready to do almost anything to see the monument finished, but he didn't want to be tripped up every five minutes by petty politics or local interference or advice. He would do the job in his own way, he said, or he would be just as glad not to do it at all. They agreed and he went to Washington.

Borglum wasted no time with professional lobbyists. His first call was on Senator Henry Cabot Lodge, of Boston, cradle of the "damyankees." Lodge thought the idea was grand and directed Gutzon to take it to Senator Smoot. Senator Smoot was chairman of the finance committee. He was also leader of the Republican party, and the sculptor was a little worried about him. He knew that he wasn't going to get votes for himself or his party in the South, no matter what he might do, and he must have been aware of possible censure in the North. But Smoot was a showman no less than Borglum.

"It is a noble idea," he said. "It will be recognized as a gesture of friendship on the part of a victorious government toward its late enemy. I shall be glad to handle it for you."

Borglum then went to President Calvin Coolidge, and what had looked like an almost impossible job was finished. Coolidge, the skeptical, taciturn and unemotional, broke out with one of his rare enthusiasms. He would give the matter his personal support, he said. And he did.

Congressman McFadden, who had helped Gutzon in the aircraft investigation, introduced in the House the bill authorizing the coin, and presently it was through both houses. But the making of a model for a coin and having it approved by the Treasury Department and the Art Commission and the Director of the Mint entails countless visits to offices in Washington, Philadelphia and New York, and it is a tedious process.

Gutzon made nine different models before he got the approval of every detail. There were arguments about the style of the lettering and the arrangement of the figures. One member of the Art Commission thought that the eagle's legs were too gaunt and lifelike and should be enclosed in feather pantalettes.

Secretary of the Treasury Andrew Mellon wanted to know why

the motto "In God We Trust" had been placed over the heads of Lee and Jackson.

"Because they did trust Him," said Gutzon, "and were sincere in their belief that they were right."

The secretary smiled. "And the thirteen stars," he went on. "What are they there for?"

Gutzon knew then that his trouble was over. "It all depends on which side of Mason and Dixon's line you happen to live," he said. "They could, of course, stand for the thirteen rebellious states." And Mellon laughed and gave in.

The first coin was struck at the mint in Philadelphia on January 21, 1925. The first model had been approved six months before, and the memorial fifty-cent piece differed from it in only one important particular. The figure of President Jefferson Davis, a part of the first group projected on Stone Mountain, did not appear on the coin. That was one concession the victorious government declined to make.

CHAPTER TWENTY

MONEY

It BECAME evident during the summer of 1924 that the Confederate memorial of Stone Mountain was on its way to a considerable solvency. The memorial half dollar would presently be minted, whatever the Yankee quarrels about the status of Jefferson Davis and the need for pants on eagles. In the meantime a new project of the inventive David Webb showed signs of lucrative popularity.

"The Children's Founders' Roll," Webb called this new appeal for cash. And all he needed to recruit the eager children to the Founders' Roll was a children's medal that he could exchange for their donations. This, he thought, didn't involve anything very difficult inasmuch as he had one side of the medal already depicted in the first model for the coin. The other side was to carry an inscription of the committee's choosing. But he didn't want the medal to cost too much, and there came difficulty.

The United States mint maintains a rigid high standard in its coinage, and Gutzon wanted the children's medals to be equally fine. He turned his model over to the Medallic Art Company of New York, whose workmanship satisfied him. The company agreed to make the medals for six or seven cents apiece. They were to be sold to the public for fifty cents or a dollar.

However, there turned out to be competition. Another company had made overtures to the Stone Mountain Memorial Association offering to do the job for a cent or two less and intimating that somebody—they wouldn't of course say Gutzon Borglum—was to profit in some way on the difference in price. Gutzon, who had put away his anger during his coin negotiations in Washington, suddenly went berserk again. He turned over to the committee all his correspondence with the Medallic Art Company, showing that he was not getting a cent. He reminded them that he had made all the models for the coin and children's medal without recompense, and pointed out one after another the things he was doing on the mountain for love alone.

"You seem to forget the promotion of your coin idea," he snapped at them. "Who paid me for that? Who paid me for the time I spent getting pushed from one office to another? Who around here ever pays for anything? Who is honest enough to think that he has to?"

Most of the directors tried to placate him, but some weren't convinced. Borglum's blood pressure was still rising when he went out.

In another week there was another bitter quarrel. Gutzon, whose view of his associates was still pretty dim, came across some publicity material designed to promote the sale of the memorial coin. He might not have liked it had he been untroubled by other things. He certainly did not like it in his present state of mind, and his criticism of the publicity director was sudden and bitter. The publicity director answered him in kind, bowed and retired, and, thereafter, the two men never got along together.

Amity was singularly lacking around the memorial headquarters for the rest of the summer. Unfortunate things just continued to happen. The Borglums, toward the end of August, went to Nantucket where, at the request of Ed Howe, the sculptor was to give some talks at the summer school for social science. They had barely arrived when Gutzon got an emergency call to get back to New York. In a heat wave of unexpected virulence the wax model of the children's medal had melted and the completion of the work had been stopped.

The records show that the Stone Mountain Memorial Association was loudly indignant and remarkably bitter. Letters subsequent to the telegrams complained about the sculptor idly vacationing while there was important work to be done.

Gutzon replied that he hadn't melted the wax and that he had previously expressed himself on the subject of the company employing the thumb-fingered medal maker who did do it. Conditions of mutual trust and good will when he repaired the damage and returned to Atlanta were no better than they had been.

Work on the memorial, however, was proceeding smoothly. Gutzon had moved his family into a house near Stone Mountain. The hard-rock men and dynamiters in the crew had learned their jobs. The figure of Jackson would be ready for unveiling in April and that of Davis in June 1925. L. M. Roberts, the Association's engineer, had examined the work and reported that everything was going along according to contract. Gutzon was ahead of his schedule.

In March 1924 the fund-raising activities of the Association began to pay their way. At the end of the month receipts equaled expenditures. In April, before the start of any extraordinary fund-raising campaign, receipts amounted to more than $28,000 and there was plentiful evidence that the flow of cash would continue during May.

The annual meeting of the Stone Mountain Confederate Memorial Association was held in April 1924 and was marked by some political maneuvers that greatly irritated the U.D.C. Officers had to be elected. A new board of directors and a new executive committee was to be chosen to act for the next twelve months. It was an understanding in the Association that the presidency would be passed around from year to year, but this year the old president made a plea for re-election. The national presidential campaign was in full progress. The Association president had been active in support of William Gibbs McAdoo and was having some friction with the editor of the Atlanta *Constitution*. If he were re-elected president of the Association, he said, he would have greater status in politics, and he would resign immediately after the primary election. His request, unfortunately, was granted. It was no help to McAdoo.

The date of the Association's election day was the same as that of the selection of a presidential primary candidate. The political meeting was held first. After it had adjourned the Association president went to the Association's annual meeting accompanied by a large number of politicians.

Up to that point the Association hadn't had many active members. The dues had been five dollars. Nobody seems to have known what the total membership was. Nobody ever counted the attendance. And most of those present were members of the United Daughters of the Confederacy.

Eighty-six politicians came into the hall with the re-elected Association president. Somebody moved to reduce dues to one dollar, and someone else slapped eighty-six dollars on the desk of the treasurer. Eighty-six new names were added to the roster of the Association. And these eighty-six, along with the president, dominated the meeting.

There had hitherto been five or six people on the board of directors. The number was immediately changed to fifty. The membership of the executive committee was increased from nine to fifteen and was to be chosen by the board of directors. A resolution was passed to bar any increase in the membership of the Association except with the approval of the president and a subcommittee of three appointed by him. The president and the executive business manager, as the result of these arrangements, were then in absolute control of the organization. The president forgot his promise to resign.

An executive committee of fourteen men and one woman was named. The men were persons of big affairs—several of them bankers whose daily routine gave them little time for benevolent causes. There was not a member to represent the U.D.C.

There has been a lot of controversy over the Stone Mountain memorial. There will, no doubt, continue to be. Nobody who ever knew Gutzon Borglum would attempt to say he was a complacent character. Decidedly he was not. He knew what he thought was right, and that is what he wanted. He wanted nothing else. Calm argument could change his point of view, of course, for he was intelligent. But he could not be browbeaten. He was honest—so he could not be bribed. His anger could be Jovian, and in his indignation he could be intolerant and insulting. No one will deny these things.

There isn't much doubt that the executive committee of the Stone Mountain Association encountered him in many moods, for he was in and about the premises from 1915 to 1925. When things went wrong with Gutzon's plans, when anybody thwarted him, the world knew about it, and few will say that the early days of the work on the mountain were without confusion.

The story is still circulated in the South that Gutzon Borglum was a genius of evil temper with whom no one could possibly get along; that he had quarreled bitterly with the ladies of the U.D.C. and, in a huff, had destroyed his models and all that it was possible to destroy of the carving on Stone Mountain, and had gone away. But none of that is true except that he did destroy a pair of models.

If anybody thinks that the carving of the Confederate memorial was a simple thing, he may consider the odd politics that took over the project at the annual meeting of the Association in 1924. There would have been nothing simple about that even if Borglum had never lived.

Little had changed in the atmosphere except that money had begun to roll into the treasury and there was prospect of more. The Children's Founders' Roll was getting a large number of members, the children's medals were being distributed in quantities, and presently the memorial coin would come out of the mint.

Gutzon Borglum, back at work on the mountain, paid little attention to the political maneuvering in the Association. If he was displeased with anything, he went down to Atlanta and told somebody about it. Otherwise he was getting President Davis and General Jackson out of the rock in shape for presentation on Davis' birthday, June 3. He was looking forward to the completion of the entire central group by the end of 1926.

He was called from this work to discuss the problem of selling the memorial half dollars. Commercial institutions experienced in such jobs wanted too large a percentage of the profit. Pseudo-patriotic associations wanted more. At a bankers' meeting in the Biltmore Hotel early in 1925 it was suggested that a number of wealthy men might underwrite the coin so that the money or some part of it might be available at once. The board of the Association authorized the proponent of this scheme to find such a group. And the man who had made the suggestion was Gutzon Borglum.

Borglum wrote to John Kirby of Houston, Texas, and got promise of $100,000 toward a fund of $500,000. With Dave Webb he went into Mississippi and got promise of more money. W. W. Fuller urged him to come to New York and there, with friends in the American Tobacco Company, he lined up a sheaf of pledges. Judge Elbert Gary promised to find more. Gutzon invited these people to meet Hollins Randolph at a dinner in Washington where the sums to be subscribed would be agreed on.

President Randolph of the Stone Mountain Confederate Memorial Association failed to show up or to answer telegrams. He was out duck shooting. Nobody, it appears, had time to go and look for him.

Gutzon considered the situation somewhat sadly. The only problem in mountain carving that he could not solve was that caused by human ignorance or cupidity. The Stone Mountain Association somehow had been happy as long as its treasury had been empty. There was now an expectation of an even two million dollars in the till.

The men of the Association formed a quick plan to abandon most of the carving program. It would be simpler, they thought, to spend $250,000 on the central group and reserve the rest of the money "for future causes and purposes."

On February 18, 1925, Gutzon was going through Atlanta from Stone Mountain to Washington with Lester Barlow, inventor of a depth bomb. Barlow had promised that if the government were to pay him his back royalties, he would donate $100,000 of the sum to the Confederate monument.* Barlow says that the sculptor was so outraged at the idea of holding up the spending of money for work on the mountain that he went straight to Washington and got an immediate interview with President Coolidge. His single purpose was to stop the minting of any more Stone Mountain coins.

Coolidge, who sat knee to knee with him in serious and intimate conversation, became incensed. He slapped Gutzon on the shoulder and declared—as Barlow remembers it—"We won't let those rebels put anything like that over on us." Barlow does remember vividly that the President promised to put an end to the issuance of the coins. Gutzon slapped him on the knee and thanked him. Of course, nothing more came of this than conversation. Gutzon had hardly reached the Metropolitan Club after his conference when Bascom Slemp, Presidential secretary, called him on the phone. The President, it seems, had not understood. The promise to stop the coin must be considered unofficial.

Things were moving fast in Atlanta. Tucker was called in from Stone Mountain to meet with some of the men who were active in the Association. Tucker refused to talk with them as a group, and Randolph met him alone.

* His claim was settled in 1940 when he was given nearly $700,000.

The conversation was what the engineer had expected. The directors were going to get rid of Borglum and were offering him $15,000 a year to carry on the building of the memorial. Tucker laughed. It was Borglum's idea, he said. He wouldn't consider taking the job even if he thought himself qualified.

Randolph seemed disappointed. "You could put *something* up there that would be satisfactory," he said.

Tucker telephoned to Gutzon in Washington and begged him to come back. The sculptor said he would. The next day Hollins Randolph gave out a statement which at least one Atlanta newspaper printed under the heading: "Borglum's Dismissal as Sculptor Is Imminent."

Gutzon was back in Atlanta twenty-four hours after receiving Tucker's message. A meeting of the executive committee of the Association had been called for the next day. But the sculptor fully believed that his contract would protect him, and he was not so worried as his friends. Virtually everybody else in Atlanta knew what the executive committee was going to do. A full copy of the proceedings of the scheduled meeting, to its climax in a resolution dismissing Gutzon Borglum, had been given in advance to the Atlanta *Journal* and was in type hours before the committeemen were called to order.

The sculptor was met at the station in Atlanta by Tucker, who drove him out to Stone Mountain. Sam Venable was waiting for him there with his sister Mrs. Mason; Mrs. Grace, of Macon, Georgia; and Mrs. Purdue, president of the Atlanta chapter of the U.D.C. The women went up on the scaffolding to view the progress of the work.

Word of what was happening in Atlanta took the sculptor completely by surprise. He listened, stunned, to the telephone message that the committee had voted to dismiss him. Quietly he broke the news to the little group about him, then considered the situation.

"I shall have to break up the models to protect my design," he said.

The plaster model of Lee's head had already served its purpose. There was a copy of the Jackson head in Stamford. He ordered these models to be dropped off the platform onto the rocks below. And, finally, he told his man Homer to break up the model in the studio, the one showing Davis on his horse. Mr. Venable said there were tears in his eyes as he took one last look at his work and turned his back.

He talked to the U.D.C. women in Mrs. Coribel Venable Orme's house, urging them to carry on without him. Then suddenly Tucker came bounding in from the road and took him by the arm.

"Quick!" Tucker said. "Kiss your wife good-by."

"But where to?" asked Gutzon.

"I'll tell you that afterward," said Tucker, pulling him toward the door.

Shortly they were gone and the people in the house heard a car roaring out the back way on a road from the city that was virtually impassable. The sound had died out and they were well on their way when the local constable arrived and sheepishly produced an order for Gutzon's arrest on a charge of "malicious mischief." The complaint declared that the sculptor had destroyed a model valued at $25.

Nobody has ever pointed out how the Association directors found out about the smashing of the models within two hours after it happened. The constable didn't know. He had just been called on to serve it, and, well, if Mr. Borglum had gone away, he couldn't do that. So he accepted a drink and sat down to enjoy it.

Not until long afterward did Mrs. Borglum discover that the head Gutzon was accused of having destroyed was the useless plaster image of Lee.

The morning after the Association meeting of February 25, 1925, the Atlanta newspapers gave roaring accounts of the affair, one of them announcing in letters three inches high: "Borglum Fugitive From Justice." There were long lists of his crimes, misdemeanors and delinquencies for which he had been driven away from Stone Mountain. Chief of these were "loafing on the job," "inordinate love of money," "wasteful expenditures," "ungovernable temper." And there was the old story of the angels of the Cathedral of St. John the Divine. Clarke Howell, editor of the Atlanta *Constitution* and Francis Clark, the city editor, were Gutzon's friends, and they sniffed at the angel story. They were the ones who telegraphed the cathedral to get the straight of it. But no matter. There was no end to such charges nor to the people who believed them. Mrs. Borglum, warned by her attorney, Albert Howell, to refrain from comment, nevertheless issued one statement: "The Greeks of old drove Phidias into exile, but his name has lived on while those who persecuted him are forgotten."

CHAPTER TWENTY-ONE

AFTERMATH

Borglum and Tucker sat down to rest on the plantation of Colonel Beniham Cameron, head of the Bankhead Highway Commission, near Durham, North Carolina, and entertained a great outpouring of their friends. Georgia made one weak effort at extradition, but the warrant was promptly thrown out by a sympathetic judge. Governor Angus McLean announced that he would call out the militia if necessary to prevent extradition, and there the matter rested. Gutzon never condescended to answer the Association's charges. On July 7, 1925, he wrote to Gerald Johnson:

It should be remembered that we undertook the building of a memorial to honor, not to war. We built it to the soul of Robert E. Lee, to his conscious martyrdom, to the valor and development of those the world said had failed. . . . Can we who have worked so disinterestedly and succeeded somewhat in reaching the ear of God for Lee and his hosts forget? Can we fail in those qualities? I am determined that history shall carry no such item in her record of our acts.

The Stone Mountain Confederate Memorial Association eventually gave the job of finishing the mountain carving to a practitioner who was at Stone Mountain only briefly and with little success in furthering the art.

Gutzon stayed at Raleigh, North Carolina, seven or eight months preparing new models for the memorial, with the aid of Captain Tucker and Hugo Villa. One day came Homer. He had walked all the way from Stone Mountain, more than 600 miles. Tucker said that he had only to shout and they would all come "a-runnin'." But there was little work, hardly any money, and no place for them to stay. Villa made and sold some violins. The others mostly had a hard time.

Gutzon's family joined him in Raleigh in a home next to that of Josephus Daniels, and they were pleasantly received.

In Georgia, the Association removed from the project everyone originally connected with the memorial except Mrs. Helen Plane. But Mrs. Plane was old and ill when the notification reached her. She commented on what had happened to the great memorial and the men who had labored for it. Then she went to bed and died.

The Association prepared statements repeating and enlarging the original charges against Borglum. Gutzon saw enough of it to convince him that masses of this material were sent to every point where any sculpture was contemplated, across the country from Texas to the Dakotas. Why all this tireless effort to discredit him? His theory was that the Association was in debt to the Atlanta banks and had to stay alive long enough to sell its half dollars and pay its debts. It must maintain the theory of its integrity by picturing Borglum as a road-company villain.

In Atlanta an active member of the U.D.C. who had friends in both camps was disturbed because neither the sculptor nor Sam Venable would take legal steps against the Association. She declared the directors were destroying Gutzon's business and would destroy him. "I cannot and will not add to this quarreling over a memorial to Lee," he wrote her. "After I got Coolidge and Smoot and Lodge, and the Senate and Congress to authorize a coin, I was further bound by my own claims that the brotherhood of America must be strengthened and preserved."

But the battle of words went on. And nobody called on Gutzon to produce his new models. The new sculptor had trouble. The granite firm of Weiblen Brothers, which had a lease from Sam Venable, refused to permit the importation of outside stoneworkers. Eventually they reached an agreement to do the stonecutting themselves on a basis of cost plus ten-per-cent profit.

The Association seized all of Gutzon's papers and records as well as his personal possessions, including art works in his studio and the machinery on the mountain. When they refused to listen to the U.D.C.'s suggestion of arbitration, which was definitely provided for in Borglum's contract, the sculptor took one step in his own defense. He sent to Georgia a certified public accountant who disproved the charge that $185,000 had been spent on his part of the project. The books showed that only $113,922.61 had gone to the mountain—and this included the sculptor's salary and every other expense of the work. The office in Atlanta at the same time had spent more than $116,000.

There was a persistent rumor through the United States that Borglum's real trouble had been a quarrel with the United Daughters of the Confederacy. That was not true if only for the fact that the political brothers in the Memorial Association's directorate had taken away the voice of these women in 1924. It was thoroughly refuted in a pamphlet issued by the Atlanta chapter telling where the blame should be placed for the monument's loss.

The pamphlet was in the precise form of the statement sent out by the Association and was distributed among U.D.C. organizations throughout the country. It never had so large a circulation as the Association's statement for the reason that the women did not have so large a fund to draw on.

How so great a memorial could have been destroyed, how the matter of the sale of the coin could have been so confused that few could understand anything beyond the fact that the money was dissipated and lost, is a complicated story. It cannot be dismissed in a few words and in fairness to all, the story of the U.D.C.

should be told. Here are some extracts from the Atlanta chapter's pamphlet:

The Stone Mountain debacle was the result of vandalism pure and simple. It is no longer necessary to defend Gutzon Borglum. Time and the course of events have vindicated him.

Borglum contracted to produce the central group in three years for $250,000, which was to cover his ideas, his designs, models, labor, a portion of his working equipment and his personal compensation. At the end of seventeen months he had produced the first model, master model and all working parts necessary to that date, removed 25,000 tons of granite, completed head of Lee, half head of Davis, designed children's medal, made model for Stone Mountain coin. Price for above, official audit of March 31, 1925, $113,922.61.

During the thirty months since the employment of his successor, the combined efforts of the sculptor, Weiblen Brothers, and the Association have produced: first models, master models, some working models, blasting of mountain side, roughing out of Lee's horse. Cost, as stated by Randolph, $171,000.

Mr. Borglum formed a syndicate to buy the entire coin issue. This would immediately have placed $2,500,000 or securities to that amount in the hands of the Association. A condition of the sale was that the money should be used exclusively in carving the mountain.

Randolph declined the offer; his reaction was as follows:

"Under the Borglum proposition, his friends could have sold the coins when they pleased, at whatever price they pleased, to whatever purchasers they pleased, and could have spent the proceeds in whatever way they pleased to carve on the mountain whatever they pleased."

Mr. Randolph has sold the coins wherever he pleased, when he pleased, to whomever he pleased, and is now engaged in carving on the mountain what he pleases against the protest of the Atlanta Chapter and hundreds of Southern people, having discarded the plans and ignored the purpose entrusted to him. The monument he is building is smaller and entirely different from the one endorsed and subscribed to by the people of the United States, whose funds he has squandered and misspent.

The document goes on at considerable length to discuss the policy of Atlanta banks in keeping the Association alive, and the piecemeal sale of coins to pay back loans that the banks advanced. The banks at the time of Borglum's departure from Stone Mountain held the Association's notes for $78,862.72. The marketable property owned by the Association including its bank balances was listed at $6,406.39. The banks in time were paid off by receipts from the coin sale. The statement closes:

Members of the Atlanta Chapter organized the original Stone Mountain Memorial Association and secured its charter.

Members of the Atlanta Chapter personally invited Mr. Randolph to become president of the Association.

Mr. Randolph has discarded the original models entrusted to him, altered the style, and reduced the size of the memorial.

He has plunged the work into a national scandal on false charges.

He has destroyed the confidence of the public in the work by false statements and lowered the standard of Georgia and Georgians throughout the United States.

And that isn't all of the story of Stone Mountain. While Sam Venable and Gutzon were quietly waiting for the group then in control to take a false step and fall, the Association's directors suddenly decided that something had to be done about Stone Mountain. Gutzon's first intimation that something was wrong came with the publication of a news story in which the new sculptor said that Borglum had deliberately left large holes in the rock to interfere with further carving. Inasmuch as Gutzon had not known that he was to have a successor and had not been in Georgia since, the accusation seemed silly.

Next came Randolph's announcement that Lee would never have worn his hat in the presence of ladies and that the Association was planning to remove the hat. Leading sculptors of the United States said that this could not be done without destroying the head. But the public had nothing to do with it anyway. There was little talk about it, and the work was done behind a canvas.

The book *Famous Statues and Their Stories,* published by Edwin Rayner in 1936, pictures Stone Mountain with a photograph of the second sculptor's designs superimposed upon it. The horses' legs are very prominent. The design is attributed to Gutzon Borglum, and there is no suggestion in the text that he had left the work.

Had Gutzon suspected what was about to be done to his head of Lee, it is probable he would have fought to retain it. It remained in his mind as one of the greatest things he had ever produced. And one close to him recalls that its destruction was caused by men who had boasted that until the end of time nothing could injure it.

CHAPTER TWENTY-TWO

BACKSIGHT

ONE OF THE most remarkable features of Gutzon Borglum's quarrel with Georgia seems to be Georgia's unawareness of it. The sculptor left Stone Mountain ahead of the constables on February 25, 1925. And he sat for a long time in Raleigh aware that a large group of worthy patriots was demanding that he be extradited to stand trial in the municipal court for breaking up a worthless lot of plaster. Then in March 1926 he received a remarkable call. The state of Georgia, which had him roughly classified as a fugitive from justice, conferred on him the signal honor of asking him to make a statue of one of her most distinguished sons, Alexander H. Stephens, vice-president of the Confederacy. The statue was to find permanent place in Statuary Hall of the Capitol Building at Washington, D. C.

Gutzon carried on conversations about this piece of work by mail and carved the figure in San Antonio, Texas. It was a striking portrait, fine, strongly intellectual features, lighted by an inner serenity and gentleness. It was a seated figure, for Stephens could not stand. And the hands, resting on the arms of his chair, were modeled to show great firmness of character. Hugo Villa, who had followed the sculptor to Texas, helped carve the statue, slightly oversize, in Georgian marble.

The unveiling in Washington in 1927 was a gala affair. A special trainload of Georgians had come to the capital with the governor of the state in the lead. The National Guard of Georgia, brilliantly uniformed, was on hand to lend color.

Most of these people were from Atlanta. Some were even members of the Stone Mountain executive committee. All seemed to ignore the tragic happenings of only two years before. It must be noted, however, that Gutzon was as good at that as they were. He was calm, pleasantly aloof and unconcerned.

In 1928 the time set for the finishing of the central group on Stone Mountain expired with only Lee's head and part of his horse completed. An attempt was made by the donors to reclaim the property. They said that the work on Stone Mountain was at a standstill and that the operating Association was insolvent.

Sam Venable circulated an open letter in which he charged that he had added together all the sums spent by the Association on bank loans, etc., and had reached the stupendous figure of $1,421,665 which, he said, it had cost Gutzon's successor to complete his model and change the bust of Lee. He added this comment:

Furthermore, Mr. Borglum's head of Lee everybody recognized. His successor's head of Lee, nobody recognizes. The nose is crooked. The left arm is withered and paralyzed. The hilt of the sword is gone and the stirrup of the saddle is broken off. The money is all gone and the carving of Lee, in my opinion and the opinion of hundreds of others, is a mutilated imperfection that cannot be rectified.

The Association was in debt to the Founders' Roll for the use of $260,800 paid for tablets, and to the Children's Founders' Roll for $35,019.91. Suits were being brought by contributors to the first of these funds. G. F. Willis succeeded Hollins Randolph as president. The Association begged for an extension of time, and the Venable family agreed to allow work to proceed until May

1931. However, nothing was done on the mountain during that period.

In 1930 the Atlanta Chamber of Commerce, under the leadership of Park Committee Chairman L. Lawrence McCord, got interested in finishing the monument. Mayor-elect James L. Key, largely celebrated for his huge Sunday School Bible Class, sent a telegram to Gutzon who was then in the Black Hills. He wanted to have Mr. Borglum come to Atlanta as his guest, he said, for the purpose of conference on Stone Mountain Memorial. The telegram was sent in August 1930. It might be mentioned that on July 4 of that year the head of Washington had been unveiled on Mount Rushmore with a great deal of publicity.

The sculptor arrived in Atlanta on the first of September and was given a rousing welcome and reception by a capacity house at the Fox theater. It was the first chance public opinion had had to express itself, and the result was gratifying to a man who had had to suffer in silence for five years. He mentioned that if he had to do it over again, he would make the Stone Mountain figures twice the size. He had learned something of mountain carving. The crowd cheered him enthusiastically, and he came home. But little came of it.

In 1931 McCord got a bill through the Georgia state legislature, giving the state right of eminent domain to take over Stone Mountain and adjacent property for a park. On this basis talks went on for years and years.

In 1933 Sam Venable with Mrs. Frank Mason, to whom he gave his share of Stone Mountain, presented a deed to Mayor Key for the portion of the cliff required for carving, and an attempt was made to get W.P.A. funds to finance the undertaking. There was a vast amount of correspondence without result. In 1936 the governor made an investigation of possibilities. In 1937 W. R. Ulrich of the Atlanta Chamber of Commerce met Borglum in Washington and they had a friendly conference.

In the winter of 1939-1940 there was another revival of interest, and once more Gutzon was called to Atlanta. The hotel men of Atlanta had suddenly become aware that tourists coming to see Mount Rushmore were dumping large amounts of cash into South Dakota. They were wondering why they had never foreseen this golden reward, and they could see that they needed Gutzon's help. They were willing to put up enough money to pay for the labor week by week if he would donate his time and use his influence to get credit with the machinery and powder companies.

Gutzon was jubilant. Dr. Ashby Jones, popular clergyman, and Preston Arkright, president of the Georgia Power Company, gave him their blessing. Success seemed so near that the sculptor wrote a letter to John Kaufman, who had succeeded Cliff Davis as stand-by on Stone Mountain, to be ready for starting work next Monday, to lay out a program for a full week. And then that too joined the futile history of the mountain. The other half-owners of the mountain wanted a million dollars which they insisted must be paid to them before work could be resumed. So this chance failed. The matter of the carving on Stone Mountain remained unchanged a year later when the sculptor suddenly died.

Despite the course of ill luck, bickering and unexplained hatred that has accompanied it, the dream of Atlanta for a Confederate memorial—or the dream of Atlanta hotel men for a popular tourist attraction—is still showing signs of life. The state of Georgia has appropriated funds for the purchase of Stone Mountain and the establishment of a park at its base. An Atlanta sculptor has been appointed to take charge of any carving that may be done on the tremendous uplift of granite. The wording of the commission is a bit indefinite as, after all popular experience with the memorial, it should be. But, somehow, the emergence of the Confederate armies from the rock seems a bit nearer than it did yesterday.

There is no recognizable trace today of Gutzon Borglum's magnificent head of Lee, or of anything else identifiable with the vision of Helen Plane. There is a disfiguring scar, the remnant of a head, part of a horse. But no matter. Some starry-eyed sculptor, somewhere, is figuring on a new supply of dynamite and drills, and some epochal work—it will start any day now, you may hear —to recover Borglum's unfortunate plan. The mark of his hand is dim, perhaps, but it is still to be found there on the rock—the reminder of what was certainly a noble and, as it turns out, continuous experiment.

The Borglum family moved to Texas from North Carolina in 1925 because the Trail Drivers' Association wanted a monument and because the Stone Mountain Confederate Memorial Association had definitely set its trail toward nothing. Texas would have been a remarkable spot for them in any case, and it was one place in the universe that they knew little about.

The romantic history of the state—its gracious women, tall men, Spanish warriors and grandees, American pioneers and land seekers, its Alamo, its victorious revolution, its statehood, Indians, rangers, ranchmen, cowboys, trail drivers—all appealed to Gutzon like a journey back to boyhood when he received the invitation of the Trail Drivers' Association to their conference in 1925. These men, now grown old, wanted a memorial. They wanted to perpetuate the heroes of an epoch when cowboys braved heat and cold, drought and flood, hostile Indians and rustlers, as they drove herds of longhorns northward across hundreds of miles of continent to Kansas or Montana.

It was disappointing to some of the newcomers to discover that San Antonio was a highly civilized city with a cultural history antedating the landing of the Pilgrim Fathers. As for their equipment, Mrs. Borglum's sidesaddle stood for years in a saddle-shop window as an eye-opening evidence of an effete custom.

A studio was improvised in a shed previously used to house floats before the annual "Battle of Flowers" parade. There, while making the first model for the Trail Drivers' monument, Gutzon was initiated into the lore of the trail. Old cowmen came in num-

GUTZON BORGLUM AND SON LINCOLN

bers and sat at ease as they yarned about how cattle behaved; how
cowboys talked, rode, ate and slept; how they dressed by putting
their big hats on; how they soothed the bedded herd by singing a
ballad of uncounted verses. When the time came for the sculptor
to make scenes in bas-relief around the base of the monument talk
rose to feverish heat over such moot questions as whether thirsty
cattle lift their tails when they scent water, or whether cowboys
squat on their heels around a campfire at night.

Gutzon tracked down the few remaining longhorn cattle in
the state and took time to witness driving, riding, roping—all the
details of the cattle business as exposed in numerous rodeos. A
cowboy known as "Red" posed for one of the chief figures in the
group. And when a question arose as to who should be pictured
in the other, there was rivalry over the claims of George Saunders,
president of the association, and another old cowman, Tom Russell, recently deceased. Russell's widow was a prime mover in the
memorial project, but she wasn't looking for a personal monument. She and her committee worked tirelessly to raise money for
this tribute to the unsung heroism of their menfolk.

As the model was finally developed to their satisfaction it
showed two riders, one pointing with outstretched arm to indicate
where water would be found, while behind them were three longhorn steers, their heads and tails raised as they scented the distant
river. To cast that group in bronze, full size, called for more
money than the women could raise at a time when drought and
low prices for beef put the cattle business in a decline. Even before
the clay model was completed, messages came from Atlanta warning the Trail Drivers to have nothing to do with Borglum. The
women seemed unconcerned. When the model was exhibited in
other cities there came lively bidding for its location. Mr. Good-
night, a famous old ranchman, offered to pay for the casting on
condition that the monument be placed in Abilene, but the San
Antonio Chamber of Commerce was determined to keep the
work where the idea originated. Only enough money for a bronze

about one-fourth life size could be raised, and the memorial was permanently placed outside Trail Drivers Hall, especially built for the purpose in Breckenridge Park. This was a great disappointment to the sculptor who had planned for an enlarged group more than forty feet long to stand under the open sky in front of San Antonio's auditorium.

As long as there was any hope of completing his work at Stone Mountain, a hope that died hard, the sculptor wanted to remain in the South, where his chief need was a roomy studio. He secured lease of space in a machine shop near the railroad tracks to complete the model of the Trail Drivers' memorial, and then began to scout around San Antonio for a more permanent location. He found it eventually in an old stone building on the edge of Breckenridge Park which had been abandoned by the local water company.

The genial park commissioner allowed him to remodel it. A new roof was built with its big skylight, an ell added, windows and doorways completely rebuilt and the interior decorated. When finished it was a delightful place for work or play, half hidden by pecan trees that shaded it from the Southern sun, with the sound of running water beneath. Here several new sculptural works were modeled, but only one was destined to stand in Texas. When it came about that Mount Rushmore demanded all his time the sculptor gave this San Antonio studio to the Witte Museum in the same park. Now known as the Borglum Memorial Studio, it is used for art classes and as a meeting place for art students.

In this city the sculptor became deeply involved in several projects promoted mostly by women, who often took the lead in civic improvements. There were women's clubs all over the state which invited the sculptor to tell his ideas on the art and beautification of one's surroundings. The Conservation Society of San Antonio interested him in their pet project of beautifying the banks of the San Antonio River, a lazy little stream that threaded its way through the city. Real-estate interests wanted to fill up the stream and use the space for more buildings, but the women wouldn't hear of it. In this the sculptor joined heartily, but his ideas conflicted with theirs when it came to restoration of old Spanish ruins.

From his experience in preserving the California missions the sculptor was keenly interested in these San Antonio ruins, one of which, the San Jose Mission, is especially beautiful. A copy of its rose window was sent to the Chicago World's Fair in 1933.

Before he arrived, its belfry tower had collapsed. Mrs. J. P. Drought, one of the most civic-minded leaders San Antonio ever had, had at her own expense hired workmen to collect the stones and wood blocks for the stairs and return them to their original places. The belfry stairs, triangular blocks of wood that unknown hands had carved out of big trees, had been carried away as relics by Mexican families, and the same Mrs. Drought had searched them out, one by one, and brought them back to the mission as a real work of restoration. Meanwhile the Conservation Society engaged a local architect to restore parts of the old church and a granary which had almost disappeared.

Seeing what was going on and knowing that such a restoration would only destroy the original character of the mission, Gutzon wrote an article in protest against what seemed to him vandalism, but never published it because he did not want to hurt the feelings of a friend who was most active in the undertaking. Instead, he sent her the typed article with this friendly warning: "I alone am honest enough to tell you that you cannot restore the lost lines of a great poem, the lost notes of a great opera, the lost parts of a great building, the lost parts of a great painting."

And there were other projects. There were two large musical societies in the city, both run by women, with considerable rivalry between them. The leader of one club came to the sculptor begging his help in building an open-air theater in an old quarry in Breckenridge Park where she could have performances by her

Civic Opera Company. "We have no money to pay an architect," she said. "Won't you design us a theater, just for the love of art and music?"

The project interested the sculptor and he went out to the quarry to study its possibilities. Mrs. Borglum vividly remembers one moonlight night when she and Gutzon were accompanied by Mrs. Drought and her guest, a professor from Dublin, Ireland, a man well acquainted with the new Irish Theater in Dublin, who had come to Texas on a lecture tour. He bubbled over with enthusiasm when Gutzon pointed out a little knoll overlooking the quarry which he had already selected as a stage. On each side of this he planned a group of columns with dressing rooms behind. For the curtain he designed something new—a barrage of water jets which could be turned on or off at will. When the curtain was down, colored lights would play on the water, creating an eerie effect and concealing the stage from the audience. All details were so carefully worked out that the only expense to the city would be for material and labor, with no fee for the designer, Gutzon, who would act also as superintendent of the work. To make sure that his architectural plans were correct, he summoned at his own expense Mr. Kimball, who had been president of the National Institute of Architects. This helpful friend not only made blueprints and drew up specifications but made a pretty water-color sketch to show how the theater would look when finished.

Naturally the members of the Civic Opera and the San Antonio Woman's Club were delighted. In a mass they went to the City Hall when the plan was submitted to the council. Without a dissenting vote a resolution was passed accepting the open-air theater as the sculptor had planned it.

And that, one grieves to record, was the end of another Gutzon Borglum dream. After a long delay a conventional design by a local architect was "unanimously approved" by the same city fathers. The theater was built at city expense. And the lady who had begged the sculptor to design the theater because she had no money to pay an architect told him that the wife of one of her leading singers was the local architect's sister. The lady accepted the tenor's brother-in-law because it made her tenor happy. "And, dear Mr. Borglum, what else could I do?" wailed the lady.

Gutzon was much taken with the appearance of Corpus Christi, Texas; however, he felt the shore line was unsightly. So he hired an aviator to take pictures of the town showing the residential portion on a plateau high above the gulf and the crowded business district along the shore line. He took the mayor and some other citizens on a motor trip to Galveston and along the Gulf Coast to Florida to see how other cities had dealt with similar water-front problems.

He built a plaster model of Corpus Christi with a fine new—and artistic—concrete promenade along the sea front, with steps down to the water's edge, and exhibited it in the rooms of the Chamber of Commerce. He designed approaches for a new bridge to replace the old drawbridge that frequently tied up traffic for half an hour at a time. And he got a Mr. Harrington of Kansas City, a reputable bridge builder, to design a bridge. The cost of this improvement, he felt, would speedily be paid by toll collected from the passing cars.

Everybody was interested in Borglum's great enterprise. A loan project was placed before the R.F.C., which turned it over to the W.P.A., which started everything all over again. In the end the whole business got into the hands of the state W.P.A. at Fort Worth, and the water-front-bridge development was changed to a sewer project. Probably the sewer was needed and anyhow it had not been proposed by a stranger.

Texas, the sculptor learned, was a place where big things were done bigly; but, nevertheless, in the accustomed fashion.

CHAPTER TWENTY-THREE

AND SO FORWARD

TEXAS OWED something to Gutzon for the suggestion of the Four-City Centennial celebration of 1936. This hundredth year that Texas had been independent of Mexican rule had to be something unique. The sculptor wrote a letter about his idea to Jesse Jones, the managing director, stating that the great fair should begin in San Antonio, the ancient Mexican capital, then proceed to Dallas and Fort Worth and end in Houston. He outlined the historical features of these cities, listed their natural advantages as exhibition towns and finished with an unusual thought: "These cities will draw enormous income from the tourist travel that the centennial will surely set in motion. For that reason all exhibition buildings should be made permanent in character, thus saving what might otherwise be considered an enormous total loss."

But though many of his suggestions were carried out, and though an art committee from each of the four cities consulted him, not one of the more than forty monuments they built was his design. The explanation is that each committee was hidebound by the idea of a competition with prizes, and Gutzon would have none of that.

He worked hard for the beautification of roads in that part of Texas where the greenery gives way to the desert. He was ap-

pointed chairman of an advisory committee to supervise the spending of the W.P.A. and the Federal Highway Department funds.
But local rivalries kept many a town out of funds, and the Federal Highway Department's $5,000,000, allotted for *road beautifi-
cation* in Texas, was demanded by an influential highway engineer who outweighed Gutzon. All road funds, he declared, must
be under the State Highway Department's control; and to this
simple proposition the federal government would not agree. So
Texas got little, and the beautification of Texas roads was left
to Texas.

Looking back over the record of those years, one can't but figure them the most disheartening in all of Borglum's life. The
sculptor himself hadn't changed much—except for the better. He
was still motivated by his love for the big things—for the projects
that would give more joy, more comfort or more safety to human-
kind. But somehow none of the plans was working out well.

Stone Mountain, as he must have known in his heart, was finished. The head of Lee would presently be an outrageous blot
on a tall cliff. He had had no part in the Texas Four-City Centennial celebration; he had been thrust out of any plans to beautify
Texas highways. He had been thwarted in his effort to provide a
sea-front development and bridge for Corpus Christi. He had lost
the job of designing the San Antonio open-air theater, which he
would have enjoyed doing. Five times in a row he had put out
his best effort and finished nowhere.

He might have been saved a lot of trouble had he known that
few outsiders ever succeed in getting anything out of the preserves
of Texas politicians—especially those busy keeping happy a Texas
tenor. But those who knew him in San Antonio say that he
showed no consciousness of his reverses. He was gracious to the
people he thought deserved his kind words. He blasted the louts
that he thought needed blasting. And on the whole all went well.
He continued to be Gutzon Borglum.

His art work was by no means neglected because of his apparent absorption in civic improvements and expositions and music festivals. Nor had ill repute deriving from the Stone Mountain Association's adverse publicity given him any lack of employment. He had not quite finished the Trail Drivers' memorial when he was given a commission for the memorial to Alexander Stephens. The armchair in which Stephens is seated was made in the San Antonio studio and cut out of marble at a local stoneyard. The marble was the gift of the Georgia Marble Company at Marietta.

The place of this model in the studio was immediately taken by a memorial to General John Greenway, of Rough Rider and earlier Yale football fame. He was a resident of Arizona, engaged in copper mining when the First World War broke out. Though past the age limit, he bought a uniform and, with the aid of Washington friends, got into the army.

His widow, Isabella Greenway, one of the most distinguished women in the country, came to the Stamford studio, bringing with her a request for the statue by the state of Arizona. Greenway had been honored as a favorite son and chosen for a place in Statuary Hall, Washington.

Unfortunately Gutzon Borglum was in Texas. Telegrams were exchanged, and he met Mrs. Greenway in 1928—at the Democratic National Convention in Houston. Mrs. Greenway brought to the San Antonio studio not only photographs of her husband but some of his clothes and favorite gear. She knew, the sculptor said, more about her husband's appearance and characteristics than any person he had ever met who tried to tell him what he wanted to know of a departed hero—and must know if he were to complete a perfect likeness.

The bronze statue was unveiled in Washington in 1930, and Mrs. Greenway ordered a replica to be placed in Arizona. The friendship between her and the sculptor which began at first sight was without a flaw during their lifetime.

From the state of North Carolina, meanwhile, came a commission for a bronze group in memory of Carolina soldiers who led the immortal Pickett's Charge at the Battle of Gettysburg, a dramatic climax that marked the high tide of the Confederacy and from which Lee's army reeled back in defeat, never to attempt another invasion of the North. The sculptor had submitted a small-scale model of the group, made in his Breckenridge Park studio at San Antonio in 1928. This was accepted and he was busy with an improved large-scale model when the same wearisome correspondence began, caused by some misunderstanding of the artist's habit of developing, that is, bettering, the original plan.

Here, for example, is a letter from Mr. Barringer, a member of the memorial committee, written to another member, Mr. Fuller, after seeing photographs of the large-scale model and noting with anxiety that changes had been made from the original. He said:

It is out of the question for me to go to San Antonio to examine the model. I am perfectly willing, however, to abide by your judgment. I confess to being somewhat disappointed, particularly in the expressions of the faces. They do not give promise of being as good as those on the smaller model. Moreover, I cannot help agreeing with the governor that the model does not seem to be completely finished.

If Borglum will put his best into this monument, as we have the right to believe he will do, it will be a great monument. I feel sure of that. Such is my confidence in Borglum I know that if he can make a good small model, he can also make a good large one.

To the sculptor this same Mr. Barringer made the following interesting comment about facial expressions:

It was Darwin, I think, who pointed out that the sneer originated in an unconscious effort to uncover the canine or fighting tooth. Most men, when very angry or about to go into a fight, have a sneering expression. I have seen somewhere the expression "a snarling grin," which conveys the idea very well. Might it not be well to put on one of your faces this "snarling grin?" For it is doubtless the characteristic of many men when they are charging the enemy.

Gutzon was quick to welcome any suggestion for improving his work from any interested source. In answer he wrote:

Thank you for your letter just received and also for the suggestion you have made. I not only think it is good, but I have just the man on whose face I would like to put that sinister expression. The man in front must be too thoughtful, too conscious of his danger and too indifferent to it, to have any emotional feelings. He is too determined. The one just back of him, the boy, will express amazement, fear—a little—but surprise and youth more. To the bearded man next to him, the one you thought was crowding him a little too close, I will give an expression of anger and supply the snarling grin. Of course, the boy back of him with the flag is too much occupied with the load he is carrying and too important to be anxious about anything but getting forward.

Because the memorial was to stand on the Gettysburg battlefield, it was highly important to locate it properly in relation to other incidents and heroes of the great battle. A special site committee was appointed, and as its chairman the sculptor had the chief responsibility. On one visit to the field he had the happy fortune to meet Mrs. Elsie Singmaster Lewars, a well-known writer who lived on Seminary Ridge, another famous part of the battleground. She was familiar with the whole historic region, knew its charges and countercharges by heart, and so gave invaluable help in selecting precisely the right site for the memorial.

The unveiling took place July 3, 1929, just sixty-six years after Pickett's Charge failed to win its objective and the Confederacy was plainly doomed. Governor Gardner of North Carolina presided, and the sculptor's old friend, former Governor Angus McLean, delivered the principal address.

A special train brought hundreds of North Carolina people to join in the dedication of their memorial. An airplane, engaged by the sculptor, dropped roses over the battleground and dipped its wings in tribute to the honored dead. By that time Gettysburg had become, as it has been ever since, a lure for tourists and sight-seers from every part of our country. Only a year after the unveil-ing of the Borglum monument C. W. McDevett published in the Raleigh *News and Observer* a long description of a visit to the battlefield, ending with this tribute:

It may be a quiet day at Gettysburg with only a few hundred visitors scattered through its tens of thousands of acres, while on other days the visitors are numbered by thousands. But the biggest group anywhere, any time, will more than likely be found around North Carolina's memorial.

That was the case on a day this summer. It was a quiet day, but there were dozens before the five bronze giants, silent dozens, studying the master's work in reverent admiration. They were from Pennsylvania, New York, New Jersey, Ohio and Maryland, as their automobile licenses indicated. They murmured praise of the picture in stone and metal. The men doffed their hats uncon-sciously. All gazed into those faces of bronze—faces that seemed filled with life—and paid tribute to the likenesses of men—strong, purposeful, clean-limbed, clean-minded men—who had been their fathers' and their grandfathers' foes. Borglum had imagined them worthy foemen, indeed, and his genius had made his hands the servant of his thoughts. Borglum carves mountains into battle panoramas. Borglum will never carve anything to equal his Tar Heel heroes at Gettysburg.

A year before the Gettysburg memorial was dedicated, a foreign-looking letter, postmarked Morges, Switzerland, came to Gutzon at San Antonio. As he was away at the time and it was Mrs. Borglum's job to oversee his vast correspondence, she opened this letter with some curiosity. She uncovered a six-page autograph be-ginning, "My great, good friend," and signed, "Affectionately, gratefully and devotedly yours, I. J. Paderewski."

The gist of the letter was that Paderewski's compatriots desired to erect a monument "to the memory of Poland's most generous benefactor, President Wilson"; that a competition had been staged; that the first prize had been awarded; that the prize winner's model was "horrible"; and that, in despair of getting a satisfactory design at home, the committee had left the decision to the writer. The letter concluded: "My decision is that the statue of that great American should be done only by the greatest American artist, by the greatest living sculptor in the whole world."

By way of explaining Paderewski's greeting and highly emotional signature, one should remember how close the two artists had become in their efforts to promote an association of mid-European republics.

Gutzon had been present when the representatives of these states had met in Independence Hall, Philadelphia. Paderewski was the first speaker at this convention, and in the few minutes of his oratory he was transformed from a civilian pianist into a soaring apostle of freedom. Professor Masaryk, who followed him with what was expected to be the key speech, could barely speak at all. He threw away his prepared address because, he said, Paderewski had said it all and said it better. "I have never listened to such an inspired speech," he said in conclusion. "I can give no explanation other than that Ignace Jan Paderewski is an artist."

Paderewski's letter to Gutzon in San Antonio begged an immediate answer by cable, inasmuch as it was hoped to have the memorial unveiled on Wilson's birthday the next year. Gutzon was in Georgia on another of his futile attempts to revive the Confederate memorial; so his wife sent him a telegram in care of the Venables:

SIX PAGE LETTER FROM PADEREWSKI WANTS MEMORIAL TO PRESIDENT WILSON BY QUOTE THE GREATEST SCULPTOR IN THE WHOLE WORLD END QUOTE. CAN YOU GUESS WHO? WANTS CABLE ANSWER.

The avowal of confidence by Paderewski, even more than his offer of the commission, was something that Gutzon appreciated. His answer was eager and quick:

MRS. MASON GAVE ME YOUR MESSAGE. SEND PADEREWSKI AT ONCE BY
CABLE QUOTE AM DELIGHTED TO ACCEPT DOUBLE HONOR FOR YOURSELF
AND WOODROW WILSON. TIME AMPLE IF WE ACT SOON. MEANS ALSO
AMPLE FOR BEAUTIFUL MEMORIAL UNQUOTE. LOVE TO YOU ALL.

Paderewski's response, grateful and sympathetic, settled the matter of the Wilson statue in a few days. Because of the early date set for the unveiling, the sculptor should first have gone to Europe to confer with the committee and to study the proposed location of the memorial. But the work on Mount Rushmore was getting critical and it was impossible for him to leave. He decided to send his son Lincoln to Europe to arrange for the casting of the bronze in Paris, Florence or Naples, and then to confer with Paderewski at his home in Morges, Switzerland.

Lincoln, accompanied by his mother, went immediately.

CHAPTER TWENTY-FOUR

TRIBUTE TO WILSON

THE TRAVELERS never forgot Paderewski as he met them at the Morges station. He was standing on the runway, a little derby hat perched on the top of his head, with his wave of hair floating out from it like a cloud. He seemed serene and happy.

"Where are your trunks?" he asked in honest puzzlement.

And they told him that they carried no trunks, that they were staying with him only between trains. His surprise was genuine and his disappointment obvious.

"I expected you to stay a month," he said. "So now you must stay for at least a week." He picked up the bags, though his butler factotum hovered around anxious to help, and led the way to his old-fashioned touring car. And they stayed at his chalet, with its wide-spreading trees, its huge garden and its vineyard sloping down to the lake shore—they stayed a week.

Gutzon had little trouble making sketches of his new subject. He had known Wilson fairly well; they had traveled the Atlantic in the same ship. Wilson had given him a degree at Princeton. They had seen much of each other when Gutzon was working on the decorations for the dormitory built by the class of 1879. And they had been close, though hardly harmonious, during the Borglum investigation of the aircraft scandal. However, to amplify his own impressions of Wilson's characteristics, the sculptor wrote to several men who had known the President: Professor John Grier Hibben, the new president of Princeton University; William Allen White; President Coolidge; and several senators. He asked them to say frankly what characteristics he should portray.

Wilson was then, as he still is, a subject of controversy. Gutzon got some amazing answers. President Coolidge thought he should be depicted as a kind of Abraham Lincoln. Senator William E. Borah thought that his features should express humanitarianism and said, "The Versailles Treaty was a cruel, destructive, brutal document. The only touches of humanity it contains were put there by Wilson." And a senator who shall be nameless said, "I feel incapable of making a suggestion along this line. If I undertook to do so, I'm afraid I should bear in mind that a man who is untruthful, no matter how exalted his position, should not be deified in sculpture or otherwise."

Gutzon decided to represent Wilson slipping out of his Academic robes and standing alongside a martial female figure of Poland on the capitol steps. Poland, helmeted, was defending herself with a sword. Forced back she stood at bay under the President's extended arm. It was a composition of great charm and historic truth. But it required more simple sentiment to be popular in Poznan, Poland, where it was to stand.

Paderewski's message of regret, contrived after he had looked at the photographs of the model, was a shock. He wired:

DEEPLY IMPRESSED. MAJESTIC GREATNESS OF YOUR COMPOSITION TRULY WONDERFUL. PRESIDENT'S FIGURE SPLENDID, SUPERB, INSPIRED. POLAND'S ENCHANTING IN VIGOR AND YOUTH. ENTIRE CONCEPTION EXTREMELY POETIC AND BEAUTIFUL. HOWEVER AM AFRAID PLACING POLAND'S FIGURE WOULD CREATE SERIOUS TROUBLE AND ADD TO EXISTING POLITICAL STRIFE. MANY MEMBERS OF PARTY NOW IN POWER, WHO HAVE BEEN FIGHTING ON WRONG SIDE, WOULD SURELY INTERPRET YOUR IDEA AS HOMAGE TO AND TRIUMPH OF THEIR DISASTROUS POLICY AND WOULD AROUSE INDIGNATION OF VAST BUT TEMPORARILY PARALYZED MAJORITY. CONSEQUENCES MAY BE FATAL. ARTIST MYSELF, KNOW WHAT IT MEANS TO PART WITH CHERISHED IDEAS, TO MODIFY PLAN CONCEIVED

IN LOVE AND MATURED BY LONG MEDITATION. AND YET AM FORCED, PRO BONO PUBLICO, TO ASK SACRIFICE IN ELIMINATING POLAND'S FIGURE ALTOGETHER. PRESIDENT'S FIGURE, NO MATTER HOW EARNEST, WILL PLEASE EVERYBODY AND HURT NOBODY. HIS NOBLE GESTURE WILL SEEM BENEDICTION GIVEN TO INVISIBLE SYMBOL OF REBORN COUNTRY FOR NEW, HISTORIC LIFE. THAT GESTURE COULD BUT ENHANCE, INTENSIFY DEEPLY RELIGIOUS, ALMOST APOSTOLIC CHARACTER OF HIS IDEOLOGY. PLEASE FORGIVE AND LET ME KNOW THAT I HAVE NOT OFFENDED YOU. SORRY TO SAY, CANNOT BE IN AMERICA BEFORE OCTOBER. MY BANK CA-BLING TEN THOUSAND DOLLARS. AFFECTIONATE REGARDS TO YOUR DEAR WIFE AND BOY.

So here was another crushing blow to Gutzon. To him it was like asking Beethoven to eliminate one of the movements of the *Fifth Symphony*. But he accepted the verdict with grace. And so he cabled Paderewski.

From Morges Paderewski had sent to the sculptor a group of photographs of the ancient square of Poznan where the statue was to be placed. Gutzon studied them closely to estimate how much light would strike his figure. Later, after wearisome correspondence with a Mr. Rucinski of the Official Council of Building Department, it was decided to move the memorial to the newly created Wilson Park.

Off and on, all winter, the sculptor worked on the model in his San Antonio studio. When completed it was generally acclaimed as a great portrait of the President. It had in it the idealism and the spiritual quality that the sculptor could give it. But he was never reconciled to the loss of the figure of Poland. He felt that the monument lacked something beautiful and significant that he could have given it.

Gutzon took his whole family abroad for the unveiling of the monument in 1931. It was his first visit to Europe in thirty years. Because he had to attend to its erection and the preparation of the pediment, they were several weeks in Poznan. One of the most interesting, and rather tragic, denizens was an old countess who had recently returned to her ancestral home. The place was more than a thousand years old, several miles out of town, and was on exhibition certain days of the week because of its historic interest.

The countess had been in exile for many years, and told an exciting tale of escape when the Germans came to her home. According to the tradition, the family fortune had started with the levying of tribute on travelers at a near-by crossroads. But most of it had been taken away by a similar process of collection. Little was left to her now. One day she invited the Borglums to "high tea," and as the family sat around the ancient table eating raspberries off priceless china, they could hear the voices and steps of sight-seers in an adjoining room. The exhibition fee undoubtedly eked out her scanty income.

Gutzon took a great liking for this aged lady in her rusty black gown and pathetic shoes. He hired a car and invited her to the opera. His attentions and the unusual experience gave her great delight, and she was sparkling.

During her exile she had cared for the Polish children in Paris. Now she was anxious to insure religious instruction for the large number of Polish orphans there. It hurt her to think, she said, that their bodies were well nourished and their souls were neglected.

As the day of the unveiling drew near, it became known that Paderewski would not be present. This seemed evidence enough that there was something rotten in Poland. The man who had been Premier; who, more than anyone else, had brought the world's recognition to Poland after the World War; who had made possible the return of territory snatched fifty years before by Germany; the man who had given most of the money for the nation's tribute to Wilson—this man alone wasn't going to be permitted to see the honoring of an American president whom he loved.

Large numbers of Polish-Americans came to share the tribute to Wilson. Three hundred priests had come from the United

States, every one carrying a wreath of artificial flowers representing his district at home. The flowers, piled about the base of the statue with the fresh wreaths of local patriots, made an impressive display.

On the morning of the unveiling day Mrs. Woodrow Wilson arrived with her niece and a group of men representing the United States. Among them were Robert Underwood Johnson, ambassador to Italy, and Bernard Baruch, who had taken the opportunity to visit the early home of his parents not far from Poznan. Mrs. Wilson went through the ordeal on the arm of General Mosciki, President of the Polish Republic, and she bore up well despite interminable speechmaking.

The crowning event of the program was a banquet at the old Royal Schloss, which at times had been occupied by Kaiser Wilhelm. After that there was a reception for a thousand or more, with General Mosciki presiding.

At dinner Mrs. Borglum was seated next to a delightful Pole whom she had met before. She asked him why there were so few at the table when she could hear the throng waiting for the reception in the next room. He seemed surprised that she shouldn't know. "But Madam," he said. "There are only twenty-four plates in the old Emperor's dining service." And he turned over a plate to show the label "W. Rex" stamped on the bottom.

Paderewski sent this telegram to Gutzon:

TODAY ON THE SOLEMN OCCASION OF THE UNVEILING OF YOUR NEW MASTERPIECE, MY HEARTFELT THANKS TO YOU, AND MY MOST AFFECTIONATE GREETINGS. YOUR PEERLESS ART HAS ENABLED MY COMPATRIOTS TO POSSESS AND PRESENT AN ENDURING PROOF OF THEIR EVERLASTING GRATITUDE FOR POLAND'S FREEDOM AND INTEGRITY TO AMERICA AND HER NOBLEST SYMBOL, PRESIDENT WOODROW WILSON.

And what happened to this noble Wilson monument? When Hitler's troops came plowing through Poland at the beginning of the Second World War it was pulled down and, presumably, turned into ammunition.

The Borglums had several other chance encounters with Paderewski. On one occasion he was to give a concert in Abilene, Texas, and invited Gutzon and his family to see him. He was in a private car and the three met him for dinner after the concert. The evening was delightful—at any rate it was delightful to Paderewski and Gutzon. They talked all night until the car was coupled to an outbound train. And then Paderewski invited them to ride on to the next stop.

Gutzon had an immense faith in Paderewski. One day in Washington during the First World War, he stated his theory to Secretary of the Interior Franklin K. Lane. "One of these days," he said, "you people will realize that imagination and disinterestedness are powerful factors in the building of a state. I believe Paderewski is capable of rebuilding Poland and of rebuilding Europe if the occasion demanded. He is capable of any sacrifice, and he has the mind and soul to keep him going."

"You artists always talk in big terms," said Lane. "So far I am with you. But there's a great practical side to nation building."

"Don't you think Paderewski has that, too?"

"Yes," said Lane, "and that's why I'm interested. That's why he's succeeding. They tell me he's abandoned music and set aside his entire fortune to arm Poland and place her on the side of the allies. Just as certainly as I'm sitting here, this great artist is going to be the liberator of modern Poland. This artist!"

"Yes," commented Gutzon. "That's what I've been telling you. He's an artist."

When the next great crisis came for Poland, there were no great artists to deal with it—only politicians.

CHAPTER TWENTY-FIVE

FOR THE PARKS

IT IS ONE of the amazing things about a sculptor that the more work he does and the more recognition he gets, the more his friends demand that he stick to his proper business. And it is probably just as amazing that the sculptor doesn't want to and seldom does. Somebody, commenting on the varied activities and interests of Gutzon Borglum, quoted a bit of apt philosophy: "I am a man; nothing human is alien to me," which was Borglum's estimate of the situation, all right. The constant urge to Art was something, he thought, that made his friends seem normal.

He might have been an aviator had his reflexes been faster at the time the Wright brothers made their test flights at Kittyhawk. His studio at Stamford was big enough to be a fine air laboratory, and for years it was cluttered with an odd assortment of things that were going to make flying better . . . and quicker, and cheaper, and easier and safer.

Gutzon was one of the observers of Orville Wright's first sustained flight at Fort Myers when the inventors were trying to prove the value of their plane to the United States Army. He saw "a little mechanism that looked like the wreck of a covered wagon" travel around a half-mile course for sixty-seven minutes. Then, after an enthusiastic greeting to the pilot, he and Orville,

Colonel Bromwell, Captain Squier and Lieutenant Selfridge rode into town aboard a streetcar. As a representative of the Aeronautical Society of America, he saw the collapse of the plane the next day and the tragic death of Lieutenant Selfridge.

Still he went on. He became acquainted with Alexander Klemin and his wind tunnel. He was greatly interested in Major Ocker's development of blind flying. He invented an airplane brake which, with modifications, was the type used in the Second World War.

In a speech before the Aeronautical Society at the Astor Hotel in New York early in 1904 he outlined his plans for a "cylindrical type of machine with the engine in the pointed nose directly behind the propeller and winglike fins to steady the flight." He demonstrated what he meant with two little models that flew gracefully over the audience. He said:

Consider the bird struggling with the power of a water freshet. The model for the aeroplane should not be the bird, but the fish. The only fish that can move in stormy water is the trout, and the trout, I am convinced, gives us an unbeatable design for an airship.

There is something in that speech to remind one of Cellini's departures from art, and the activities of Da Vinci when he was looking most clearly at the patterns of a future life. But his friends weren't impressed. Mrs. William Brown Meloney of the *Herald-Tribune* and *This Week* magazine, with whom he carried on a ceaseless correspondence, gave him a sharp rebuke and told him that art needed him more than the airplane business. And he sent her this prompt answer:

Dear Missy: You regret as many of my friends do that I am not eternally astride a ton of clay, constantly modeling. On the other hand, the insistent application of a man's mind or his body to one activity creates lopsidedness.

I was hardly out of my teens before I discovered that it was only men of varied interest in life, men of varied capacities, whose minds survived middle age. . . .

I mean the sort of men who can turn from the study of an orchid to the building of a fortress, to mending a sewer, to designing a fleet, to colonizing a continent.

Gutzon spoke a lot. He liked public speaking and he was good at it. Any good cause was his cause, and, inasmuch as he never seemed to be looking for any personal reward from his public fighting, he made a lot of friends in unexpected places.

He loved children and he was disturbed by New York's lack of room for them. He remembered his own childhood—so much of it in the fresh, open air—and he campaigned vigorously for playgrounds or parks or unplanned pieces of the outdoors that would give them a chance to stretch their legs. He began to write on such subjects for the newspapers and spent most of his days in wordy controversy. He wrote largely on political subjects and was rated among the country's foremost essayists on the subject of world peace. His peace article, "An Essay on Economic Boycott," was one of twelve selected from 20,000 for publication in the book "Ways to Peace." It was widely reported in the newspapers, widely discussed, and carried abroad by President Wilson when he went to make his futile treaty of Versailles.

The park controversies pleased Gutzon for two reasons. He thought they might bring about a little better living for the children. And they might promote a general love for flowers—bring a new generation into the open air and give it a consciousness of nature. He loved growing things—green trees, soft grass and the smell of aromatic shrubs. He never forgot his chase to capture the moon in Fremont.

In his early life he wished to be a horticulturist. Years afterward he found at the door of his New York studio an opportunity to practice his green thumb and at the same time to put his play-spot theories into practical development. In 1907 he was invited to join the board of directors and serve on the executive committee of the Metropolitan Parks Association which became the Parks and Playgrounds Association of the City of New York. His membership was one of his special interests for twenty years. He was appointed chairman of a subcommittee which later became an independent body looking after the affairs of Central Park.

Gutzon was highly pleased with his work as permanent chairman. Forty years had passed since the country's two pioneer landscape artists had made one of the most famous parks in the world from some rocks and a swamp in the middle of Manhattan Island. They had brought in hundreds of tons of soil and thousands of rare trees and shrubs. They had laid out driveways for carriages and winding paths for pedestrians. They had provided lakes and playgrounds for children. In 1907 Samuel Parsons, the landscape architect under Mayor Green, was begging uselessly for better park equipment and a new watering system. The sculptor felt that he had been cast in the right role. An appropriation of $100,-000 for improving the water system was passed that year.

The sculptor gathered the curses of the old school of artists when he joined the parks association to keep the Academy of Design from putting up a building in Bryant Park. He won a taxpayer's suit against the city in 1911 to prevent the slovenly extension of Riverside Drive in the Washington Heights region. In 1918, in a similar action, he prevented the building of an unsightly pumping station in Morningside Park. And routine park business, outside of the courts, amused him continuously because it was so full of trouble.

In 1910 Mayor Hylan appointed Charles Stover, who had worked under the direction of the park association, his Commissioner of Parks. Stover promptly turned the park into a playground, principally by digging swimming pools and wading puddles wherever there was room for them. He came into direct opposition with Parsons the landscape architect. They quarreled. The commissioner held up the architect's salary on the ground that he was absent from his office too much.

Gutzon entered the fight with a letter to the New York *Sun,* pointing out that the new commissioner had "not rotted enough manure to fertilize a ten-acre lot, nor mustered enough courage to contract for a single manure pit." He reminded his readers that "Last year a $100,000 high pressure water system remained absolutely idle for the lack of a little hose, and $100,000 worth of property was allowed to go to ruin." He arrayed himself against a movement to impeach Stover and put his own report on the needs of the park before the Board of Estimate and Apportionment. With him on the committee was a fine array of talent— Jacob Schiff, Francis Lynder Stetson, William J. Gibson, George W. Perkins, Charles L. Burmeister and some others. They got a respectful hearing.

The sculptor submitted with his report sixty samples of Central Park soil that had been analyzed by the U. S. Department of Agriculture. The budget committee gave him hearty approval and allotted enough funds to save the park.

During the years Gutzon served on its board of directors, many important questions were discussed by the Parks Association, such as what to do with the old Arsenal building, what about additions to the Metropolitan Museum, what about monuments and statues, what about Riverside Park and the New York Central Railroad tracts. He deplored the usual attitude of the Association which in its zeal to "save the park" objected to almost every new proposal, regardless of merit. He took most of his indignation to the newspapers.

In 1922 he fought for the request of the National Sculpture Society to hold an open-air exhibition near the Metropolitan Museum, although he was not a member of the society. The Association opposed him. He declared in the New York *Times:*

The charm of Central Park lies in the development of its original, natural contours. The National Sculpture Society should be allowed an area of fifty to one hundred acres and there place their exhibit to suit the natural conditions, precisely as they would place it if it were permanently located. I feel certain if some such plan is inaugurated, it will be successful. . . .

And he took an active part in the city's big stir about the proposed development of Riverside Park in connection with the New York Central's right of way along the Hudson River front. It was part of his plan that "The park from the Drive, with its river glimpses, should be the most tempting in Manhattan, and every walk into it should possess a separate individual interest." And so in February 1917 he wrote to Mayor Mitchell.

The First World War put a stop to many of the plans of the park designers. Mayor Mitchell went into a training camp in Florida and was killed in an airplane crash. Gutzon resigned from the Association in 1922, but he listened to the plea of George Gordon Battle, the president, and reconsidered. He remained active for many years.

One of Gutzon's last appearances in New York was in 1939 at a dinner party given by "Missy" Meloney. Present were the new Park Commissioner Robert Moses, and Mayor Fiorello La Guardia. He was surprised to see them and obviously pleased.

"I've been anxious to see you fellows," he said as he sat down. "I've been wanting to tell you about my new plan for the development of Central Park. . . . Now what I've had in mind is this——"

CHAPTER TWENTY-SIX

THE CZECHO-SLOVAK ARMY

MANY PEOPLE on the Borglum visiting list figured that Gutzon was a Czecho-Slovak merely because he ran a Czecho-Slovak army on his front lawn in Stamford. He wasn't, of course, but nobody got any evidence of that from the highway.

The sculptor's interest in the Czecho-Slovak cause came about in a purely natural manner. For some years he had had working with him, on and off, a young Austrian sculptor's assistant named Micka (pronounced Michka) and Micka had some odd ideas about the European war. There was need for reapportionment of some parts of Austria, he mentioned. And presently he began to talk about an independent republic that was to be formed by a group of Bohemians and Slovaks.

Gutzon was interested in this, as he was in all new republics that were brought to his attention. He looked into the matter and shortly found himself in spirited correspondence with its leaders. The republic makers, he discovered, called themselves Czecho-Slovaks, and with them, as a sort of motivating influence, was Thomas Masaryk. The cause seemed to be popular. Large numbers of these foreigners who had found security and freedom in the United States were now volunteering to go back and fight for their countrymen in Europe, and, since the draft law had not yet gone into effect, nobody stopped them.

Masaryk was mostly in Washington trying to get the United States to aid his cause. There Borglum met him and helped him to get a $12,000,000 appropriation from the U. S. Treasury. The two then collaborated in writing a constitution for the new Republic of Czecho-Slovakia. In Gutzon's files was found a parchment-bound copy of this document with Masaryk's signature on it, together with a letter expressing the leader's gratitude for Borglum's help.

That's how it came about that the sculptor offered a part of his property in Stamford to serve as a military post. The land was vacant, there was plenty of space, and there the Czech volunteers could be trained while they waited for transports to carry them across the Atlantic. As headquarters Gutzon donated an old farmhouse. The volunteers built their own barracks and cleared a parade ground across the woods.

The first recruits to arrive at the camp looked a little confused. As a military force they were a lonely lot. The United States had nothing to do with them. They were under command of the French and were to be sent to a French sector when they reached the front. But there wasn't any French control of them in this country. Whatever military control they had was purely theoretical.

The Czecho-Slovak organizers in New York and Washington were pleased by the patriotism of the men who volunteered to fight. But, once they had expressed their satisfaction, they forgot all about the army. It was easy to send passage money to worthy young men all over the country and move them on to the camp in Stamford. As a result of this carefree policy, most of the business of handling the volunteers fell automatically to the Borglum family.

Frequently a batch of recruits would be sent from New York without advance notice or arrangements for provisions. The Borglums would then have to scour the neighborhood to borrow blankets and appeal loudly to the Red Cross for a quick food supply. Once in 1918 when the painter George Luks was spending the summer with Gutzon he and the sculptor painted posters which were sold at auction to raise funds for the camp. The boys needed some adequate kitchen materials, such as a stove, knives and a collection of pots and pans.

The Czechs, after a little pushing by Borglum, put on a sort of pageant which showed an attack on an Austrian village by a band of the new republic's troops. It was realistic, and press reports said that it was very thrilling.

The soldiers had hurriedly put together a few thatched-roof cottages and hung up a background to give the illusion of the Austrian village. Everyone who came to Wire Mill Road that night was in Czech costume, and that included the Borglums and their guests. It was a gala night, and it brought another tide of volunteers.

On another evening there was an impressive musical program. Masaryk came with his daughter Anna and one of the Benes brothers presently to become famous in Europe. Miss Kitty Cheatham, a singer who had made many concert tours in Europe, was present also. She heard the massed male chorus of the soldiers sing her composition "America" as it probably would never be sung again. The boys were born singers, and they meant what they sang.

Gutzon telephoned one night that he had heard important news and would deliver it to the camp in person. So the Czecho-Slovak army stayed up late that night. There was no radio. The late evening papers would arrive with Gutzon Borglum. So there was nothing to do but wait. About 10 o'clock the sculptor arrived. The boys stood at attention in dead silence. "I won't keep you long," he said. "But I have heard good news and I wanted to tell it to you myself. . . . President Wilson this afternoon announced that the United States has recognized the independence of the Republic of Czechoslovakia." The boys were enthusiastic that night. They built a huge bonfire on the parade ground. They marched around it and over most of the neighborhood singing and shouting for a large part of the night.

The camp commander, a Czech, was a professional agnostic. He said it hurt him to look at any sort of religious observance. This made things difficult for him because the greater part of the Czecho-Slovak volunteers were deeply religious. They were always aware that they were going into danger, and until they came to Stamford they had always been able to go to church when and if they wanted to. The conflict between the commander and his troops was rapidly approaching a state of open mutiny when Borglum intervened. He arranged to have mass celebrated in his home whenever a contingent of soldiers was due to go abroad. Father Kubacec would come up from Yonkers on the eve of their going, to hear confessions. In the morning he would celebrate mass on the open terrace. And everybody in the camp would attend except the commander.

When the first group left for the front they wanted to carry the new republic's flag, which, so far, they had seen only on the camp stationery. Gutzon requisitioned one from the headquarters in New York, but there was none there, either. So he toured the New York shops for suitable flag material and brought it home. It was cut by a Bohemian tailor from Chicago on the table in the Borglum dining room. Four stars, representing four provinces, were eventually stitched to the field. The camp commander said that very likely there was no other flag like it anywhere in the world. He was probably right.

A hundred men marched with this flag down Wire Mill Road to entrain in Stamford for the boat from New York. They were dressed in blue-gray uniforms with berets of the same color. And somehow, they looked like soldiers. Gutzon frequently wondered how many of them had survived the war.

Every few weeks a similar pageant rolled out of the Borglum estate. Altogether several thousand volunteers learned squad drill and the manual of arms on Gutzon's front porch. Several hundred were still there on Armistice Day and went roaring to town to join in the general celebration.

In the meantime the sculptor and some other Americans had formed an association of independent mid-European nations. Leaders of the nations and American aides assembled on October 25, 1918, in Independence Hall, Philadelphia, where they drew up a declaration of common aims. This much-bandied declaration of independence was signed by Paderewski for the Poles, Masaryk for the Czechs and five other lesser lights for nations in being or about to be.

A preceding Victory Meeting had been held in Carnegie Hall with Masaryk and Paderewski as principal speakers. It was a conclave volcanic in its enthusiasm for two nations that now have been allowed to die. It is remembered chiefly for Paderewski's remarkable speech.

Much of the labor of getting these ill-assorted people together for the Philadelphia meeting was the free gift of Lieutenant John Townsend, a young American. He had learned his Europe while living with his father who was in the diplomatic service, and he had given his time day and night to the campaign for the unity of the small nations. He worked too hard and on the evening of the ceremony at Independence Hall, he suddenly collapsed. He never recovered. Gutzon was impressed by him. To a group of Czecho-Slovak officers he had this to say:

We can all take lesson from his shining example. He was one of the young Americans who gave their lives to save Europe . . . eager to help, uncomplaining, self-sacrificing. He was an example of the Western spirit that seems always to be at the disposal of the rest of the world. I, for one, will pray to live my life in the copy of his generous spirit.

Everybody was touched. Nobody said anything about Gutzon's part in the raising of the Czecho-Slovak army.

CHAPTER TWENTY-SEVEN

THE NOBLE SPORT

AND THEN there was the matter of The International Sporting Club. It was among Gutzon Borglum's most altruistic endeavors and certainly one that can be viewed without any reference at all to his art.

It may seem to some readers that there is something of a retrogression when an artist involves himself in a sporting club—that the whole effort militates against his ideals of his craft. But that doesn't seem to be the way Borglum felt about it. Boxing was just another odd subject that interested him and one with which he believed he could do something. He may even have fancied himself as a fighter—and, in view of later conduct, it seems that he did.

Critical opinion being what it is, three propositions should be noted as a sort of prelude to what follows:

1. Many physicians agree that boxing, or, as it is sometimes called, "The Manly Art," is an excellent physical exercise, particularly for those who win at it.

2. During the First World War, the United States Army made boxing an important part of the training of two million young men as soldiers.

3. After the war an extraordinary number of returned veterans (the estimate of the trade is 20,000) wanted to take up boxing as

a profession because they liked it, or because there was a living in it with big money for those who reached the championship in any grade from bantam to heavyweight.

There was no tangible evidence that the sculptor had gone very deeply into the study of these matters. But as a man who had raised an army on his own grounds he was one who undoubtedly would listen to any harangue about what was good for soldiers being just the stuff for virile men who were not soldiers. And the appeal came to him without his making any move to ask for it.

One Sunday afternoon in 1917 there came strolling up the driveway to the Borglum home in Stamford a stranger somewhat noticeably costumed. As he alighted from his cab and started a leisurely march to the terrace the Borglums were conscious of a broadly checked suit, a flaming tie, a monocle and a bright-yellow cane. The man's face may have shown a hint of Irish, but otherwise he was unmistakably British and impressively advertising it.

At the door he introduced himself as William A. Gavin of London. "But I have come originally from old Ireland," he mentioned. "I was taught to love the arts at my mother's knee. I have never forgotten the precepts she laid down for me. . . . 'A great artist,' she always said, 'must live very close to God.' And I have come here, sir, as a humble pilgrim. I have seen some of your magnificent work and I stand in great awe of it. I should esteem it a great privilege, Mr. Borglum, if I could go home and tell some of my friends that I have had the chance to shake your hand. . . ."

Mr. Borglum invited him in.

Whatever else Mr. Gavin may have been, he was a finished worker. He has been described by some of those who knew him best as a somewhat small, round, dapper gentleman with an amiable manner who was stiff enough to be nearly pompous. But he knew how to take his time.

In due course he mentioned what had given him his interest

LINCOLN AND GUTZON BORGLUM IN HOIST

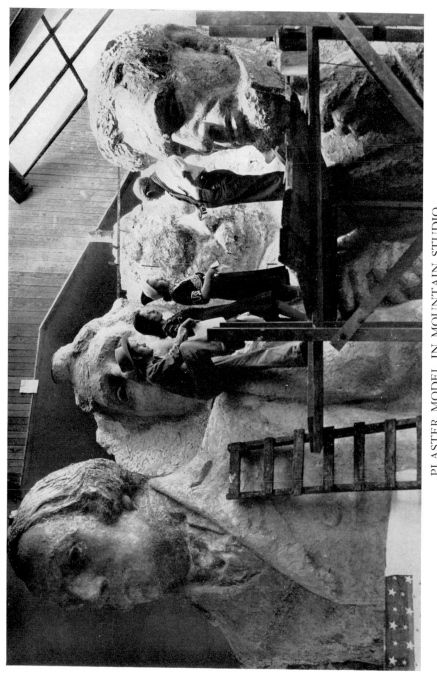

PLASTER MODEL IN MOUNTAIN STUDIO

in sculpture. "I have learned," he said, "what the human body looks like in motion. I know there must be strange techniques in the art that permits the transfer of this motion to blocks of stone or metal. I can sense it. I can see it although I cannot comprehend it. I have been able to recognize master productions. I have never failed to see that they were master productions—and I may say that so far I have never seen any that move me the way that yours do."

"And you are not an artist?" inquired Mr. Borglum.

Mr. Gavin sighed. "Ah, no," he said. "I wished to be. As a child I haunted the art galleries. But there were financial difficulties in the family and I was discouraged. I have given much of my life to sports."

"Interesting," murmured the sculptor.

"Yes, indeed," returned Mr. Gavin. "In a way it has been an odd path—and not one, perhaps, that I should have chosen if I had been given the selection. But I feel that I have done a worthwhile thing. The strength of the nation may be said to depend upon its horses, rifle shots, swimmers, tennis champions, boxers, and, of course, cricket players. I have tried to make these people constantly better—and, in my small way, I have succeeded."

"I like boxing," admitted the sculptor.

"I had believed you would," said Gavin. "At the moment boxing is my own principal interest. That is one of the reasons why I have come to talk with you. Unfortunately few people in New York have ever seen a boxing match. They do not know what it means to watch the effortless movement of a pair of skilled boxers —to note the extreme precision with which their effort is controlled." To him, he said, such contests were the most beautiful thing in the world—expressive of the fundamental male instincts, inspiring. And after that he got around to the reason for his visit.

It had occurred to him, he said, that Mr. Borglum might be of help to him in raising the level of boxing in the United States. He had come from England because he hoped to do what Lord

Lonsdale had done over there to get outstanding people interested in the art instead of the heedless ruffians who now controlled it. Gutzon's name had been given him, he said, as that of a man whose integrity was well known to the community and who had expressed some sympathy with the people who were trying to make ring contests legal. If Gutzon would join his list of sponsors, he said—and he named several highly respectable men of Gutzon's acquaintance—he would form an immense club, restore the manly art and form a national association to promote it. He, himself, he mentioned, would advance all preliminary expenses.

The sculptor joined this crusade without further pressure. Nobody connected with him could have doubted that he would. Boxing had some of the artistic appeal for him that it theoretically had for Gavin. He had known about fisticuffs since boyhood, and, as his sculpture progressed, his continuous swinging of the tools had broadened his shoulders and put power behind his punch. Boxing had become one of the things that he thought he might learn to do better than anybody else, and he had tried to prove it. His friend Bob Davis had brought the world's heavyweight champion Bob Fitzsimmons to the sculptor's studio just as a test. Borglum had made a somewhat secondary showing against the champion, but that hadn't hurt his enthusiasm. Maybe he didn't know as much about ring mayhem as a champion, but he still knew as much about the theory of boxing as anybody else. That's what he was thinking when he signed Gavin's prospectus —which was quite a prospectus.

It turned out that there was a lot of business about the boxing reform movement that Gutzon had not suspected. In September 1919 there came into being The International Sporting Club, Inc., of New York, an organization that was to show the National Sporting Club of London how sports really should be conducted. According to the plan ably outlined by Mr. Gavin, there would be 2,250 members. Each member, to get the great movement started, was to buy a gold-debenture bond for $500 as a sort of initiation fee. The bond was to pay six per cent annually. After that the dues would be $100 a year.

Land was bought and plans were drawn for a magnificent club-house at Lexington Avenue and Forty-ninth Street. Excavators came with suitable tools and began to dig a hole for this great temple of sport. Members rushed in to buy their gold debentures. The hole deepened and presently was surrounded by a high fence to keep New York's enthusiasts from falling into it.

By the end of 1920 Gavin was beginning to be one of the most talked-about men in New York. He, of course, was managing director of the club. He was mentioned in press reports as the man in control of "organization and development," which seem to have been his chief concern.

Major A. J. Drexel Biddle was first president of the organization. Gutzon Borglum, still eager for the return of boxing, suddenly found himself treasurer. The Army and Navy were well represented in the membership by people who had been active in the First World War—admirals and generals, and commanders and colonels. And there were so many more figures from financial and social eminences that the roster was a sort of *Who's Who.* There was quite a sensation when this list of magnificent members moved into the struggle to get boxing back again.

Whatever may be said about Gavin's effort to raise the level of the boxing industry, it is certain that the club presently began to make some headway. Senator James J. Walker, presently to be known as New York's playboy mayor, led the fight at Albany and presently won it when the Walker Bill (Chapter 714, Laws of 1921, N. Y.) was passed. But he had a lot of amateur assistance. Biddle made an impassioned plea to Governor Alfred Smith and later broke through Tammany obstructions to lay the matter before Boss Murphy and demand his support.

When the bill was passed, as nearly everybody thought it would be, a testimonial dinner was given to Gavin. Jimmy Walker declared that the legalization of boxing in New York was due to

Gavin's skill in organization and to his tireless energy. He read a letter to the banqueters that Borglum, still full of crusading zeal, had written to him:

> You have recounted some of the obstacles Gavin surmounted in the passage of the bill. They were great, no doubt, but they were small compared with those he has encountered in the founding of the International Sporting Club. And these are small compared with the obstacles that stood in the way of convincing the governors of twenty commonwealths of the wisdom and necessity of forming a national body. It seems that boxing, which has become the black sheep of the family of sports, and of which Maeterlinck says, "It is not a coincidence that the nations who love boxing do not know the knife," is at last destined to come into its own.

Gavin went on. While the eager members were still peering through the fence at the empty hole at Lexington Avenue and Forty-ninth Street, he began a series of gorgeous entertainments for celebrities. At one of them, entitled "Ladies' Night at the Commodore Hotel," the women leaders of New York's society looked at a prize fight for the first time in their lives. Gavin was a good promoter. The homeless club staged, in all, three bouts—Fulton *vs*. Wills, Carpentier *vs*. Levinsky, Herman *vs*. Lynch.

Georges Carpentier, the French championship contender, was the chief attraction and got considerably more publicity than he deserved. Champion Jack Dempsey, who, a few months later, was to knock out M. Carpentier, was present at the Sporting Club bout and was applauded with dignified acclaim. With all this enthusiasm roaring through New York, Gavin got some new ideas for his building. He arranged with Gutzon to carve marble panels for the main room and to produce a large piece of sculpture for the entrance. Borglum started to make models of the specimens required . . . but it is hard to find any record of what became of them.

The third prize fight sponsored by Gavin was between Pete Herman and Joe Lynch at Ebbets Field, and it was not much of a success. It ended in a riot that caused the club to lose its license to promote private bouts and something like $40,377.32 in cash. Major A. J. Drexel Biddle walked out and trouble began to pile up.

In May 1921 some of the members who were no longer impressed by the empty hole in the ground on Lexington Avenue formed a committee and asked Mr. Gavin to give an accounting of the International Sporting Club's finances. He did so suavely and willingly. There were 1,700 members on the list, he said. That was because of his care in selection. Some of these had paid only part of the $500 due on their debentures, but a total of $742,000 had been paid in and quite a lot had been paid out. The price of the building lot had been something like $250,000. There had been a charge of $105,000 for the digging of the hole. He had made an advance of $120,000 for steel, contractors' fees and architects. And then there had been some expense—about $126,000—for "organization and development."

There was further inquiry. Borglum became president of the club to succeed Major A. J. Drexel Biddle, and to the end he looked upon Mr. Gavin as a much maligned man.

It was discovered, during what remained of 1921, that Gavin had incorporated two organizations—The International Sporting Club and The Army, Navy, and Civilian Board of Boxing Control —which everybody knew about, and also The International Sporting Club Corporation. The International Sporting Club Corporation was a holding company designed to control the real estate —and the money—of the other two. When the membership investigating committee found out about it, it was in "an unhealthy condition."

In November 1921, after he had spent another $62,000 for "organization and development," Mr. Gavin got tired of all the mistrust and bickering. One night he and his attractive wife quietly slipped out of New York. They left no word of explanation or farewell. They left no purse to pay the current bills of the International Sporting Club. The investigators found that the membership had paid in a total of $1,013,478. Before the report was completed they received a nice letter from Gavin saying good-by to everybody, but they found no way to include it in the valuable assets which consisted chiefly of the hole in the ground. They found $149.69 in one bank. In another there was $3.52.

There were those who believed him incompetent to handle money, and those who thought him extremely competent—in his own interest. There were some, like Gutzon, who still believed in him. Nobody sued him; nobody charged him with any crime; no crime was ever proved against him. The money was spent. The members disagreed whether he had given them their money's worth in excitement and novelty.

Gutzon got words of sympathy from Charles Dana Gibson, Postmaster General Hitchcock, Senator Coleman Dupont, Major General Leonard Wood and others. But nothing came of his efforts to retrieve the Sporting Club. Gavin was gone. The Club was gone. After a while the hole in the ground was filled by another building, the anguished creditors ceased their crying, and presently nothing remained in New York to mark the regime of Gavin except the boxing act. Borglum was never quite sure that it was worth bragging about.

CHAPTER TWENTY-EIGHT

FRIENDS AND HOME

ONE OF THE chief errors in the life of Gutzon Borglum was his belief that everybody loved him—or nearly everybody. As a matter of fact, he wasn't quite that popular. His record for a public career that lasted just about half a century is, of course, the continuous story of a crusader who didn't mind the noise. He was a positive, stubborn character who could never see why some people didn't want his ministrations. But it must be admitted that what he wanted to do for human beings was all intended for their own good—and not, particularly, his. He was interested in beauty, and in other people . . . and emphatically!

Lester Barlow, the inventor, who knew him well, said that Gutzon's ambition was to show that he could do anything better than anybody else, from sculpture to tightrope walking. In a way he was right, for Gutzon was a perfectionist with unbounded confidence in himself. If he had gone in for tightrope walking, he would have tried to do it better than it had ever been done before, and, possibly, would have succeeded—possibly not. But the point that Barlow overlooked was that Borglum was always a critic of method and never of results if the work showed progress in technique. If a thing was better done, he never cared much how.

Many of those who knew him well thought he was a man of

great humility. He accepted criticism with great calm and respect. He was an ideal father and husband and a pleasant, unexacting friend. That's what those closest to him say—which is one of the things that makes Gutzon Borglum so difficult to understand.

There were hundreds of people in the United States who weren't so close to him—the ones who thought he talked only about tons of rock, and man hours, and A-rigs, and dynamite—and many of them figured him for a hard businessman with a Class "C" temper. That, unfortunately, is the picture of Gutzon that he left for himself in so many parts of this calm and pleasant land. And the worst part of it is that in many particulars it is authentic.

Gutzon was intense in his work. He believed in himself. And when he ran into opposition in what he considered a perfectly obvious course, he had a devastating vocabulary and a voice like the crack of doom. He was afraid of nothing.

It is odd, of course, that such a man could be a dreamer and a poet. Those who stood up to him toe to toe in bitter wrangles would never be convinced that he could see both sides of any-thing—that he could be tolerant and kindly. But he was a poet, and those who put flowers on his grave remember him for soft-ness and gentleness.

Once he said that a man who wasn't a great poet could never become a great artist. He had a reverence for a child's unspoiled outlook on life, and when asked what was his favorite poem he frequently cited Francis Thompson's essay on Shelley and the lines that begin: "Know you what it is to be a child?"

For all that he was still the man whom the hard-rock worker epitomized with the comment that he was a good stonecutter but he didn't talk pretty.

He made a lot of remarkable friends, about half of whom never knew a thing about art. They liked him personally, and when he talked they listened. Otherwise, you can't very well explain the financing of Stone Mountain, and Mount Rushmore, the work of liaison between two great political parties, the fantastic air investigation.

He knew countless people—politicians, artists, travelers, writers, soldiers, actors, cowhands, drillers, bankers—who would turn a hand for him if he asked them to. Quite likely he didn't talk sweet to them either.

"Any man, in any walk of life, has something to tell you if you'll listen," he once explained. And he listened.

"It would be a godsend," he mentioned when his bank balance was down nearly to zero after the Stone Mountain fiasco, "if every man had enough money so that he could do what he wanted to do." But even then he was never able to keep what money he got. Somebody else always needed it.

Of his conflicting characteristics his friend "Missy" Meloney, the editor, once wrote this to him:

Dear Gutzon, Heaven bless you. What a glorious time God had of it when He made you. A glorious thought that, seeing the Infinite Hand reach down and gather up the dust of the mighty and the great and mold it with terrific force into the hardest— and softest—soul I have ever known. Out of Milton and a speck of Angelo, and a grain of Napoleon, an atom from Paul and a flame from the Immortal Redeemer. It is a thought to play with. Such a strange, complex, unlimited person you are . . . counting a line of vital importance, throwing away a fortune, soothing a crying baby, harboring an army, fighting for peace, loving a friend. You and Mary are destroyers of weak faith, and I love you both.

"Missy's" picture of him is the one that his friends knew best. He never felt that he or anybody else had been endowed at birth with superior talents, though he always felt that he had done well with what he had. His ability to be successful as an artist, he declared, was due to trained observation and hard work. As a matter of course, he never talked down to an individual or to an audience. Once a Texas friend of his, Ralph Bradford, remarked that he was going to a "little hick town" to give a speech and didn't need to prepare for it. Gutzon disagreed with him. "You never know the brains of an audience by the size of the town," he said. "How do you know you won't be talking to some 'king maker' who's just there waiting for a train?" So Bradford, who presently moved on to an important post in Washington, did so because he stopped to prepare what he had to say—and the ambient "king maker" was in the audience.

"If there hadn't been any 'king maker,'" Gutzon commented afterward, "it would have been just the same; somebody, if it was only Bradford, would have known that the orator was doing a good job."

Among the sculptor's oldest friends was the painter Martin Borgord, a man of Norwegian extraction whom he had known in California and France. Borgord received honors in Paris and late in life returned to California. He stopped to visit Gutzon in South Dakota. Through him Gutzon met another well-known painter, William Singer, and his wife, and visited them in Norway. Mrs. Singer bought two of his marbles for her museum in Hagerstown, Maryland.

Another friend of the early Paris days was the Belgian sculptor Paul Nocquet, who came to New York to be near Gutzon and lost his life in a balloon ascension. After his death Gutzon collected his art works, had some of them cast in bronze and arranged an exhibition. The sale netted several thousand dollars for Nocquet's mother and sisters in Belgium. Among the patrons of the show, whose names appeared in a handsome catalogue, were President Theodore Roosevelt, Sarah Bernhardt, and the French and Belgian ambassadors to the United States.

Gutzon took care of Nocquet's burial in Mt. Kisco and prepared a calf-bound volume, *In Memoriam,* which contained, among other mementos, prints of the first air photographs of

Long Island. Nocquet had taken a camera on his final trip, and the films were found in his pocket. Though wet, they were successfully developed and are probably the first pictures taken from the air to be reproduced in the public press.

Gutzon, after his return from Europe in 1901, met the Herbert Wadsworths of Washington and the Genesee Valley. They were horse enthusiasts. So was Gutzon. Martha Wadsworth was a dominating personality, and she was a social power in Washington. But once she motored all the way to Hermosa, South Dakota, and again to Stamford, Connecticut, just to visit with the Borglums.

Herbert Wadsworth's attitude toward his wife's activities was one of whimsical tolerance and his view of Gutzon's enthusiasms was much the same. In 1912 he wrote this to Borglum:

Any indication that you are recovering from the Too-Many-Things-at-Once disease is most gratifying. Once I wanted to reform the world and now I'm too exhausted to reform myself. By and by, when you can take a long time off, come up to Ashantee— The Dawdlers' Do-Nothing Roost—and do nothing with me. Say, where is home, anywhere? . . .

Another equally old friend and brilliant woman who also motored out once to Texas to spend the winter near Gutzon was Edith Cornell Smith, wife of Sydney. She and her husband lived in Thirty-eighth Street, near Gutzon's studio. They were old New Yorkers to whom tickets at Carnegie Hall and the Opera House, and various club memberships, were as much a part of the annual budget as taxes and rent. Edith was deeply artistic and after her husband's death spent most of her summers in Stamford where she was a welcome part of the Borglum family. There were many such travelers. In time Gutzon came to look on their arrivals as he did the rains or the rising of the sun. But he was overcome with wonderment when Julian Lee Rayford, then an obscure young artist, thumbed his way from North Carolina to Texas just to talk to him. "I don't think I ever meant that much to anybody before," said Gutzon. And he meant it.

During his bachelor days in New York, Gutzon occupied a quaint brick apartment on 104th Street where other artists lived, including the Boardman Robinsons. It had been built by a strange woman who, in her youth, had gone abroad to study art and life. She had come back with strong distaste for the respectability of her well-to-do relations. After erecting this flat building, she had taken up her abode in the basement amid an assortment of art treasures gathered up in Europe. The sculptor admired what he called her wild streak, by which he meant her defiance of the conventions, and they got along quite well.

She would allow him to do what he pleased to the second-floor rear apartment, she said. So he rented it and transformed it completely and extravagantly, equipping it with furniture built from his own designs. The dining room had a round mahogany table six feet in diameter. Around it were twelve circular chairs all painted green and rubbed to a soft patina. There was a sideboard to match.

Gutzon passed out twelve keys to twelve friends who could come when they pleased and find a place at his table. Among them was Adolph E. Borie, called "Billy" by Gutzon and "Doppie" by everybody else. As president of the Savage Arms Company he was of considerable help in the aircraft investigation and in settling the affairs of the Sporting Club. He was an ardent fisherman, and, therefore, one of Borglum's own kind.

The sculptor would go almost anywhere fishing with anybody he trusted. But now and then he would decline to make a second trip. Bob and Madge Davis once invited him to fish with them in a Canadian lake. He didn't like it. Sitting in a boat and trolling was too tame a sport, he said. "You might as well be pulling a suitcase aboard the boat as one of those lake trout." The trout stream near Hermosa was the chief reason for his buying the Black Hills ranch. It was expensive and brought more debts and embarrassment. But the fishing was a compensation—or so he said.

In the duplex apartment where he lived in New York before moving to Stamford, close friends, Charles Rann Kennedy and his wife Edith Wynne Matthison, occupied the flat upstairs. Gutzon became acquainted with them through a neighbor, Henry Miller, who first staged Kennedy's play *The Servant in the House.* Edith was leading lady, and in the cast were Walter Hampden and his wife and the elder Tyrone Power. The sculptor engaged the company for a special performance in honor of the Howard Lodge at the Masonic Temple. A special edition of the play bound in vellum with the Howard Lodge emblem stamped in gold on the cover was presented to each of the players and to distinguished guests.

There wasn't much privacy about Gutzon's home life. At Stamford there were usually more outsiders than he had room for. He lived too far from town for studio assistants to go back and forth. At least one of them lived with the family all the time. And because he liked to do his writing after work hours or on holidays, a secretary was another permanent member of the group. A few of the outstanding ones came to be friends.

In the earlier days there were Eugenia Flagg and Helen Johnson Keyes, daughter of the historian. In Georgia, Lillian Taylor, who fought through the Stone Mountain war, was always on Gutzon's side and frequently stayed with the Borglums in Stamford or out at Rushmore. Jean Philip was also ready to take up cudgels for the chief and was frequently called.

When the barracks of the Czecho-Slovak volunteers were vacated the Borglum part of the community was enlarged to care for casual visitors and studio staff. In looking after all these tides of people Banks, the chauffeur, became an invaluable help and seemed so much like one of the family that Mrs. Borglum's nieces and nephews referred to him in their prayers as "Uncle Banks." Another indispensable person came to Stamford in those early days—James Reilley, the Irishman who has now been there for thirty years. His children grew up with Gutzon's, and one of them reached a position of importance at Rushmore. Old Reilley is still there, still keeping count of the empty acres.

The sculptor was likewise a dutiful son and brother. Very often some member of his family was living with him. With the first large amount of money he received for a monument commission he sent his father and others on a six-month trip to Denmark. Again he brought to New York a younger brother and his family, to keep them for a whole year while the brother was taking a medical course. There are many letters to show that moments of crisis were not infrequent in the Borglum family and that Gutzon was always ready to aid.

When his son Lincoln was born Gutzon's happiness was touching. This was his miracle, he virtually announced, and his alone. Within a week he was quarreling with the trained nurse because she would not let him pick up the baby when he pleased, day or night. There was also some resentment about the timing of the boy's appearance. He had arrived on April 9, 1912, and, in keeping with the name the sculptor had in mind for him, his birth date should have been Lincoln's birthday. Some friend fixed up this worrisome situation by mentioning that April 9 was Appomattox Day.

In due course the baby was taken to Bridgeport to pose for the baby faces spouting water from the rim of the Wheeler Fountain. In that same fountain he was christened by his uncle, Rev. Marshall Montgomery, after which he was registered in near-by St. John's Church, for which Gutzon had made the reredos.

The child, apparently, was the most important thing that had yet come into the sculptor's life. He took him everywhere he was allowed to, presented him to friends up and down the Atlantic coast, and presumably was grateful that the child's mother was a calm and tolerant woman. Once, when Lincoln was four years old, Gutzon picked him up suddenly and said they were going

to Boston on a two-day trip. But they weren't back in two days—
or in thirty days. By that time the anxious mother was telegraph-
ing to every place where she thought Gutzon might have
chanced to go. And from Atlanta she got an answering wire:
"Don't worry. Both boys here. And well."

When his daughter Mary Ellis was born on her father's birthday, March 25, 1916, he began to make plans to have her with
him wherever he went. But he learned that the arrangements
were not so easily taken care of. However, by the time of the
Stone Mountain break, Mrs. Borglum had learned to drive a car
and the four Borglums were constantly on the go, exiles from
home, but, wherever humanly possible, together.

Life at the Stamford home and studio is recalled by those who
took part in it as a continuous carnival. Michow Ito, Japanese
dancer, moved onto the old campsite of Mrs. Lanier and the
Greenwich girls with a summer school. He taught dancing and
listed classes in history and provided some art theory, taught by
an old American artist. His men pupils and his staff, including a
Japanese cook, lived in tents. The girl students were billeted in
the old Czech barracks. One of the girls, Angna Enters, stayed
on after the rest had gone. She wrote several books and became
famous as a dancer, but is known best locally for *Silly Girl,* in
which the days of the fantastic summer school are recalled.

Ito, who was an odd character, is now known to history principally because one of his pupils posed for the leading figure in
Gutzon's "Wars of America" group. Ito had plans for establishing
the peace of the world through the promotion of fine arts. But he
wasn't consistent at it. One day, when he heard that a Japanese
envoy had arrived in Washington to take part in the 1922 naval
conference, he borrowed a Bible and hurried down to the capital
with a message. There he created something of a sensation by
arguing with the Japanese delegate that it would be better to throw
away the sword altogether than to haggle about its relative
length. The envoy thanked him kindly and paid no attention.

Probably because of friendship with Henry Miller, Gutzon knew many actors. They were in and out of Stamford for years. When Margaret Anglin was rehearsing her play *The Bronze Woman* she sent her leading man, who was playing the part of a sculptor, to the Borglum studio to pick up local color. He borrowed some authentic stage properties such as a mallet and chisel.

Later Gutzon, who knew Edgar Davis, tried to get a part for Miss Anglin in *The Ladder*. This play was about Davis' thoughts on reincarnation, but that is not what one remembers it for now. Its Broadway record was established chiefly by the fact that nobody had to pay to see it. The tickets were given away free. And it went on almost to a performance record with virtually nobody in the house. Miss Anglin, however, never played in it.

With much interest the sculptor liked Laura Hope Crews. She played in *The Great Divide* by William Vaughn Moody, another of Gutzon's favorites. Gutzon found a resemblance between Moody's philosophy and his own, particularly as shown in the poet's *The Fire Bringer*. Gutzon frequently talked of Shelley's *Prometheus Unbound* as he might have concerned himself with somebody living, breathing and immortal. He was a glamorous, free spirit, and anyone who had anything to do with his chronicle was a demigod.

Another seldom chronicled trait about Gutzon is the fact that he was passionately fond of the violin. He had to give it up in order to find time for his modeling, but he cherished an old fiddle for years until vandals broke into his Stamford studio and smashed it and other things to bits. Toward the end of his life Congressman Kent Keller gave him another violin which is somewhat remembered by those about him. He received the gift on the ranch in Hermosa and, thereafter, it was his custom to rise at five in the morning to practice before the day's work began.

Whatever one's criticism of this almost secret work as a virtuoso, it must be conceded that he liked good music and probably tried to learn to play it. He knew and loved the great classics—and also the country's folk tunes. He hated grand opera, but he liked brass bands.

He had a remarkable love for motion pictures. This was partly due to the fact that at Rushmore there was hardly any other diversion. But it was likewise because actors who first appeared to him only as people who moved about the screen suddenly became real and interesting to him. Anyway, he used to go to the theaters in Rapid City several times a week whether they changed programs or not. He saw Jeanette MacDonald seven nights in succession in *Naughty Marietta,* and Grace Moore, Irene Dunne, Greta Garbo, Marlene Dietrich and others of the sisterhood with less concentration.

Almost as much as the glamour girls he loved the pictured cowboys. Not that he cared whether the cowboy was a good hand or bad, but he liked the horses.

For more quiet relaxation he enjoyed Wild West stories of the good old dime-novel kind. He and Mrs. Borglum used to read them aloud to each other on long cross-country trips. Although there are countless Wild West story magazines on the newsstands, they discovered that only one is recognized by connoisseurs. In the sparsely settled regions of the West—even in San Antonio—this magazine was hard to find, and Gutzon sometimes used to lay out a trip so that on a special day he would be at a place where it would be available. Thus he would miss no time getting to the next installment of some continued story.

Gutzon used to look for stories by Max Brand on the ground that his literary style was superior. Long afterward he discovered that Max Brand was actually a well-known writer who had made a fortune writing under different pseudonyms.

In meeting friends new or old the sculptor's outstanding trait was his unworldly attitude, totally unaffected by praise or blame, by newspaper gossip or radio commentators. This is exemplified in a story that he used to tell on himself.

During his early days in New York the actress Blanche Bates, who had known him in California, invited him to a matinee where he found himself the lone male in a box of women. He noticed that opera glasses were being turned on the box, presumably because of the exceptional beauty of the woman beside him, and tactfully he withdrew into the background.

As he was filing out after the performance he overtook Miss Bates and asked, "Who was that striking woman sitting next to me?"

Her laugh was spontaneous as she called to her friend, "Oh, Lillian, here's one man in the world who never heard of you!"

He had been spending the afternoon with the most glamorous woman in the world, Lillian Russell, and he hadn't realized it. He was not embarrassed. He never liked to be told in advance the names and positions of people he was likely to meet.

"I don't care to be hampered by other people's opinions—or guesses," he said. "I like to discover people for themselves. And I do."

"You certainly do," conceded Miss Bates.

And, of course, he did.

CHAPTER TWENTY-NINE

SHRINE OF DEMOCRACY

A monument's dimensions should be determined by the importance to civilization of the events memorialized.—GUTZON BORGLUM.

BACK to the mountains came the boy who had felt kinship for them more than half a century before, to put into form a dream that was as yet nebulous and disturbed. Vaguely he felt that he was going to preserve forever some symbol of a great national ideal. The trouble was that he did not yet have an inkling of what the symbol looked like or how he was going to keep it intact for future generations to look at. And he had the granite—the living rock of the mountains—that would turn the weather as it had been turning it for thousands of years. It would keep what he carved on it down through time to the rim of eternity.

It sprang from the Stone Mountain conception, this project. But it wouldn't be the same thing. There would be no army of horsemen riding across the white face of a cliff. For this, as he knew but found it hard to express, must provide a quick glance at the history of the whole republic, and not until he had accomplished it did he find the words. He said:

The Shrine of Democracy, carved on Mount Rushmore in the Black Hills of South Dakota, is the first of its kind in the Western Hemisphere and perhaps in the world. It is a memorial to the conception and organization of this great government. Monuments have almost never been built deliberately to make note of the intellectual or political acts of a people. The great memorials of China, Angkor, India, Egypt and Greece were incidental to the life and religion of the nations. None, I believe, was deliberately so conceived, so designed and so located that it would remain an understandable message to posterity ten thousand, a hundred thousand, or, if the material survived, a million years hence.

Each succeeding race destroys or buries its predecessor, appropriates what it can and throws the rest to the winds. Only the most enlightened of human beings revere the remains of others. So it was thoughts of this sort regarding the failure of mankind to make suitable, indestructible records of its attainments that led me to carve our national record on a cliff, on rocks that are of communally useless material. Therefore our sons will not pull them down.

Gutzon Borglum arrived for the first time in Rapid City, accompanied by his son Lincoln, then 12 years old, on September 25, 1924. He was met by State Historian Doane Robinson, who had invited him on behalf of the Black Hills and Yellowstone Park Association, and was taken to the Harney Peak region by a group of citizens including Dr. Cleophas C. O'Harra, president of the South Dakota School of Mines. The road led into a region of rising plateaus, then past rocky spars that were called the Needles, and to the Sylvan Lake, where they spent the night. The next day they climbed Harney Peak. Gutzon observed several locations suitable for carving, and he said so. But there was nothing so fine in that area as the Stone Mountain cliff. He reserved decision pending further inspection and went back East.

The result of this short visit was that Mr. Robinson proceeded to get the permission of the government to undertake the carving in the Harney Forest area, which was federal property, and to try to get an appropriation from the South Dakota state legislature.

There was no difficulty about his first effort. He got his governmental permission through the Congressional delegates from South Dakota, led by Senator Peter Norbeck and Congressman William Williamson, whose support and interest were valuable assets. Mr. Robinson almost as quickly discovered something that is undeniably true about mountain-carving projects: They cost a lot and it is almost impossible to get anybody to donate money toward them. The state authorized the formation of the Mount Harney Memorial Association, but could find no money. The state of South Dakota, as an organization, never did find any.

The Stone Mountain storm burst in the spring of 1925 and was responsible for a lot of Robinson's troubles, for the desks of the legislators were shortly piled high with literature sent out by the Stone Mountain Association trying to discredit Borglum. The only result of this warning call was a temporary delay. Senator Norbeck reported that Gutzon was a friend of the President and was known and respected as an artist and a patriot by both senators and congressmen. So the legislators of South Dakota figured that the gentlemen in Atlanta were kindly but mistaken.

Gutzon came back to the Black Hills in the fall of 1925 to look for available granite. He was piloted on a camping trip by Theodore Shumaker, an old bear hunter and former man-hunting sheriff. Before meeting Gutzon he had been well acquainted with Theodore Roosevelt, "Wild Bill" Hickok and "Calamity Jane" Burke.

They entered the Hills near Harney Peak through pathless, rugged, almost impassable timber and tree falls. What Borglum wanted was a granite cliff, four or five hundred feet in height and towering that much above neighboring cliffs. It must lie in such an angle that the main wall would face the southeast, and there should be enough of fairly even, unbroken stone to provide at least an acre of upright surface for carving.

The wall facing southeast was a necessary condition because

on it the figures would be cut to face the sun. It looked almost like an impossible requirement.

The party had been two weeks in the open, clambering up and down over seemingly inaccessible mountains, when they suddenly came face to face with Mount Rushmore. Gutzon was too tired to try to scale it in the waning day. But he knew that, barring serious cracks in the rock, this cliff was the one he'd been seeking. They camped in a quiet ravine in the mountain's shadow, preparing for supper and a comfortable night's rest.

"This looks like what I want," said Gutzon. "Where is it?"

One of his guides shook his head. "About due east of Harney Peak," he said. "But I never saw it before. There's probably never been a man within miles of this place."

So the next morning they started to climb and presently came to an entrance to the great dike they hoped to surmount. Wear and tear of wind, water and ice had cut this opening, piercing the cliff to half its depth. The climbers were still 150 feet from the top —the top that became the heads of Lincoln and Roosevelt. The heads of Jefferson and Washington were placed 200 feet farther south and higher.

They surmounted this last perpendicular wall by pyramiding one man on the shoulders of two others and using a lariat over a projecting sliver of rock as a hoist line. With torn hands and broken nails they reached the upper floor and looked down on the mining town of Keystone, about three miles away. The sculptor related his impressions thus:

When I first saw the shoulders of Rushmore I knew instinctively that I was a doomed man. I knew that while the years and I reshaped the mountain, I must be reshaped myself.

Once before I had something of the same intense, emotional shock. That was when I stood in front of Stone Mountain and listened to Helen Plane pleading with me to cut into the wall the story of Lee and his associates.

Such thoughts passed through my mind as we lay prostrate to

rest in the sun on the top of Mount Rushmore. Here great masses of rock of new dimensions, of greater hardness, rose above and about me. I was conscious we were in another world. We could imagine clouds moving over us and around us in stately dignity, or driven by hurrying winds out of the north, or falling as rain or snow against the chill white cliff. And there a new thought seized me—a thought that frightened me and was to redirect me and dominate all my carving: the scale of the mountain peak!

We were 6,200 feet above sea level—500 feet above the surrounding cliffs. We looked out over a horizon, level and beaten like the rim of a great cartwheel, 2,000 feet below. We had reached up toward the heavenly bodies; we were looking at the forms removed from the detail of earth in the valleys, with crude colossi piercing the sky. I had worked seven years on Stone Mountain without real consciousness of this changing relationship of lofty mountain forms isolated in space. And it came over me in an almost terrifying manner that I never had sensed what I was planning. Plans must change. The vastness that I saw here demanded it.

The Rushmore elevation is the highest elevation of granite, except near-by Harney Peak, between the Rocky Mountains and Europe. It is a hard formation called pegmatite, peculiar to the Black Hills, and on Rushmore it is of a finer, more even grain than that of surrounding rocks.

Once there was a sea in this region, then rising tracts of sediments compressed into complicated folds. At some remote time the earth's interior intruded upon the sedimentary folds, pushing steadily upward beneath the surface, and so formed in time the granite batholith of the Harney Peak region. The overload above the granite must have been of great height before it was destroyed by erosion. It was torn down and now lies scattered across the Bad Lands and in valleys all the way to the sea.

There is no telling when Mount Rushmore was exposed to the sky. Dr. O'Harra believed it to be one of the oldest mountain formations in the world—older than the Alps or the Apennines or the Pyrenees or the Caucasus—older, even, than the Himalayas. Said Dr. O'Harra:

Mount Rushmore, placed near the center of the Black Hills, in the heart of the continent, midst a galaxy of the world's profoundest splendors, where every stone shows an imprint of sanctity and every bush is aflame with glory, for thousands of years, yes, for millions of years, has surveyed its entrancing surroundings and with uncovered head has looked into the benign face of a kindly creator.

So now a mountain had been discovered such as the sculptor had never hoped to see. There remained the twin problems of getting the means to carve it and a majestic design to put on it. Senator Norbeck, notified the next day, was cautious. He declared flatly that the location wouldn't do. It was inaccessible. There were better cliffs and he could point them out. He and the sculptor met in Keystone, twenty miles from Rapid City, and spent another day in the hot sun looking for the cliffs that Norbeck remembered. After that the senator gave in.

The parks of South Dakota were Senator Norbeck's hobby. He had antagonized farmers by including their lands in park areas, and he had schemed to find money in the state and national treasuries that could be used for landscaping them. Virtually every road in the Black Hills and Bad Lands is his creation. If he needed a new one, he could make it. So he wasn't much worried about the remoteness of Rushmore.

"We'll get a highway up to it," he said. "Now, what are you going to put on it?"

It was Robinson who gave the clew. Years before, in the shale hills west of old Fort Pierre on the Missouri River, some children had found a leaden plate left there in 1743 by the Vérendrye brothers, French explorers. They had claimed the region for the French king as part of the Louisiana Territory. And it was brought out that Dakota was linked with the little colonial republic on the Atlantic seaboard in 1803 when President Thomas Jefferson sent out the Lewis and Clark Expedition. Considering these two episodes, Gutzon Borglum in his own stepless way decided what he would do. He would build a memorial to symbolize the creation and extension of the great republic, the forming of its government, the saving of its political union, and the completion of the dream of Columbus—a water route to India—by the cutting of the Panama Canal.

The characters he chose for the carving were obviously four: Jefferson, author of the Declaration of Independence and our political gospel; Washington, who made the visions of Jefferson practicable; Lincoln, who preserved the union; and Theodore Roosevelt, who was chiefly instrumental in the building of the Panama Canal. When the design became clear in his mind Gutzon said:

Our forefathers wrote in the canon of human government that a man has the right to be free and happy. They formed a sisterhood of states on that simple creed, and their challenge became the tocsin cry of the world's oppressed souls. Those words have changed the philosophy of the world's governments. They are the motive, spirit and purpose back of the Rushmore memorial.

We have not created a monument to Washington or Jefferson or Lincoln or Roosevelt, but to the meaning of those eleven words as maintained in our government by those four great leaders. Those words—man has a right to be free and to be happy—hold the Western experiment as the guide that leaped out of medieval Europe, more important to humanity's immortality than creeds and governments.

So the names of the Presidents to be carved on Mount Rushmore were agreed on by Norbeck, Robinson and Borglum as early as the fall of 1925. But that wasn't the end of it. Of course not. From press reports it was difficult to see that any two people agreed on any man as a possible candidate for the super carving. The women's clubs got turned into a movement for Dr. Susan B. Anthony, the noted feminist. And they argued bitterly and earnestly. Somebody introduced a bill in Congress for her support.

Gutzon, however, wasn't to be shaken. He said that the men

selected might not be the greatest the United States had produced, but they exemplified the four great periods of the country's progress and so deserved their places in the memorial. He would carve other figures later, he said, in some places where they would not be crowded.

He went to work first on the head of Washington and studied long in an attempt to find out what kind of man he was. Of the familiar Washington portraits he said:

I have examined all the available portraits of value—the Stuart and Trumbull portraits, and the Houdon portrait which I consider best of all. Not the statue by Houdon in Richmond, the figure of which is poor, but the unretouched mask by Houdon which is now in the Corcoran Art Gallery. It is unquestionably the most valuable evidence of the appearance of Washington extant. I choose to represent him before retirement. In retirement a certain fulness of cheek becomes apparent as in Stuart's last picture. His face, definitely masculine, takes on a more rugged form and reminds one of Cromwell at forty-five. There is much of the robust Britisher, the country squire or nobleman. There is none of the prettified Virginia gentleman that Stuart always produced. I recall a story to the effect that Martha Washington once told him that Stuart had said he had an awful temper, and that he must warn Stuart not to circulate such stories. Washington is said to have pondered a moment and replied, "My dear, I'm afraid Mr. Stuart is right."

The sculptor made a small model of the group in San Antonio in 1926. When he returned to Rushmore that same year he made an enlarged plaster model of Washington's head on a scale of an inch to a foot. By this time he had determined to make the heads sixty feet high; his previous thought of thirty-foot heads he found to be completely out of scale with the mountain. To make sure of the size he had gone down over the face of the cliff, located the nose line perpendicularly and the eyebrows and chin horizontally. From those lines he was able to calculate the scale. For the next several days he crawled about the cliff and valley studying the points he had marked on the mountain in red paint with a six-inch brush.

The enlargement of the Washington head was made in an old log cabin more than two miles away from the cliff of Rushmore. Plans were afoot to raise money for the vast work, he was told. But that summer, at least, nobody was able to find it. Gutzon and his family lived until September in Keystone. Their living quarters were typical of the mining boom that had cluttered the valley with shacks in the late seventies.

"Compared with the setting of the rest of the project," said Gutzon, "they were ultramodern."

CHAPTER THIRTY

DEDICATION

ONE OF THE favorite jibes of the scoffers who didn't think the Shrine of Democracy would ever amount to more than a big scar on a hill was that the workmen spent all their time dedicating it. Gutzon listened to these charges gravely and without heat. "People like to go to dedications," he said. "And if you don't get people out here, nobody is going to know what you've got." In addition to being a top sculptor he was also a good showman.

One remembers that the enterprise had virtually no friends in the summer of 1927—certainly no friends with ready money. The citizenry knew about it. That is to say, the citizenry of the Hill towns knew about it. They had heard it was buried somewhere out in the *bosque* near Keystone. Gutzon Borglum and a couple of aides went up there each day on rented horses and surveyed and measured. In Keystone Gutzon talked with representatives of the power company and salesmen from machinery companies. But certainly nobody was cutting any rock off the surface of Mount Rushmore.

And then, in one of the most fantastic journeys that the history of the Presidents records, Calvin Coolidge came out to look at the West. The White House Correspondents' Corps has never reached a decision about why Coolidge chose the Black Hills for his vacation that year. He caught trout with bait. Somebody should have advised him not to put on Sioux eagle feathers. He played a weird game of golf on a private course that was nearly vertical. And the best thought of the Washington press on the subject was that he was just a New Englander who had learned how to be a tourist. Now it is permitted to wonder.

Coolidge came out to the Game Lodge, thirty miles southwest of Rapid City, chiefly because Peter Norbeck suggested it and carefully laid the way for him. Norbeck was one of two South Dakotans who was really enthusiastic about making the Harney Peak region an object of national interest. Norbeck and Gutzon were friends who believed in each other's magic, and Gutzon was a friend of Calvin Coolidge. You may make out of these premises anything you like. But there isn't any doubt that the carving of Rushmore ceased to be idle conversation when the President arrived and slogged three miles up the hill through the dust to raise his hand and give the project its sacred quality.

The President was rolled out over a new road from Rapid City to the Game Lodge, a hostelry on Squaw Creek, handed a fishing rod and assigned to a preserve that had been packed with specimens from the state hatchery. Indian chiefs came and made obeisance. The grumbling correspondents installed themselves in Rapid City. Then, on the second day, Gutzon Borglum paid his respects to the distinguished visitor. He hired an airplane—which nobody else had thought of—and flew over the Game Lodge to drop a huge bouquet of mountain flowers on Mrs. Coolidge's lawn.

The next day he arrived more formally at the President's picnic plot to arrange, as he afterward reported, "a visit of dedication to Mount Rushmore." And it is significant that the interview seems to have been previously arranged and the subject of the discussion well understood. Nobody was surprised when the date for the dedication was set—August 10, 1927. By that time everybody near enough to see was convinced that the President was just doing the things he had his heart set on. Recalling his interview with President Coolidge, Gutzon wrote:

It was a fine interview. Coolidge was a silent man. But he always talked with me—fishing, politics, even a little about art. He was happy he had come to the Black Hills for his summer outing. He said they reminded him of the Vermont mountains.

When the day arrived for the dedication we drove up as far as we could and walked the rest of the way. The President was mounted on a safe horse, led by an orderly on each side on foot, until we reached the cabin I had taken over as a studio. It was about 1,500 feet from the cliff.

There were lots of specially invited guests who had struggled up the hill. It was something new to see the consecrating of a mountain by the President of the United States. Nothing had been left undone to make this an official act. Everything was done with the greatest of dignity and decorum. Coolidge was really impressed.

"We have come here," he said, "to dedicate a cornerstone that was laid by the hand of the Almighty. On this towering wall of Rushmore in the heart of the Black Hills is to be inscribed a memorial that will represent some of the outstanding events in American history, and portraying the features of four of our Presidents.

"The progress of America has been due to the spirit of the people. It is in no small degree due to that spirit that we have been able to produce such leaders. If coming generations are to maintain a like spirit, it will be because they continue to study the lives and times of the great men who have been leaders of this country, and continue to support the principles those men represented. It is for that purpose that we erect memorials. We cannot hold our admiration for the historic figures which we shall see here without growing stronger in our determination to perpetuate the institutions that their lives revealed and accomplished."

That, for the most part, was the dedication. And, singularly enough, it was very effective. The hot and weary witnesses who had made the march out of Keystone had suspected it would be, and they had no reason to complain. Calvin Coolidge, for once in his life, had been deeply moved.

The little crowd stood quiet and motionless for a minute. Gutzon was called over to the President's side.

"Look," said Coolidge abruptly, "who's paying for all this?"

"Well," answered Gutzon, "the Rapid City Commercial Club has been taking care of preliminary expenses. And since the Mount Harney Memorial Association has been formed, some money has been raised in the Black Hills and the state generally. We've got donations from the Homestake Mine and the railroads and from people outside like Charles Rushmore, Herbert Myrick and Coleman Dupont. We are very grateful."

The President sniffed. "You'll not go far on that," he said. "The people of South Dakota can't even pay the interest on their farm mortgages."

"They've had a dry year west of the Missouri River," explained Gutzon. "We can hope for more water next year."

"Nonsense," declared Coolidge. "They never get water out there. When I get back to Washington I want you to come to the White House. You know Secretary Mellon?"

"Yes," said Borglum.

"All right," pursued the President. "He and you and I will sit down and figure out what can be done to promote this work. I know great governments do things like this."

The President then handed the sculptor the drills and Gutzon climbed to the top of the mountain. The engines were turned on for the first time. The huddled, silent witnesses caught the sudden chatter of the drills. The carving of Mount Rushmore had begun.

Gutzon came down and presented the first drill in use to President Coolidge. The next two went to Doane Robinson and Peter Norbeck, and he kept the fourth. Then everybody plodded back down the hill to Keystone.

"See me in Washington," repeated Coolidge as they said good-by. And that the historian might record as the beginning of Rushmore financing.

Norbeck and Borglum disagreed as to the proper approach to the problem. Borglum said that he would ask the federal government to donate as much as the memorial promoters were able to collect from other sources. Norbeck said no, that money was hard to collect privately, that you couldn't run drills on promises and that Mellon could be made to pay the full cost. Gutzon, remembering how he had raised more than a million dollars for Stone Mountain, refused to listen to this argument. But, it turned out, Norbeck was right.

Toward the end of 1927 Borglum was in Washington. He laid his plan before Mellon just as he had said he would, and Mellon was pleased. So was President Coolidge, for Gutzon's modesty was something unusual at the time.

Norbeck was not pleased. "You could have got it all," he said. "Now I don't know what you'll get." He put a bill through the Senate, while Congressman Williamson was doing the same thing in the House, providing for a twelve-member commission to take over the drawings, contracts and material now held by Borglum, to be held and owned by the United States government. The $50,000 fund in the Rushmore treasury was exhausted in the middle of December 1927; so work was abandoned and nothing was done in 1928 while everybody in the Black Hills waited for Congress to act.

Norbeck was discouraged in 1928. In a letter to Gutzon he wrote:

Previous to this, public sentiment has held up pretty well under our repeated assurances that everything would go right along. But the fact that neither you nor I could scare up a few dollars for the work during the summer of 1928 has led people to believe that we were just talking hot air. Very few people in South Dakota take the matter seriously any more. Doane Robinson tries to, but it keeps him awake nights and he needs sleep. . . .

This letter came to Gutzon in San Antonio, where he was working on the memorial to Woodrow Wilson destined for Poland, and he was a bit put out. To this letter he replied:

Photo by Lincoln Borglum

VIEW OF RUSHMORE SHOWING HEADS OF THE FOUR PRESIDENTS

F.D.R. AT THE UNVEILING OF JEFFERSON, AUGUST 1936

My dear Senator, if I didn't love you and sympathize with the difficulties you have had to face in the past year, I would get cross. But no one can respect you more than I do, know you half so well, agree with you so much and fail to feel that anything you write would be written in the best spirit. If I say anything a bit harsh, I am going to ask you to treat my remarks in the same spirit.

I have a feeling from your letter that you feel I have not raised the money that should have been raised; that I have not carried through the matters I should have carried through. Now let us clear up a few of these points. First, because it was with great reluctance that I took up the Black Hills work, for it is a terrific undertaking and I found the country and the people utterly uninformed in such matters and without funds. I agreed to go to the Hills and make a survey for a fixed sum. That was accepted; a bill was introduced in your state government with the result that nothing was paid for that service by the state. I found, in other words, that whatever I undertook, I had to carry much of the load all the time, in financing and developing interest, in engineering and production.

Finally when the work was in hand it was always in South Dakota that the inertia was felt most. While I was there, everything was promised; immediately I left, everything was put off until I returned. I have made at least three complete rounds of the cities in the southwest of South Dakota, feeling out gatherings for the purpose of informing and interesting the people and securing help for the memorial. I have been informed, time and again, at each of these gatherings, that the necessary funds were available provided your committee, or someone you designate, would either be with me or go and collect the money.

This was told me even at the Homestake Mine, where I talked for a solid hour to the manager and legal head of the concern, and secured from them the statement that they were completely sold on the proposition and would do their part. You yourself secured their contribution. I am not blaming you for anything. I have never questioned your wisdom, or your politics, or the reasons for delay in Washington. But I do think, and you must bear me out in this, that if the bill had been passed, the past year would have been one of energy, action and production, with the head of Washington completed on the mountain.

Less than a month after this exchange of letters the Rushmore bill was passed; $250,000 was appropriated on a matching basis and more than $50,000 released to match sums previously subscribed. Considering the carving program, this fund was still nothing to cause much celebration. The making of monuments has always been expensive. One such group alone—the Jefferson Memorial in Washington—had an estimated cost of $3,000,000. But one takes what one can get, and Gutzon was cheered again.

In one of his last Presidential acts Calvin Coolidge appointed ten men and one woman as the Mount Rushmore National Memorial Commission: John A. Boland, Rapid City, South Dakota; Charles R. Crane, New York City; Joseph S. Cullinan, Houston, Texas; C. M. Day, Sioux Falls, South Dakota; D. B. Gurney, Yankton, South Dakota; Hale Holden, Chicago; Frank O. Lowden, Oregon, Illinois; Julius Rosenwald, Chicago; Fred W. Sargent, Evanston, Illinois; William Williamson, Rapid City, South Dakota; and Mrs. Lorine Jones Spoonts, Corpus Christi, Texas. At their first meeting, called by President Hoover in the White House in June 1929, J. S. Cullinan was elected president of the commission and John A. Boland chairman of the executive committee. Work on Mount Rushmore began at once.

Some people remember 1929 because of renewed hope that the great memorial would be finished. But most of the rest of the United States recall it as the year that started the big depression. Contributions came in slowly; then they stopped. Cullinan, with the blessing of President Herbert Hoover, organized the Rushmore National Memorial Society of the Black Hills to handle advertising, fund raising, memberships, management of concessions, maintenance of the park area, publicity and other matters not directly connected with the building of the memorial. Memberships were set at $100 apiece, which brought in $6,000, and that was the biggest sum that anyone in the undertaking saw for a long time.

Then there was the matter of a suitable inscription. The idea of such explanatory matter to accompany the carved figures had been set forth in the Congressional bill. It had been discussed by the sculptor and President Coolidge in the summer of 1927 and again when the pair met two years later in Texas. Borglum asked of the ex-President some eight or nine terse paragraphs covering the territorial expansion of the republic and starting with the Constitution and the Declaration of Independence. The available space on the mountain gave room for about 375 words in letters three feet high. If reduced to two and a half feet, there would be room for 475 words. Reporters spread word throughout the country that Coolidge was writing a history of the United States in 500 words. He denied it.

Gutzon wrote a letter to Mr. Coolidge after that restating what he wanted. He was about to dress the mountainside for the entablature, he said, and would appreciate some copy. Mr. Coolidge sent the two paragraphs which read:

The Declaration of Independence—The eternal right to seek happiness through self-government and the divine duty to defend that right at any sacrifice.

The Constitution—Charter of perpetual union of free people of sovereign states establishing a government of limited powers under an independent President, Congress and Court, charged to provide security for all citizens in their enjoyment of liberty, equality and justice under the law.

Gutzon changed the wording slightly. He cut out the word *through* before *self-government* in the first paragraph. In the second he eliminated the phrase *under the law* after the word *justice*. Mr. Coolidge objected to the editing. The newspapers raised another storm. Coolidge complained of the publicity. The sculptor assumed all blame and got this somewhat annoyed reply from Coolidge:

I know that you are a great artist. What I meant to convey is that I do not wish to be engaged in putting up a monument to myself. I wished my name kept off the mountain. I do not see any reason for your committee giving the press any statement of any kind in relation to me. I wish you every success. . . .

Then there were letters to the *Times,* and essay contests in the newspapers, and speeches by high-school students, and resolutions by the Rushmore Commission. But in the end there was not one single contribution of the required length. Flaws in the granite caused a shift of figures that left no room for the entablature; and the Commission set the whole matter aside for future reference.

CHAPTER THIRTY-ONE

CARVING THE MOUNTAIN

Some sons of God must stand upon the mountaintops
And there through all the deathless generations guard
The continents, and guide the gracious stars of fate:
So God made mountains for the throne of these.
Upon this mountaintop America enshrines
Her sturdy sires, exalts her noblest knight.
Where children of the earth may lift appraising eye
And feel his virtue while his strength invests their souls.
—DOANE ROBINSON

GUTZON BORGLUM carved a mountain. And as the years went by he became a dynamiter, a geologist, a practical miner and, very definitely, an engineer. He got used to crawling about on the face of a cliff, and in time he used to say that his sculpture was not greatly different from the cutting of a large block of stone in a studio. But, of course, the stone of the mountainside wasn't dressed or prepared. It couldn't be shifted into the light or away from it. The amount of stone to be removed was prodigious, and injury of the material left for carving was always a serious possibility. How one of these projects ever got itself done is something that he wasted thousands of words trying to explain.

When Gutzon first used dynamite for carving on Stone Mountain it had been taken by the world as a fantastic idea. But there was no coyness about its use when it came to Rushmore. It was laid out there in all proportions and all quantities. The sculptor had experts who knew what could be done with a six-inch stick, or half an ounce of it, or with a percussion cap alone. And they had to be in touch not only with the drilling of the moment but with the design of the whole monument to avoid the chance of an overcharge at one point injuring stone at a distance.

Such drilling skill was developed that the sculptor could depend on them to block out a nose to within an inch of the finished surface, to shape the lips, grade the contours of the neck, cheek, brow and all round areas. He could even shape the eyeball as a whole, but the defining of the eyelids and the pupils was done by drills, air tools and by hand.

The sculptor's first concern was the position of Washington. He put in days studying the surfaces, shadows, reflections and the course of the sun; and eventually he chose the place where Washington's head rises today. It was the best spot on the mountain.

He began to make models to suit the cliff. He discussed the angle of the head with Carothers, one of the literary secretaries of the Hoover administration, and he had long conferences about the character of the first President with Hoover himself. They decided that *uprightness* should be emphasized in Washington's statue. The head should not incline to right nor left, nor forward nor back, but should be set on the shoulders so that it would show dignity and poise. Carothers drew a straight line down the middle of a paper, put a ball on the top of it to indicate the head and remarked quite gravely, "This is the way it should be drawn."

And that is the way it was drawn. The center of Washington's head was fixed at the point where the horizontal line going across the brows met the vertical line through the chin. In roughing off they had to remove fifteen feet of rock before they found a hard, undamaged surface. This was done late in the summer of 1927. Blasting was not resumed until 1929.

Work on Washington taught them how to proceed quickly with other figures. It established methods, determined tools, temper of steel, arrangement of scaffolding for hoists and a labor gauge on the men who were to perform most of the rough toil on the monument.

The first preparation for carving was to draw in its proper position on the mountain an oval of the required length and width. This oval was divided into three sections—one at the line of the eyebrows, one at the end of the nose and a third at the end of the chin. These measurements were in the scale of the model; in other words, a model sixty inches in height had an enlarged outline sixty feet in height.

The work on Rushmore was done from swing harnesses developed at Stone Mountain. They were made of a leather-covered steel frame and were quite strong. The men were buckled into them. Thereafter they might be bumped or fall, but they could not get out without unbuckling themselves. The swings were suspended at the end of a 300-foot steel cable from a winch on the top of the cliff. They were housed in a shack on Washington's head.

Ordinarily the practical method would have been to determine precisely where in the cliff the head was to be located, then fix the model at the same angle; next, to begin at the top, peel off the rough stone and finish as you went down. That's the way any good mechanic or engineer would carry on such work, relieving the features, finishing as he descended and using the stone shelf that the work always left under his feet to stand on.

But this was a work of art, not of mechanics. The revelation of the face by the sculptor was as if he were releasing a living thing. Each drill hole must pierce the stone with certainty, so as not in any way to injure what was below. Gutzon said he could not allow mechanical methods to reduce his art production to a lifeless form.

Each day they carefully surveyed the rough-blocked face. When they reached the chin line they were thirty feet in from the original granite cliff. There they stopped and built a scaffold from chin to forehead, and the sculptor sent to Texas for his old friend and assistant Hugo Villa. It was then June and an unveiling was scheduled for July.

No man on the Rushmore project had ever carved a mountain before. But no matter. He had less difficulty with them than with any other phase of the undertaking. Most of them were the so-called forgotten men of Keystone—veteran miners, the one-time workers of the idle Holy Terror Gold Mine. They were hard-rock men; they were used to explosives; and they did not need many instructions.

In the end the sculptor had several experts on the mountain as adept as any in the country, and a loyal group of helpers. Gutzon established a boardinghouse near the blacksmith shop, engine room and other buildings at the foot of the cliff, and frequently came with his guests to eat with them. He knew them all.

Gutzon's original contract with the Mount Harney Memorial Association had specified that Captain Jesse Tucker of Stone Mountain be named superintendent of the work at Rushmore and given a fixed salary of $10,000. To make this sum possible the sculptor reduced the amount to be paid to himself. The reason for Tucker's position, he frankly stated, was that he must give part of his time to other sculptural work, and that while he was absent from Rushmore he needed someone to take his place.

But presently the Rushmore Commission hadn't any money to pay to anybody. There were arguments and misunderstandings, and Tucker resigned. After that the full burden of the work fell on Gutzon. He moved with his family to the Black Hills and built a studio some distance from Rushmore at Hermosa.

Gutzon probably missed Tucker more than anybody else with whom he had ever worked. Correspondence between them during the first few months of construction on Rushmore shows the great concern of both of them for the safety of the workers. Tucker, who thought the men careless, was certain that they would contrive some bad end for themselves. But the years went on and the carving got done and somehow there were no serious accidents.

The nearest approach to disaster came when a lightning flash exploded a percussion cap just as the worker was making an artificial electrical connection. The man in the swing harness was shot out into space but by instantaneous muscular reaction flexed his knees as he was hurled back against the side of the mountain. He was badly bruised but not otherwise hurt. The sun was shining when the accident happened. Thereafter no blasts were set off without the advice of the weatherman.

The other accident occurred when a steel wire controlling the hoist broke. The open box in which three or four men were riding came hurtling down. The quick wit of a young man from Stamford, the assistant superintendent, prevented a serious crash. He stuck an iron rod between the hoist wheel and the cable that retarded the descent of the car. Only one worker jumped out as the car hit. He was treated for a minor chest injury.

Some unknown friend whom Gutzon always identified privately as Sam Insull set out a Diesel engine for him at a town in the western part of the state. For two years it furnished all the power needed not only to run the air compressors and drills on the mountain but the pumps of the Holy Terror Mine as well. A Wyoming company was started and Gutzon, on the promise of electricity for less than his own plant would furnish it, agreed to shut down. Shortly before the day scheduled for the unveiling of the Washington head the power company informed him that he must sign a contract to use the company's electricity for twenty years or be cut off. Gutzon snorted and turned to the Diesel engine. But there was no hope from that source. Somebody had dismantled it and carried away most of the movable parts.

Commissioner John Boland rushed out from Rapid City and thereafter Gutzon bought power from the new company. But he refused to sign the twenty-year contract. The cost of the power was a matter of bitter discussion forever after.

Lincoln came to the mountain in 1932 and worked two years without pay. Gutzon trained him to do the "pointing," which consists of measuring the models and locating their enlargements on the rock. It is the direct translation of the work of the artist from studio to the material which he will cut, and Lincoln was carefully prepared.

Gutzon declared that Lincoln was a master of this work, understanding its complicated mathematics, and father had confidence in son. Under him a staff of three assistants served as a "pointing crew" for the measurement of all models to be enlarged on the mountain. When not measuring they acted as aids and guides to the drillers. The instructions given to Lincoln at one period when the sculptor's arrival at Rushmore was delayed indicate the dramatic quality of the work. The sculptor instructed his son thus:

I want you, in beginning the work and allotting the positions to the men, to avoid the two finished faces completely. Do not touch the hairlines around the face of Washington or his chin, or under his chin. Do not approach the face lines of Jefferson, or to the side of his face or under his chin.

On Photograph No. 1, I have drawn a circle where you can locate Payne [a driller] to begin down-drilling under what will be Washington's ear and the left-hand lapel of his coat. Put one or two men on the lapel, which I have marked No. 2. Put two men on Washington's shoulders and work carefully from the top, which I have marked No. 3. That will dispose of five or six men.

I have marked Lincoln's eye. You can put two men in cages in each of the eyes. I would use Anderson on the one side and Bianco on the other, putting Bianco where the feldspar streaks run down, and Anderson on the outside. I would give Payne, with Bianco, a position on the nose and have them begin to take off stone by drilling in squares and breaking it off down to within six or seven inches of the finished surface. But do not try to cut the eyelid or eyeball. Make a round mass for each of these. Lincoln's face in that way will take up probably six more men.

You can put about three men on the Roosevelt stone, marking carefully the contour of Lincoln's face so that none of that is disturbed, and going back into the hole next to Jefferson's face as deep as you can. If you can put any men down on the block that I have marked No. 8, without any danger of tools and stone falling on them, all right. I would put about three men down on the big crag. We still have seventy or eighty feet to take off that. I think this will keep you busy until I get there.

It did.

CHAPTER THIRTY-TWO

CONVERSATION

•

IN THOSE DAYS Gutzon Borglum found time to smile once in a while, although anybody who knew the trials of mountain carving might have wondered why. He had been written down for a comfortable part of a million-dollar memorial project. Seldom, during any one carving period, did he get much of it. Some years he got none. People were donating toward Rushmore begrudgingly in nickels and dimes. He was always shorthanded. The experts he needed couldn't exist on the cash available. Somebody raised the price of electricity. Somebody dismantled the Diesel engine. There were wrangles over concessions and concessionaires and small-town politics. There were road troubles, and supplies were late. And there were other things. The question of why anybody should wish to become a topflight sculptor seemed unlikely to be answered—ever.

The head of Washington was officially unveiled on July 4, 1930. The rest of the cliff was unchanged, and Washington's chin seemed to rest on the ledge from which it had been carved. But when the great flag swung aside to reveal the sculptured face the witnesses, strangers to Stone Mountain, felt that from then on the memorial would never die.

J. S. Cullinan, first president of the Rushmore Commission, presided and gave the monument its name: "The authority of

Congress to carve colossal portraits of these great men in the granite of the Black Hills has created a perpetual *Shrine* for political *Democracy*." And Borglum, tired, dejected, almost conquered by a world where nobody ever seemed to want to do anything, was pleased with that. A head was finished on Rushmore, and the dullest of these laymen looking at it knew that it was a finely done piece of sculpture. He heard someone saying that it would be there forever, and he hoped that it would last longer than Lee's at Stone Mountain.

The crowd at the unveiling got safely back to Rapid City with no trouble at all. And nobody thought of Borglum's connection with the district's good roads.

In the spring of 1930, trying to get from Rapid City to Keystone with two cars and tow aids, he had been ditched six times. He never got to Mount Rushmore that week. However, he did get to the telegraph office and sent word to President Hoover that the roads were impossible and that he would shut down the project unless conditions were improved and men could get to their work. Hoover sent the message to Governor William J. Bulow, who in turn made an appointment for his state road commission to meet the sculptor that week.

Meanwhile the governor telegraphed this message to Mr. Cullinan:

BORGLUM HAS THE TEMPERAMENT OF ALL GOOD ARTISTS, GETS MAD WHEN HE CANNOT CONTROL WEATHER CONDITIONS. NOTHING SERIOUS EXCEPT THAT HE GOT A NEW EXPERIENCE AND A NEW TOUCH OF LIFE. AM SENDING HIGHWAY ENGINEER TO SEE WHAT CAN BE DONE. WITH GOD'S AID AND PATIENCE HOPE TO GET HIM SMOOTHED OUT.

Within three days they had planned the beautiful road now leading from Rapid City to the memorial. Strange as it seems, South Dakota spent $480,000, plus a quarter of a million on other roads, to reach a monument on which she had not spent a dollar. Meanwhile Senator Norbeck with his Custer State Park Commission was working on a road approaching Rushmore from the opposite direction by way of Iron Mountain.

Iron Mountain Road is one of the country's finest examples of what can be done with economical engineering. Engineer Charles E. Smith who laid it out hadn't much money to spend. The highway runs along part of its highly beautiful journey between Keystone and Grace Coolidge Creek on two lanes that are widely separated. It climbs terrific grades on corkscrew uplifts built of pine logs. It is well paved, well graded and safe.

One of the features of the highway is said to have come by accident. Work was started from the south end and presently struck a mountain that had to be tunneled. The hole was surveyed with no plan save to keep it in line with the approach already built. When the miners finally broke through they were looking into the face of Washington on Rushmore. The two remaining tunnels were cut at the same angle, framing the memorial with a showmanship worthy of Gutzon Borglum himself. Borglum was intensely pleased. "Norbeck's Iron Mountain Road," he said, "is as much a work of art as the carving of the mountain."

Another Norbeck road over the so-called Pine Creek route between Rushmore and Hill City, again a masterpiece of scenic road building, was the cause of the sculptor's abandoning his original plan of placing Jefferson on Washington's right in the Rushmore grouping. There was a contributing factor in this decision due partly, he thought, to poor work. Up to summer of 1931 Gutzon had been trying to place the figure of Jefferson where he believed he belonged—on Washington's right. Work had continued after the unveiling until the fall of 1930 and was resumed in the following spring. In July of that year the sculptor went to Poland, taking Lincoln Borglum with him, to erect his statue of Woodrow Wilson. He left Tallman and Villa in charge.

There was no way of testing the stone in the location for the Jefferson head, so he had quickly roughed out the block and left Villa pointing the face.

When he returned from Europe and motored out to Rushmore he noticed while still a mile away that something was radically wrong. He exclaimed to Villa, "What's wrong with the Jefferson head?" Villa answered by turning to Tallman: "Didn't I tell you the master would notice it from a long way off?" Then he said, "Well, there was a little difficulty about the pointing." The trouble, he explained, was too deep a depression under the eye and there was not enough stone to push the head farther back.

The sculptor did not wait to find out what had gone wrong— rock or work. He was almost too angry for words. Gutzon thought he had taken all precautions. About half the work was finished and it wouldn't do. Who or what was to blame did not matter. The damage was done. There was not enough stone to allow free modeling of Jefferson's face, and Norbeck's new road, exposing the back of the head, made a change in the composition advisable. The sculptor made a bold decision to abandon what had been done on Jefferson and place his figure on Washington's left. This necessitated a change in the whole grouping, while the flaws in the rock in Jefferson's new position were so deep that he had to go back sixty feet before he found good stone for the carving. Senator Norbeck, the only one consulted in the matter, gave complete approval.

Villa left shortly after this incident, but came to see his old master in Texas a year or so later and greeted him with his old-time affection. Nothing ever came between them again. Subsequently he flitted in and out of the Rushmore studio at unpredictable times. But Villa was a city man and was not at home in this rugged community. Gutzon missed him, for he brought to the studio a breath of the charm found in the Old World wherever art is active.

The year of Washington's bicentennial, 1932, witnessed the shutdown of work at Rushmore for lack of funds, which to the sculptor seemed an unforgivable disgrace. However, there on the mountain was the portrait of the first President, which Mr.

Cullinan had declared was the best in existence. The face seemed to belong to the mountain, having taken on its elemental courage, and Gutzon figured it as vital as he could make it. He occupied himself with regrouping the models in the studio. It had disturbed him to have the figures as close together as in the original composition, and now this had been opened up by putting Jefferson so far inward that it gave room for the sun to pass back of Washington and light Jefferson's face. The flaws in the rock which made this necessary began to appear a blessing in disguise.

The recomposition also involved changing Washington's shoulders in relation to his head. The left shoulder was moved back seven feet and then another seven feet, while the right shoulder was moved seven feet forward. When word got around that Borglum was moving Washington's head there were loud alarms. Norbeck was flustered. Monument lovers from Rapid City rushed out to the mountain to see how a head that weighed several tons could be transported. There was some disappointment when they saw nothing more novel than the chiseling of the shoulders; but they talked, and the story, it is said, made good publicity.

John A. Boland of Rapid City, chairman of the executive committee of the Rushmore commission, was charged with the hiring of workers, purchase of materials and payment of salaries and bills. And it must be said that these worthy endeavors were seldom fraught with any sweetness and light. Boland's office was in Rapid City—too close to Rushmore, he thought—and he could not move it because of his statewide business. He sat there quietly and never interfered with the carving operations. He felt that Borglum was a great artist and that the carving of Mount Rushmore was a noble undertaking. He may one day be considered a great patriot.

One of Boland's handicaps in the situation was his unwillingness to spend any money that he didn't happen to have. This attitude was, of course, diametrically opposed to that of Borglum, who never could be convinced that money really mattered. And it is said that these two stalwarts had "occasional clashes." "Occasional clashes," one regrets to say, is a highly erroneous and short-weight title for what they had.

Gutzon once said that he could feel his blood pressure rising when he got within 500 miles of Rushmore and faced the prospect of seeing Boland. Boland's blood pressure went up only when Borglum needed money. But the men met, discussed the Shrine of Democracy, swapped observations about the current financial situation and brought the language of toe-to-toe wrangling to a new high.

Gutzon declared, of course, that he never took these arguments seriously. No row, he said, was ever worth remembering after its cause was gone; and that, probably, is a true report on his reactions. The last time he and Boland met he was pleased with the course of the world and mellow toward Boland. He had his arm across the chairman's shoulder and was calling him "Johnny."

What Boland thought about these goings on is, of course, an entirely different matter. He never talks much about his struggles in behalf of majestic art. "Borglum was a great sculptor," he sums it up. "He certainly was that."

The matter of concessions on Mount Rushmore bothered Gutzon considerably more than most people interested in the project realized. Continuous importunities for jobs and for permission to sell souvenirs and postcards and photographs near the work were petty annoyances with which he found it hard to cope. He knew that some such items had to be provided as part of bringing knowledge of his work to the attention of faraway people, but he would not tolerate cheap workmanship or poor taste in anything sold near the carvings. He got along for a while by keeping this trade under supervision in the Rushmore studio, but the relief was only temporary. A resurgence of what he called "local petty politics" presently involved him so that he called on the Department of the Interior to send someone to protect him.

The Department of the Interior complied and Gutzon learned

that nothing is so bad that government intervention can't make it worse. The unimaginative, bureaucratic routines taught to Washington office workers were wholly out of place in a work so constantly changing and so free from fixed rules. The protector sent by the department turned out to be an earnest young man who started out to confuse the South Dakota politicians and did well at it. But he wished to do greater things. He became aloof and secretive.

After some weeks he was discovered to be corresponding with an engineering company in Switzerland known chiefly for its construction of cog-wheel railroads. He thought the company might be interested in building such a funicular line up and around the face of Rushmore so that visitors might walk under Washington's nose or sit in Lincoln's eye. Gutzon's indignation set the young man right and was long remembered.

The Park Service of the Department of the Interior had formulas for all of its functions. Its personnel with whom Borglum came into contact believed that the heads should be carved in orderly fashion. First, the figure of Washington should be completely finished; then the workers should move on to Jefferson, and so on. This, they pointed out, would give people something to look at.

Once more the sculptor who had asked only that he be protected from the harangues of would-be postcard peddlers made a protest against the continuous suggestions of ignoramuses. Harold Ickes, head of the department, understood Borglum's position clearly and told him in forceful language to ignore such suggestions. But the subordinates never seemed to comprehend. One of Ickes' engineers went so far as to offer to relieve Borglum of all worry. "Why don't you finish your models and give them to us to reproduce on the mountain?" he inquired. "We have plenty of men who can do that sort of work—and quickly, too."

"Somebody has to put the life and expression into carved faces," Gutzon began to explain as he had been explaining since his first days on Stone Mountain. "That's why more good mechanics don't turn out to be good sculptors."

There was also the question of "hiring and firing" workmen. The bureaucrats could not understand that the sculptor had to discharge anyone who refused to obey orders, or that he might suddenly need a certain type of workman for a particular job and then need him no longer. It was such a complicated procedure to get a worker placed on the government payroll that it was no wonder they didn't want to discharge him again in a few days. There are many letters to show that the sculptor's relationship with the various heads of the Park Service was most friendly. Difficulty was due to a misunderstanding of what an art production of this unprecedented character required.

Even the Rushmore Commission suggested impractical sculptural plans and picked out certain parts of the work it would "like to see finished." And while Gutzon was pushing the work, begging more funds to get more power, more workmen, skilled carvers, so that the work might be finished in his lifetime, it was irritating to be told that certain commissioners and local interests would like to keep the project going as long as possible because more tourists would come if they could see the sculptor at work.

After 1932 the work dragged on with frequent interruptions and without sufficient funds. Workmen were complaining of the daily climb to their stations—1,500 feet with a rise of 500 feet, which the sculptor himself made several times a day—resulting in a working time loss of from an hour to an hour and a half every day for every man on the job. To date, approximately seventy per cent of the roughing out of the entire surface to be carved had been completed and thirty-five per cent of the finishing, within a total working time of twenty-two months and an average of four to six drillers at work.

The personnel of the Commission was so changed by illness, death and lack of interest that it became increasingly hard to get a quorum at the semiannual meetings. Mr. Cullinan had resigned as president to be succeeded by Fred Sargent of the Chicago and North Western Railway. Only Gutzon could not resign. As he remarked, the rock of Rushmore was riveted to his neck.

A new phase of the work began in 1934 when the federal government assumed the burden of financing the memorial. Frequent stoppages, constant lack of sufficient power and skilled workmen, plus the unpredictable condition of the stone, had greatly increased working costs. Congress first voted to remove the fifty-fifty matching restriction attached to the first appropriation, making it immediately available, and next passed a second appropriation of $200,000. There were those near Mount Rushmore who said it was about time.

CHAPTER THIRTY-THREE

— AND FINAL PEACE

So THEN there was no trouble at all save bureaucratic misunderstandings and the vagaries of Rushmore rock. Accurate estimates of the time required to finish the work were impossible because of the constant shifting and reconstruction of design. The stone on Mount Rushmore, although the best in the Black Hills, offered interesting surprises. Some new reddish substance appeared on Lincoln's cheek. Silver and tin crystals were found at the end of his nose. The feldspar crystals on Rushmore are unusually large and add to the difficulties. This was especially true on the lapels of Washington's coat where no powder could be used. Finally Jefferson's head had to be slightly turned so that the poor stone came in the hollow between his cheek and nose and could thus be removed entirely.

An unfailing support to the sculptor through these difficulties was President Franklin D. Roosevelt, who wrote a dozen or more sympathetic letters. One of them he closed by saying, "I am very much interested in the work you are doing, and will be glad to remove any drawbacks that may handicap you. . . . With best wishes always. . . ."

So it is not surprising that he was present at Rushmore on August 30, 1936, for the unveiling of the head of Thomas Jefferson. He had been touring the West to see for himself the results of desperate drought and had been routed to reach Rapid City on time.

At the President's request the exercises were informal. Flags of Bourbon France and Hapsburg Spain, fluttering from the top of the mountain, were lowered as the huge American flag was swung back to reveal the face of Jefferson. In a few words Gutzon asked the President to dedicate this memorial as a shrine which for years to come would bring people of all the earth to see what manner of men struggled here to establish self-determining government in the Western world. Mr. Roosevelt responded:

On many occasions when a new project is presented to you on paper and then later you see the accomplishment, you are disappointed. But it is just the opposite of that in what we are looking at now. I had seen photographs. I had seen the drawings. I had talked with those who were responsible for this great work. And yet I had no conception until about ten minutes ago, not only of its magnitude but of its permanent beauty and of its permanent importance.

Mr. Borglum has well said that this can be a monument and an inspiration for the continuance of the democratic-republican form of government, not only in our beloved country but, we hope, throughout the world.

This is the second dedication. There will be others by other Presidents in other years. When we get through there will be something for the American people that will last through not just generations but for thousands of thousands of years. And I think that we can perhaps meditate a little on those Americans ten thousand years from now when the weathering on the faces of Washington and Jefferson and Lincoln shall have proceeded to perhaps a depth of a tenth of an inch, meditate and wonder what our descendants—and I think they will still be here—will think about us. Let us hope that at least they will give us the benefit of the doubt, that they will believe we have honestly striven every day and generation to preserve for our descendants a decent land to live in and a decent form of government to operate under.

Doane Robinson, Senator Norbeck and William Williamson occupied seats in the front row of the platform, with John Boland immediately behind. The President remained in his automobile throughout the ceremony, with his party, including Governor Berry of South Dakota, around him. It was Senator Norbeck's last public appearance. At the end he smiled and handed to Gutzon a note of a few lines reminding him touchingly of the satisfaction he must feel to see this accomplishment.

At this time, the summer of 1936, the work on the Lincoln face had advanced enough to show his eyes and part of his nose. It was pushed on so that on September 17, 1937, the 150th anniversary of the adoption of the Constitution, this head also was ready for unveiling.

For years Gutzon had been undecided whether to carve Lincoln with or without a beard. He had tried it both ways in other carvings with almost equal effect. But he had a feeling that a beard added strength to the face and that the world was more familiar with a bearded Lincoln. That was the face he finally decided to carve. He sent a small model of it to Franklin Roosevelt, carrying out his promise that Roosevelt would be the first to know.

The Lincoln head was dedicated on schedule and for the first time a Rushmore program was carried by radio broadcast to the entire country. Former Congressman Williamson, a member of the Rushmore Commission, presided. United States Senator Edward R. Burke was chief speaker. There was an impressive moment when the sculptor called the roll of "all those friends of Rushmore whose understanding sympathy and instant aid made this great memorial possible, and who are now with the gods— Calvin Coolidge, Peter Norbeck, James Cullinan." Then taps sounded from the distant heights. The trooper who blew the call was suspended from the side of Washington's head, a quarter of a mile away.

During the rest of 1937 much work was done on the Roosevelt head. Gutzon wanted it in condition to photograph for the appropriations committee. He himself had to spend much time in Washington worrying about the financing. He also made a brief trip to France to look after the erection of his statue of Tom Paine, modeled in the Hermosa studio.

As a model for Roosevelt he used a bust of the President that he had made during his lifetime. There was trouble finding stone enough for the head. He had to go back 120 feet in the rock before the model could be fitted. This was trying work.

All in all, 1937 was a typical Borglum year. His contract with the Commission was due for revision. The matter dragged along for months before an agreement could be reached. The sculptor got no pay for all that year, and he had to pay his lawyers a quarter of what he would have received to get any contract at all. The new contract was, in the main, satisfactory. It provided that the sculptor working with the Commission should prosecute work on the memorial to a successful conclusion. Gutzon felt that nothing but his death could stop it now.

In 1938 there was a tremendous rush of tourists who could hardly be accommodated. Congress appropriated $300,000 for the comfort of visitors and the finishing of the carvings. In the same year the Rushmore Commission was reorganized. Senator Key Pittman, long a friend of Rushmore, became chairman, succeeding Fred Sargent, who had died. Kent Keller, chairman of the House Library Committee, became vice-chairman. An executive office was established at Rushmore for the handling of accounts and materials.

The new commission met at Rushmore in August 1938, and the sculptor made a report. He wasn't worried about the statues any more, now that he'd hit enough rock to take Roosevelt's face. But his plans for the future included a lot of other things, including a big storehouse, more electric power, an adequate water supply to replace the trucking of water four or five miles in cans.

He said it was time to begin work on the Hall and Stairway under the figures as specified in the original contract. And he got everything but the Hall and Stairway.

The President's reorganization bill of 1939, which conferred additional control over Rushmore to the Department of the Interior, caused havoc. Work on the Hall was immediately discontinued over Gutzon's protest. Construction of the storehouse was stopped. Lumber and materials were left strewn about to be ruined by the weather. He complained to the President and got a compromise order. The Commission was authorized to control carving and finish the storehouse. But the Commission still refused to permit Gutzon to dig his Hall.

It would have been an amazing thing, this Hall, and one day possibly will be. It was to be a room cut out of the solid rock 100 x 80 x 32 feet to an arched ceiling, finished in dressed granite. Here Borglum had planned to store the records of electricity beginning with Franklin—light, heat, music, radio, telephone, telegraph and controls of power as they were used in the spread of the republic. Man's accomplishments were to be preserved here, sealed in airtight glass cases. If such an exhibition could be provided, he declared, the world a thousand years from now would have something interesting and educational to look at.

In 1939 South Dakota celebrated the fiftieth anniversary of its statehood, and a meeting of the people was held at Rushmore. Governor Harlan J. Bushfield, later U. S. Senator, said, "At this time, when freedom and democracy have been challenged in so many parts of the world, no better place for this ceremony could possibly be selected than the Black Hills and particularly this Shrine of Democracy."

The Sioux Indians were there under Chief Henry Standing Bear, camped in wigwams around the base of Rushmore cliff. Some 15,000 people had come from all parts of South Dakota and neighboring states. Doane Robinson appeared in the same suit of clothes and the same hat he had worn on statehood day fifty years before. It seemed to be a fitting contribution to Rushmore's most enthusiastic celebration.

Across the country in Washington, Congressman Francis Case, now Senator, of South Dakota, whose home at Custer was virtually in the shadow of the memorial, was carrying on the old fight for funds. To a Congressional committee he said:

> The best answer to every question about Rushmore is to see it. . . . I have seen it grow from a dream to a reality. . . . The soundness of Doane Robinson's idea, the dogged persistence of the late Senator Peter Norbeck, and the ability of Gutzon Borglum to inspire people with the works of his hands and with his vigorous exposition of American ideals, have kept the project going on. . . .

And Mr. Case read into the record a letter from John Boland which said in part:

> Mr. Borglum is an artist. I am a businessman. Therefore it is only natural that we should at times disagree regarding the business functions of the commission. Such differences, however, have never been serious and an amicable understanding has always been reached. My only desire is to have the Mount Rushmore memorial completed in the best possible manner and to have Mr. Borglum carry on his great work with the assistance of his son, Lincoln, the continued co-operation of the commission and the efficient supervision of the National Park Service.

So presently all human troubles had been wafted away from Rushmore, and briefly the atmosphere was filled with the sweetness and light that Gutzon had foreseen. As the park was landscaped and the carving of the mountain went on with effortless speed, nobody could remember the charge that Gutzon Borglum had an ungovernable temper. He was a keen observer, but he was temperate and he was polite.

One remembers the day when Walter Travis of the Rapid City

Journal paid one of his routine calls at Rushmore. Gutzon beamed on him. Travis knew that Gutzon had recently been in a long and futile argument with Rapid City's administration on the desirability of straightening and decorating Rapid River. But he smiled, too. It was none of his business.

Gutzon pushed out his hand for a hearty greeting. "Welcome, Speedy," he said. "And how is everything in your backward and objectionable little village?"

"Only a Borglum could say," answered Travis, "because Borglums never forget."

People whose contacts with Borglum spread over a long time know that in his own opinion he was indubitably *right*. But looking back over the years they realize that most of the time he really was right, and for the rest of the time, however reluctantly, he would listen to reason. He wanted to get things done and he had a great impatience with people who stopped him. But no one of his friends who knew his generosity and gentleness ever hinted that his most vocal indignation could be classed as ungovernable temper. Temper, possibly . . . but not ungovernable.

He was one of this generation's most accomplished showmen. He took the jibes of the newspapermen with good grace. And he gave them back the same way. You may remember the matter of Washington's nose. Some reporter, trying to spur him into a grand speech, asked him if he would call the figures on Rushmore as *perfect* as they might be. The great sculptor shook his head. "Not today," he said. "The nose of Washington is an inch too long. It's better that way, though. We are slowly approaching perfection. It will erode enough to be exactly right in 10,000 years."

Borglum, possibly, was not the man that a dullard could understand. It is not enough to say that he was a great sculptor—perhaps the greatest of his generation. He had to be many more things to get the Mount Rushmore memorial finished. Looking back over his story one is definitely confused. Should he be given world honors for his art, or for his remarkable aptitude for getting money out of smooth and experienced politicians, or for his incredible knowledge about the weakness of stone, or for his skill as a dynamiter, or for his absolutely unbreakable will? You may take your choice and be partly right. If he had lacked any of these attributes, Rushmore would still be back in a wilderness with dead trees piling up about its base.

Borglum died suddenly on March 6, 1941, in Chicago. He had spoken a few nights before for Dr. Harry Kelly, a friend of many years' standing, in Park Ridge. He was in severe pain, yet he stood for more than an hour to deliver an impassioned plea for faith in America and the principles of personal liberty on which the government was founded. He was plainly ill at the close. He was taken to a hospital the next day and eventually failed to survive a coronary thrombosis. The years on Rushmore had done his heart no good.

Despite the fact that he was supposed to have been making his fortune in the Black Hills, he died thousands of dollars in debt. It was years before the hospital and doctor bills could be paid. Lincoln Borglum knew what details were still lacking on the almost finished figures on Rushmore. The Commission, with the concurrence of the Park Service, designated him to finish the work. Lincoln refused to make any changes or to carry the work any farther than indicated by his father's models.

Congress passed a resolution for Gutzon Borglum's interment in a tomb to be carved in the rock at Mount Rushmore. But Gutzon, some time before his death, had extracted a promise from Lincoln that he should be buried among the flowers in California. His friends, led by Commander E. F. McDonald, Jr., decided with the family that his wishes should be carried out.

So he was buried in a memorial court of honor with the inscription composed by his lifelong friend Rupert Hughes close by him:

His birthplace was Idaho; California first taught him art,
Then France who gave him fame;
England welcomed him: America called him home.
His genius for the exquisite as for the colossal
Gave permanence on canvas, in bronze,
In marble, to moods of beauty or passion,
To figures of legend and history.
Nations, cities, colleges paid him tribute.
As patriot he stripped corruption bare. As
Statesman he toiled for equality in the
Rights of man. At last he carved a
Mountain for a monument: He made the mountain
Chant, "Remember! These giant
Souls set America free and kept her free.
Hold fast your sacred heritage, Americans!
                    Remember! Remember!"

So, for a time, there is a pause in the story of Gutzon Borglum. You may still rouse an argument about the art of mountain carving. Some relics of the Stone Mountain Association are still convinced that he was angry-tempered and erratic and that nobody could get along with him. What they do not see is that all such things make no difference. The Four Faces of Rushmore stand looking into the sun. And Gutzon Borglum seems likely to live as long as any human man who ever trod this earth, except the four he helped make immortal.

INDEX